HUMAN RIGHTS: CONFLICT TO BUILD PEACE

HUMAN RIGHTS
Conflict to Build Peace

GOPAL BHARGAVA

Publications
KALPAZ PUBLICATIONS
DELHI–110052

HUMAN RIGHTS: Conflict to Build Peace
(Human Rights)

Rs. 790

ISBN: 81-7835-203-6

Published in 2003 in India by
Kalpaz Publications
C–30, Satyawati Nagar
Delhi–110052
E-mail: kalpaz@hotmail.com

Laser Typesetting at: Varsha Graphics, Delhi
Printed at: Mehra Offset Press, Delhi

Contents

Preface

Human rights are based on respect for the dignity and worth of all human beings and seek to ensure freedom from fear and want. They are rooted in ethical principles and usually inscribed in a country's constitutional and legal framework. The promotion of human rights is of particular relevance in the context of globalisation and its potential for excluding and marginalising weak members of the international community and people with limited resources. It is the responsibility of every individual and every organ of society to promote respect for human rights and to secure their universal recognition and observance. All human beings should act towards one another in a spirit of brotherhood.

At a very basic level, the proclamation and acceptance of human rights norms inherently involves majoritarian morality. Human rights are agreed to exist because a majority says they do. Specific goods and benefits are treated as human rights because a majority says they do. With either an invented or natural genesis, human rights are meant to protect some aspect of humanity. Human rights may be those entitlements that we have by virtue of being human, but there are real difficulties in determining which attributes of human life require protection under human rights standards.

Violations of human rights is one of the most worrying problems of our times for the entire world civilisation. The responses to the worst human rights violations of the twentieth century, to totalitarian oppression have created a veritable human rights culture. This culture focuses less on the punishment of transgressive behaviour than on establishing a broader discourse of rights. International human rights has come to offer nothing short of a global language by which to represent violations of human dignity. The discourse of international human rights has become a medium for the condemnation of local abuses, regardless of how these abuses may otherwise be characterised or rationalised within domestic political schemes. Rights talk can affect local dialogue and in this way structure domestic political developments.

Editor

1

Democratic Governance

From the human development perspective, good governance is democratic governance. Democratic governance means that: People's human rights and fundamental freedoms are respected, allowing them to live with dignity. People have a say in decisions that affect their lives. They can hold decision-makers accountable.

So, promoting human development is not just a social, economic and technological challenge: it is also an institutional and political challenge. Accompanying this new consensus is a growing conviction that many persistent development problems reflect failures of governance. Studies in a range of countries and regions hold weak governance responsible for persistent poverty and lagging development.

The governance crisis is evident in widespread corruption, inefficient public services and a host of other failures. These studies have also shown what poor governance means for ordinary citizens -schools without teachers, courts without justice, local bureaucrats demanding bribes at every turn. All are important for human development -especially since ineffective institutions usually cause the most harm to poor and vulnerable people. But just as human development is about much more than growth in national incomes, governance for human development is about much more than effective institutions and rules. Participating in the rules and institutions that shape one's community is a basic human right and part of human development.

Governance for human development is partly about having efficient institutions and rules that promote development by making markets work and ensuring that public services live up to their name. But it is also about protecting human rights, promoting wider participation in the institutions and rules that affect people's lives and achieving more equitable economic and social outcomes. Thus governance for human development is concerned not just with efficient, equitable outcomes but also with fair processes. Governance for human development must be democratic in substance and in form -by the people and for the people.

Essential Goals of Human Development

Political freedom and participation are essentail goals of human development. Political freedom and the ability to participate in the life of one's community are capabilities that are as important for human development as being able to read and write and being in good health. People without political freedom such as being able to join associations and to form and express opinions -have far fewer choices in life. And being able to participate in the life of one's community commanding the respect of others and having a say in communal decisions -is fundamental to human existence.

That political freedom and participation are crucial to human development is not always well understood. Indeed, there is a widespread misperception that human development is only about economic and social outcomes such as reducing income poverty and improving health and education. Though these are important for human development, its aim is much broader -to promote the freedom, well-being and dignity of people everywhere.

Economic growth is a means to these broader ends. The success of the human development index (HDI)-itself only a partial measure of the economic and social dimensions of human development -has contributed to this misperception because it leaves out so many aspects of human development.

People are not only the beneficiaries of economic and social progress, they are also its agents, both as individuals and by making common causes with others. That is one reason strategies for promoting human development have traditionally emphasized investing in education and health and promoting equitable economic growth. These are two pillars of development because they mobilize individual agency by strengthening productive capacities. Political freedom empowers people to claim their economic and social rights, while education increases their ability to demand economic and social policies that respond to their priorities. Putting participation at the heart of human development strategies raises a question about the scope of human development.

Human development is certainly broader than education and health. Many other capabilities are also important in expanding human choices. But public policy is about setting priorities. And the human development approach requires deciding which capabilities are most important for public policy. There can be no single answer: societies and people value capabilities differently depending on their situation. Human Development Reports have applied two criteria in identifying an important capability. First, it must be universally valued by people the world over. Second, it must be fundamental in the sense that the lack of it would close off many options in life. Other than that, the basic concept of human development has remained open-ended.

The political shifts of the 1990s built greater consensus on the value of political freedom and human rights -consensus reflected in recent intergovernmental declarations such as the Millennium Declaration of the UN General Assembly and the consensus document of the March 2002 UN Conference on Financing for Development. In an era of rapid globalization, markets and political liberalization -not government planning -are often the main drivers of economic and social change.

But a decade ago, with the legacy of the cold war still alive, the world was divided on the importance of political freedom and participation. And 1990 was the tail end of the planning era of development, with the state as the primary actor. As a result human development strategies emphasized the need to reallocate public investments in favour of human development priorities, especially the two pillars of expanding primary health care and education and promoting pro-poor growth. Changes in the world have shifted human development priorities and made political freedom, participation and collective action much more important as public policy issues.

Alongside the economic entrepreneurship that drives markets, social entrepreneurship now drives policy debates on issues that matter for people. In addition, consensus is emerging on the importance of collective action by people and civil society groups in shaping the course of human development. Other capabilities might be considered important today -such as personal security or the capability to be free from physical danger or violence.

The human development approach to development has fallen victim to the success of its human development index (HDI). The HDI has reinforced the narrow, oversimplified interpretation of the human development concept as being only about expanding education, health and decent living standards. This has obscured the broader, more complex concept of human development as the expansion of capabilities that widen people's choices to lead lives that they value. Despite careful efforts to explain that the concept is broader than the measure, human development continues to be identified with the HDI -while political freedoms, participating in the life of one's community and physical security are often overlooked.

But such capabilities are as universal and fundamental as being able to read or to enjoy good health. They are valued by all people -and without them, other choices are foreclosed. They are not included in the HDI because they are difficult to measure appropriately, not because they are any less important to human development.

Democracy and Human Development

The word democracy, from the Greek, means "rule by the

people". It sums up well the human development approach to governance because it expresses the idea that people come first: governance must conform to the needs of people, not vice versa. Whether there can be such a thing as "will of the people" in a world with disparate and competing interests, the basic democratic principle - of the equal concern for all people in the formation of governance structures -captures a key part of what human development should be about. The democratic system of voting in elections adds another crucial element of governance from a human development standpoint, because elections are the paradigm of enforceable accountability.

When a government fails to live up to the needs and desires of the people, the people can throw it out of office. No form of accountability is more direct. There is also no more egalitarian form of participation. The principle of "one person, one vote" gives every individual an equal say in the choice of government -in theory if not in practice. Other forms of participation can also be important for ensuring the accountability of state and non-state actors when, for one reason or another, the ballot box fails to do the job. But there is always the risk that particular groups and interests will wield undue influence, as those with more resources, or simply more determination, impose their views.

Democracy also requires functioning institutions. It requires a legislature that represents the people, not one controlled by the president, prime minister, bureaucrats or the military. It requires an independent judiciary that enforces the rule of law with equal concern for all people. It requires well-functioning political parties and electoral systems. It requires security forces that are professional, politically neutral and serve the needs of people. It requires an accessible media that is free, independent and unbiased, not one controlled by the state or by corporate interests.

And it requires a vibrant civil society, one that can play a watchdog role on government and interest groups -and provide alternative forms of political participation. These institutions, underpinned by democratic values and respect for human rights, provide checks and balances against the risks of tyranny -and of populism, because in democracies populist politicians can mobilize support by using propaganda and appeals to racism and other forms of intolerance. In 1995 the Inter-Parliamentary Union assembled experts from various regions and disciplines to develop an international standard on democracy.

The Universal Declaration on Democracy was adopted in 1997, starts with basic principles. Democracy is a universally recognized ideal, based on values common to people everywhere regardless of cultural, political, social or economic differences. As an ideal, democracy aims to protect and promote the dignity and fundamental rights of the individual, instil social justice and foster economic and social development. Democracy is a political system that enables people to freely choose an effective, honest, transparent and accountable government.

Democracy is based on two core principles: participation and accountability. Everyone has the right to participate in the management of public affairs. Like wise, everyone has the right to access information on government activities, to petition government and to seek redress through impartial administrative and judicial mechanisms. Genuine democracy presupposes a genuine partnership between men and women in conducting the affairs of society. Democracy is also inseparable from human rights and founded on the primacy of the law, for which judicial institutions and independent, impartial, effective oversight mechanisms are the guarantors. The declaration sets out the prerequisites for democratic government, emphasizing the need for properly structured, well-functioning institutions.

The capacity and willingness of citizens to influence the governance of their societies should not be taken for granted, and is necessary to develop conditions conducive to the genuine exercise of participatory rights. Society must be committed to meeting the basic needs of the most disadvantaged groups to ensure their participation in the workings of the democracy.

Indeed, the institutions and processes essential to any democracy must include the participation of all members of society. They must defend diversity, pluralism and the right to be different within a tolerant society. Democracy must also be recognized as an international principle, applicable to international organizations and to states in their international relations. Democracy is always a work in progress, a state or condition constantly perfectible.

Sustaining democracy means nurturing and reinforcing a democratic culture through all the means that education has at its disposal. In democratic societies people participate in the public sphere in many ways - debating issues with friends and neighbours, writing to newspapers on the rights and wrongs of government policies, marching in protests, becoming members of political parties or trade unions giving them a say in the decisions that affect their lives. Participation involves engaging in deliberative processes that can bring people's concerns to the fore.

In representative systems of government, decision-making is delegated to officials. But informed decisions require input from the people affected by them and cannot rely solely on "expert knowledge ". Democracies take different shapes and forms -because political systems vary, they may be "differently democratic " on many fronts. For the world's parliamentarians the essence of democracy lies in its basic principles.

In democracies people have a voice -underpinned by freedom of speech and thought, freedom of information, free and independent media and open political debate - that allows them to be heard in public policy-making. Public pressure can influence the decisions and actions of public officials as well as private agents, as with environmental pollution or abusive labour practices. These democratic processes are clearly related to three aspects of development:

— First, democracies are better than authoritarian regimes at managing conflicts, because the political space and the institutions that provide for open contests give opponents hope that change is possible without destroying the system. Some politicians argue that democracy leads to political instability, undermining development. But empirical studies show that the reverse is true. Sociopolitical unrest and handovers of power occur more often in democracies than in dictatorships, but they do not disrupt development. Between 1950 and 1990 democracies experienced twice as many riots and demonstrations and three times as many labour strikes. But such events -as well as changes in government -did not slow economic growth in democracies. Under dictatorships they did. Dictatorships were also more prone to violent political upheavals, experiencing a war, on average, every 12 years, compared with every 21 years in democracies. And wars caused greater economic hardship in dictatorships than in democracies. Democracies can mitigate internal conflicts so that they do not develop into political crises and economic turmoil. The same relationship holds in the opposite direction that is, higher incomes help democracies survive once they emerge, and the likelihood of reverting to authoritarianism declines as incomes increase. Higher incomes also contribute to political stability.

— Second, democracies are better at avoiding catastrophes and at managing sudden downturns that threaten human survival. In India famines were common under colonial rule -for example, 2 -3 million people died in the 1943 Bengal famine. But since independence and the establishment of democratic rule, there has been no recurrence of famine -despite severe crop failures and massive losses of purchasing power for large segments of the population, as in 1968, 1973,1979 and 1987. Each time the government acted to avoid famine. For example, food production fell sharply during the 1973 drought in Maharashtra, but famine was averted, partly because 5 million people were quickly put to work in public works projects. In contrast, during 1958 -61, famines in China killed nearly 30 million people. Political incentives in democracies also seem to help societies avoid other disasters, especially economic ruin and the collapse of development. The worst economic crises in democracies have been much less severe than the worst under dictatorships. True, some of the highest economic growth has been achieved under non-democratic rule, notably in the East Asian tigers between the 1960s and 1990s.

— Third, democracies help spread the word about critical health issues, such as the negative implications for women of a large number of births, the benefits of breast feeding and the dangers of unprotected sex in the context of HIV/AIDS. In these areas open dialogue and public debate can disseminate information and influence behaviour. Sharp declines in fertility in highly literate Indian states such as Kerala were due not only to high literacy but also to its interaction with public debates on the benefits of small families.

Social injustices are widespread in democratic and authoritarian regimes alike, whether deliberate or otherwise in the allocation of public services or in discrimination against squatters, street children, migrants and other socially marginal groups. Discrimination against ethnic minorities, women, the elderly and others continues even in long-established democracies, as the Commission for Racial Equality recently reported in the United Kingdom.

According to one study covering more than 50 countries, countries with higher income disparities have lower tax revenues and government spending than countries with more evenly distributed incomes. Such biases occur in both authoritarian and democratic regimes. Democracies range from those with highly uneven income distributions to those that are more egalitarian. The same is true for less democratic regimes.

Similarly, there is a wide range of achievements in key human development indicators such as the under-five mortality rate or the net primary enrolment ratio. Mali has progressed further than Togo in stabilizing its democratic structures but has done no better in spreading primary schooling, raising literacy or reducing infant mortality.

Bahrain and Syria have done as much to spread primary education as more democratic Jordan -and more than Morocco. Some democracies have huge, often growing inequalities in income, wealth, social advantage and power. Consider Brazil and the Russian Federation, with some of the world's widest income disparities.

In many Latin American countries disparities in income and education rose in the 1990s after democratic rule was restored in the 1980s. Income inequalities also jumped in the former Soviet Union, Central and Eastern Europe and the Baltics. By contrast, Indonesia, the Republic of Korea and Malaysia achieved solid economic growth and reduced income inequalities under non-democratic rule in the 1970s. So, while democracy can promote equitable development, the goals of democracy and equity should be considered largely independent - with both requiring dedicated effort and political will.

Democracy may not automatically secure equitable social and economic development, but poverty does not prevent democracy from taking root: Costa Rica, Jordan, Mozambique and Senegal have expanded people's freedoms and participation much more than their less democratic neighbours with similar incomes. The lesson is that democracy is not a luxury for developing countries.

On the contrary, democracy has intrinsic value for human development because it has strong links to political and civil freedoms and can contribute to social and economic development. But these links are not automatic, and strengthening them is the challenge of democratic governance -making democratic institutions serve human development.

Today, societies can be more or less democratic, just as people can have broader or more constrained choices to lead lives they value. But there is no defined end point. No society is ever completely democratic or fully developed. What matters is moving forward, and not slipping back. People everywhere want to determine their destiny. The kind of democracy they choose need not follow a particular model -the North American or the Western European, for example. The model must be adapted to local circumstances and history. But everywhere, democracy requires a long process of political development.

Threats to democracy come not only from political parties that are personalized and unable to represent people, but also from intolerance, extremism and a lack of respect for human rights and human dignity. The implication is that priorities for advancing democratic principles vary according to the social context, just as priorities for human development vary over time and across communities. Promoting the equal concern for all people in the formation of governance structures meant something different in an era of state-owned industry and the transistor radio than it does in an era of transnational corporations and the Internet. Democratic governance in this fast-changing environment is about more than people having the right to vote. It must be about strengthening democratic institutions so that they keep pace with the changing distribution of economic and political power.

ICTs in Democratic Governance

Two years ago, at the United Nations Millennium Summit, the common ground upon which information and communication technologies (ICTs) and human rights can be analyzed was forged, which resulted in a declaration that affirmed common global commitments to the protection of the vulnerable, the alleviation of poverty, and the rectification of corrupt structures and processes - particularly in those countries in which there is a dearth of 'rule of law'. The current period of preparation for the upcoming World Summit on the Information Society (WSIS) - in which the International Telecommunication Union (ITU) has a leading managerial role - offers an excellent opportunity to address tensions that exist between national, regional and global models of governance - particularly where hotly debated topics like human rights draw to the forefront of discussion key issues like transparency, accountability, and the universality of human rights principles.

The way in which new communication technologies may be able to help realize some of the goals of the 2000 Millennium Declaration will be explored. The convergence between telecommunications, broadcasting multimedia and information and communication technologies (ICTs) that is driving the development of the global 'Information Society' is responsible for the transformation of a variety of economic and political sectors, as well as the socio-cultural strata of nations around the world.

The benefits of information and communication technologies (ICTs) lie not purely in the range of their functionality, but in the variety and versatility of their application. Much has been written about the potential of ICTs to 'revolutionize' society, particularly in the context of their role as catalysts of the 'Information Revolution'. This 'revolution' is often juxtaposed with its predecessor, the Industrial Revolution, usually for the purpose accentuating the idea that communication networks are as integral to the process of development as was the birth and development of industry in the 19th century.

While it is the question of access that has risen to the forefront of development agendas in the context of the famed 'digital divide' , much work remains to be done in analyzing and understanding how these technologies are utilized and applied to bring about expected revolutionary societal and economic changes and improvements.

While the conventional wisdom is that new technologies contribute to economic development, and that this in turn trickles down to the whole of global society, it is relevant to bear in mind that such diffusion depends on relatively equal patterns of income distribution , as well as a variety of other variables that are not necessarily prevalent in the developing world.

The subject of how modern communications alter the way in which various entities of the private sector, the public sector and civil society interact has spurred much debate. More specifically, such debate targets the underlying theme of whether they are conducive to fundamental shifts in the distribution of power towards the dissolution of strong, centralized political hierarchies.

Across different phases of policymaking and information dissemination, they can be applied in various forms as database technologies, decision support technologies, networking technologies, and personal identification and tracking technologies.

The idea that ICTs, in the process of empowering people to exchange information, may help to effectuate change by supporting decentralized, participatory development. Conversely, lower levels of functional interactivity are more likely to render a technology supportive of more centralized power structures. The unit of analysis is a subjective measure of each technology's capacity to support an 'ordinary' individual's activities, with darker shading indicating greater capacity for reciprocity in each of the five major categories:

(i) makes multi-directional communication possible,

(ii) allows for control over the communication act by the participants and

(iii) supports an exchange of roles between participants in a communication process. Two more characteristics of multi-directional communication are

(iv) the possibility of feedback and the speed with which feedback can be communicated and

(v) its requirement for synchronicity in time.

E-mail unequivocally stands apart from its predecessors as being more conducive to reciprocity in communication. The idea that new communication technologies may bring about social change - here defined as the enhanced awareness and protection of human rights in the international system - is "... one of the theoretical underpinnings of the positive perspectives on the benefits of the communications revolution." At the same time, it appears that a decisive factor in the way human rights are asserted and protected lies in the way power is governed and managed by those who control and regulate various communications apparatus.

ICTs have indeed permeated the structural workings of the international system, often challenging top-down 'command and control' power hierarchies by facilitating the de-centralization of information vital to the workings of national and international governance.

Vertical relationships between governments and society are being replaced by horizontal network relationships between public, semi-public and private agents, and ICTs are revolutionizing the internal workings and external relations of public administrations. This is in part because information has become itself a resource and commodity, surpassing its traditional role as mere facilitator to political and economic decision-making.

In many ways, the sensitivity of governments to the potential use of information and communications systems against them is itself a sensitive subject area, in part because historically, the deployment of telecommunications networks and informatics have been closely related to the workings of the military complex and the realization of political, ideological and military goals. In light of this generalization, it seems that where the lines of the dissemination of information, the diffusion of culture and activism, and access provision to new markets cross with those of national security, it is vital that 'Information Society' imperatives are treated with paramount diplomacy.

It goes without saying that communications networks facilitate the broadening of scope and perspective in a way that empower all those who utilize them, and a realistic vision and discussion of the Information Society must be inclusive of this phenomena. Held is indeed one author who argues that nation-states are drawn together by complex processes of interdependence on problems such as AIDS, migration, human rights, crime, trade, environmental pollution, and new challenges to peace, security, and economic prosperity which spill over national boundaries.

Once considered to be the sole territory of sovereign states, the protection of human rights is now viewed as a universal concern, as evidenced by the recent conviction for genocide, rape, war crimes and crimes against humanity handed down in the International Criminal Tribunals..." The rise in transnational human rights networks has been referred to by some as the 'third globalization' - and has helped to develop a global civil society capable of working with governments, international institutions, and multinational corporations to promote internationally accepted standards of human rights and democracy.

Examining the economics and politics of ICTs is an integral part of understanding the broad development agendas espoused by a variety of institutions, and a rights-based approach to this development upon the basis of equality and participation is a constructive one. While the World Summit itself is likely to incite just the beginnings of collaboration and cooperation between the 'powers that be', it is possible that through it, global civil society and international organizations may together successfully emphasize "...the relationship between the global citizenry and the state, whereby the former is seen not as the passive object of the latter's machinations but rather as an active participant in shaping not only immediate policies but also long-term parameters of legitimacy of the state."

The private sector and governmental institutions are vital to any study of the international system, and while the roots of state-centered governance are alive and well, due attention must be directed towards those which comprise the key component of civil society.

The definition of global 'civil society', according to Lipschutz, refers to the trans-nationally organized political networks and interest groups that are largely autonomous from any one state's control. The broad array of nongovernmental organizations, clubs, societies, trade unions, and political parties that are the domestic counterparts to transnational networks, have a vital role in illustrating how new transnational networks of common interest are effectively leveraged.

They often represent the social interests of individuals and the protection of basic human rights, and are usually not motivated by profit or power. Civil society uses the same tools that commercial organisations and mass media institutions use to influence their audiences: publishing technology, mailing lists, collaboration technologies, conferencing, virtual communities, and electronic polling and surveys. Examining the resonance of such voices in global fora is vital to the appraisal of shifting power dynamics in the international system.

The emergence of an international civil society seem[s] to be taking place due to the so-labeled 'democratization' movements in Eastern Europe, Latin

America, Africa and Asia and new international communications technologies seem to be giving the promotion of these ideas more force than might have been the case 50 years previously. Overlooking the importance of this group of stakeholders risks compromising not only the richness and integrity of the 'global knowledge networks' facilitated by ICTs, but also their ultimate utility and purpose.

The consultative status of various non-governmental organizations (NGOs) at high levels in many international organizations ensures their participation in processes and institutions of global governance, and the fact that they spill across national boundaries forces a certain re-casting of general notions of political participation and citizenship.

The dependence of international bodies on NGOs is such that an absence of unhindered NGO activity in a particular country may very well mean that international attention may not be drawn to the situation in that country, even where human rights violations on the ground might merit it. This is because it is easier to focus attention and resources on those states about which information is plentiful. The practice of the accreditation and participation of civil society in UN conferences and special sessions has evolved and developed during the 1990s, when many of the major UN conferences took place.

In the Millennium Declaration and its follow up resolution, enhanced partnership and cooperation with civil society as a whole was called for to ensure its contribution to the implementation of the Declaration. "The United Nations has had a relationship with civil society since its establishment. The first NGOs were granted consultative status by the Economic and Social Council (ECOSOC) as early as in 1948; the first set of rules on this relationship was adopted in 1950 by the ECOSOC in resolution 288 B(X), and were reviewed by the General Assembly in 1968 in resolution 1296, which became the basis for establishing criteria for the participation of NGOs at the UN.

The role of NGOs in the wider processes of international 'ICT-decision making', which refers essentially to the range of technology-oriented development and policy coordination activities of key players. According to the report, the ICT policy 'universe' is categorized into three main groups, comprised of the UN family organizations (the ITU, the World Intellectual Property Organization (WIPO), the UN Educational, Scientific, and Cultural Organization (UNESCO), the United Nations Development Program (UNDP), and the UN Conference on Trade and Development (UNCTAD)), the international trade and finance organizations (the World Trade Organization (WTO), the World Bank Group (WBG)), and various private sector bodies.

The main kinds of issues upon which international decisions are made lie upon the horizontal axis, while the main types of decision-making process lie upon the vertical axis. As new governance arrangements are forged in conjunction with more traditional arrangements, partnerships are developed between various private and public entities, and the increasing role of non-governmental fora emerges strongly. NGOs are indeed among the newer players with clout in the international arena and continue to be a major reason why ICTs have emerged to challenge existing development and power paradigms.

While on the macro level there continues to be debate vis-à-vis the ultimate cost effectiveness of ICTs in development given other contending priorities, on the micro level, there appears to be near-universal acceptance of the fact that development strategies should be based on partnerships between government, the private sector, and civil society as well as the creation of human capacity. Despite 'revolutionary' notions associated with ICTs, there appears also to be a collective acceptance of the fact that governments should be the appropriate policy-makers and leading users of ICTs.

The Millennium Declaration

The Millennium Declaration was adopted by 147 Heads of State & Government members of the United Nations in September 2000, with close consultation and collaboration with the UN, the World Bank, the IMF, the OECD, and other regional experts. The Declaration sought to identify and document 48 social and economic indicators, listed by country and spanning a twenty-five year period, giving each country a profile of progress towards development and the eradication of poverty.

"The Declaration acknowledged that progress is based on sustainable economic growth, which must focus on the poor, with human rights at the center" ; indeed, social, cultural and economic rights are at the heart of its goals. The Declaration itself is structurally comprised of eight major sections, starting with 'Values and Principles', and including 'Peace, Security, and Disarmament', 'Development and Poverty Eradication', 'Protecting our Common Environment', 'Human Rights, Democracy and Good Governance', 'Protecting the Vulnerable, 'Meeting the special needs of Africa', and 'Strengthening the United Nations'.

Strategies for moving forward include the fostering of national human rights institutions, support for the practical application of a rights-based approach to development, the provision of electoral assistance to help the consolidation of new and restored democracies, and progress toward the implementation of democratic principles through institutional reform programs.

They also incorporate encouraging the continued ratification and implementation of the Convention on the Elimination of All Forms of Discrimination against Women, working to protect the rights of migrants and their families, and helping to ensure the freedom and independence of the media. A very basic critique of the Millennium Declaration touches upon the question of credibility: how much can credit can it be afforded, given that in the past 55 years and countless declarations, half the world's population continues to subsist on less than $2 per day?

The Declaration sets out to attain several specific human rights objectives, including upholding the Universal Declaration of Human Rights. And yet, of the 190 UN member states, only a few over a hundred have signed the existing protocol to the International Covenant on Civil and Political Rights. This chasm between the Declaration's espoused values and reality is a troubling one. An attempt to provide redress for these resounding doubts is the articulation of the Millennium Development Goals (MDGs).

Article 9 under Section II of the Millennium Declaration is particularly focused on strengthening international respect for the rule of law, bolstering cooperation between the UN and regional organizations, ensuring implementation of treaties in areas of human rights law (among others), and striving toward the elimination of the global drug problem and international terrorism. In each one of these areas, ICTs can and do play a vital role if national governments allow for the development of networks that enhance transparency and impose accountability on those who may seek to evade it.

Article 20 under Section III is also particularly amenable, whereby the development of partnerships between civil society and the private sector can be initiated, strengthened and confirmed via their utilization. Herein also lies the specific delineation by the United Nations of the benefits of new technologies and ICTs and the importance of their availability for all.

Articles 24 and 25, also under Section III, focus specifically on the other main areas namely the promotion of democracy, rule of law, and above all the collective agreement to uphold the Universal Declaration of Human Rights and to strengthen the capacity of all nations to implement human rights practices and principles. Also cited in this article is a crucial reference to the importance of more inclusive political processes, allowing for the participation of the citizenry, as well as the right of the public to have access to information through the workings of a free press.

While the Declaration supports the notion that globalization is a positive force, it is important to note that for each success story, there have been setbacks - in some places, mortality rates for children under-five have increased, school enrollment ratios have dropped, gender gaps in primary education have widened, and malnutrition has not been conquered. One main question that remains is whether or not measurements of progress toward the MDGs - which stem essentially from averages - actually include or bypass the poor and the disadvantaged, given the fact that much demographic data is not sufficiently disaggregated.

When this is the case - whether by region, gender, ethnic group, human development data reveals discrepancies that are not acceptable from a human rights standpoint. A key application of ICTs in this context is the way in which they can be used to elucidate the plight of those who may be overlooked - bringing their voices, their stories and their images into the realm of global networks even when they fall below the averages.

States [that] respect human rights are more likely to seek cooperation and not confrontation, tolerance and not violence, moderation and not might, peace and not war. States [that] treat their own people with fundamental respect are more likely to treat their neighbors with the same respect. From this proposition, it is clear that human rights—in practice, as in principle—can have no walls and no boundaries. Justice breaks out beyond the bounds of particular cultural traditions and territorial boundaries.

According to the "Road Map towards the implementation of the UN Millennium Declaration", all human rights - civil, political, economic, social and cultural - are universal and interdependent; they comprise the foundations of human dignity. Human rights are a central part of UN reform, which emphasizes the centrality of human rights in all activities of the system. "People throughout the world remain victims of summary executions, disappearances and torture

Accuracy on numbers is difficult to ascertain because violations take place in too many countries of the world and are rarely reported." Where there are major violations of human rights, there is also often a lack of democracy, poor governance, negligible rule of law, as well as general conflict and injustice. Pervasive poverty and broad disparities in the distribution of power also often go hand in hand with human rights violations, which include transgressions against cultural, socio-political, economical, and civil rights.

Universalism and Cultural Relativism

Over the past several decades, there has been the conflict between the two major perspectives on human rights: the universalist and the cultural relativist. The former holds that an individual is a social unit, possessing inalienable rights and driven by the pursuit of self-interest. In fact, universalism is used by many Western states to negate the validity of more 'traditional' systems of law, and posits that more 'primitive' cultures will gradually evolve to espouse the same approach to rights and law as Western cultures.

In the latter cultural relativist model, a community is the basic social unit, and concepts such as individualism, freedom of choice, and equality are relatively absent. Cultural relativists tend to believe that a traditional culture is unchangeable, and implicitly that there is no unanimity across the determination of that which represents the rights of all individuals everywhere. As an approach, it appears to be in itself a rather arbitrary idea, as cultures are rarely unified in their viewpoints on different issues. It has become evident over the past several decades how mechanisms of supranational governance and intergovernmental collaboration have facilitated progress towards a universal system of human rights.

The recent adoption of the International criminal court in June 1998 is an important step in the direction of enforcing and promoting the values agreed upon by the member nations. International organizations/committees "... are responsible for using the implementation of the international system for the protection of human rights - it is through them that it is possible to invoke a state's obligations under international law in order to obtain a formal or official response to allegations of torture and obtain some form of remedy." The International Bill of Human Rights is comprised of the Universal Declaration of Human Rights (UDHR), the International Covenant on Economic, Social and Cultural Rights (CESCR), and the International Covenant on Civil and Political Rights (CCPR).

The Commission on Human Rights - a prime example of a non-treaty mechanism/body - drafted a preliminary international bill of human rights in 1947. The Commission consists of the participation of about 3,000 delegates from 53 member and observer States and from various NGOs. Originally, the Commission on Human Rights sought an International Covenant on Human Rights (CHR) in order to vivify the Universal Declaration of Human Rights; many drafts of this document were created in the nearly two decades between 1949 and 1966.

The Universal Declaration of Human Rights

In Decemebt 10, 1948, the Universal Declaration of

Human Rights came into existence. The Declaration's thirty articles universalized global concern for a set of inalienable human rights, including the basic right to life, to safety from unfair persecution, to the freedom of thought, expression and religion, and to more culturally based rights pertaining to marriage, employment, education and shelter.

Although adoption of this Declaration was limited to the UN General Assembly and has thus been non-binding and un-enforceable, the document itself has served as a basis for the development of other regional human rights agreements, including the European Social Charter, the African Charter of Human and Peoples Rights.

Article 19 of the Universal Declaration of Human Rights (1948) is particularly important to note in understanding global human rights. It states that everyone has the right to "... hold opinions without interference and to seek, receive and impart information and ideas through any media regardless of frontiers. It was further stipulated that news personnel were to have the right to "... the widest possible access to sources and information, to travel unhampered in pursuit thereof, and to transmit copy without unreasonable, or discriminatory limitation, [and] should be guaranteed by action on the national and international plane.

Needless to say, NGOs played an important role in the development, adoption and publicizing of the UDHR, starting with the International League for the Rights of Man, one of the earliest NGOs to practice the tactic of 'shaming' of totalitarian regimes, military dictatorships and even democratic societies.

The main purpose of the International Covenant on Economic, Social and Cultural Rights (CESCR) that came into force in 1976 was to further clarify rights declared in the Universal Declaration, protecting specifically the rights of workers and families (to paid leave for working mothers, and protection of children, etc.).

Broad rights to health, to protection from discrimination and to an adequate standard of living were also a major part of this covenant, and are monitored by the Committee on Economic, Social and Cultural Rights. The International Covenant on Civil and Political Rights (CCPR) came into force on March 23, 1976, also clarifying rights stated in the UDHR, and elaborating upon new rights associated with the protection of the sanctity of life, rights protecting accused persons and criminals, mobility rights, and civil rights.

These fall into the realm of the right to be free from capital punishment, the right not to be unfairly arrested or detained, the general right to free movement, the right not to be tortured; and the freedom of thought and expression. The CCPR bounds signatory countries to the protection of their inhabitants, and is monitored by the Human Rights Committee established in 1977.

On the international level, there are a variety of predominantly non-violent means employed by the United Nations to deal with violations of human rights among member nations, the majority of which tend to fall under the category of 'sanction'. These include suspension (deferring the privileges of a member state), embargoes (limiting or halting a country's economic activity or communications flow), expulsion and force.

UN Commissions on Human Rights now takes place on the margins of formal sessions, in informal networking among governments, and between NGOs and other stakeholders.

Other UN bodies, such as UNICEF, UNIFEM, and the offices of the UN High Commissioners for Refugees and Human Rights often seek out the counsel of networks of like-minded governments, NGOs, and regional organizations such as the European Union, the OSCE, the Council of Europe, the Organization of American States, and the Organization for African Unity.

The Paris principles, which were endorsed by the Commission on Human Rights in 1992 and the General Assembly in 1993, have become a particular reference point for UN activity in the area of human rights.

More than 50 national human rights institutions have been established according to them, and nearly 40 countries have undertaken the process of adopting national plans for human rights. Up until the present, most members of the United Nations have become either participant or signatory to existing major human rights conventions. Indeed among the most important milestones in advancing human rights through the United Nations system occurred at the World Conference on Human Rights, held in Vienna, Austria, in June 1993.

Previously, NGOs played a crucial role, organizing an effective worldwide campaign to ensure their participation; along with governments, they were able to achieve a number of major breakthroughs, including winning unanimous endorsement for the creation of a UN High Commissioner for Human Rights and a declaration reaffirming the universal nature of human rights.

ICTs and Human Rights

The use of ICTs in the realm of human rights can be broken down broadly to four main realms whose level and quality of interaction - amongst themselves and with one another - has been vastly heightened as a result of the deployment of communications networks. Individuals, NGOs, national governments, and supranational institutions have all been empowered insofar as they have the means to effectively communicate their stories, agendas, laws and agreements, respectively and with maximum impact.

Indeed, the ICTs like the Internet may facilitate the networking and mobilizing functions of many NGOs working across national borders, as a countervailing force to the influence of technocratic elites and government leaders running traditional international organizations, and may be even more effective as a force for human rights, providing a global platform for opposition movements challenging autocratic regimes and military dictatorships, despite government attempts to restrict access in certain countries.

This changing dynamic has contributed in many ways to the development of a new 'diplomacy of human rights, which highlights the alleged tension between power and morality, and which supersedes the predisposition of organizations like the UN to focus 'selective morality' on certain areas of the world over others. Whereas national governments and supranational institutions have long been positioned to guide, respectively, the formation of national/international policies through various well-oiled gears of public diplomacy - individuals and civil society representatives have not.

While ICTs have contributed greatly to the enhanced transparency and accessibility of information from the 'top', particularly insofar as legal and administrative information is concerned, they have done even more to improve the administrative, organizational and management skills of the 'bottom', and thus to tip the scales of power slightly back toward an equilibrium. A wide range of governments throughout the world continue to utilize a variety of tools, including licensing, limits on access to newsprint, control over government advertising, jamming, and censorship, to inhibit independent voices.

The growth of new, Internet-based media did help facilitate public access to a wide range of information, but some governments continued to develop means to monitor e-mail and Internet use and restrict access to controversial, political, news-oriented, and human rights web sites. Other governments have chosen to prohibit Internet access or limit it to political elites. For those who subscribe to a 'technological determinist' approach, these types of examples are indeed supportive of the idea that communications technologies are fundamental drivers in the transformation of society at every level - including social interaction between institutions and individuals.

The importance of general information sharing and more transparent and accessible knowledge management systems are being emphasized through ICT coordination in the promotion of humanitarian aid. Most notably, the UN Office for Coordination of Humanitarian Affairs (OCHA), which coordinated a symposium in February 2002, has called for: information systems driven by operational needs; the development of standards of information quality; the identification and dissemination of successful technology applications; the establishment of ways to connect disparate information systems; and general improvement to preparedness, including baseline data for high-risk areas and rapid response humanitarian information centers.

The idea that ICTs can help to avoid the duplication of work and enhance the organizational efficiency of those working in the field of humanitarian aid is only just beginning to be explored. Information gathering as far as 'human rights data' is concerned is in itself a tremendous challenge, for prior to the actual sharing of information between various organizations and networks arises the question of how to quantify and represent acts of violence.

The design of information management systems that provide quantitative analysis for large-scale human rights projects for truth commissions, grassroots human rights NGOs, monitoring missions, etc. ICTs thus obviously play an instrumental role - not only in terms of spreading 'the word' about human rights violations and protection through communication networks between civil society, national and international entities - but also in terms of formulating what 'the word' is, and determining how real world incidents can be communicated to the realm of factual, accessible information and data. While there is precious little 'hard' data that effectively measures the extent to which human rights are defended/protected on a relative country-by-country level, there are proxies that can help to get a general idea of what is happening on a comparative basis.

The relationship between ICTs and the Millennium Declaration goals associated with human rights, democracy and good governance, statistical analysis was undertaken to determine whether or not a quantitatively based correlative relationship exists between the deployment of communication networks and the above-mentioned principles across 161 countries.

Several dependent variables were tested as proxies for the growth of ICTs, including the year-to-year growth of main telephone lines per 100 people, the year-to-year growth of mobile subscriptions per 100 people, and the year-to-year growth of Internet subscribers. These were run against the weighted rankings of Freedom House, which can be considered as a general proxy for measuring the likelihood of a national environment to be amenable to acceptable standards of human rights protection, given a reasonable ranking of protected civil and political liberties.

It is important in such analysis to control for GDP levels, given the strong likelihood of a positive relationship between the wealth of a country and the capacity of its population to adopt use of mobile technologies and the Internet. Year-to-year growth numbers were used in favor of absolute penetration numbers because of this same issue of high positive correlations; the extremely high correlation between absolute penetration numbers and the GDP variable lends to problems of multicollinearity in the analysis if absolute numbers are used. Running a regression analysis yielded interesting results, which were not entirely surprising.

Despite the fact that the data did not yield significant results for the impact of mobile and Internet subscriber growth on Freedom House rankings, the increasing growth of main telephone lines per 100 people - combined with controlling for higher GDP levels - did prove to reasonably explain corresponding lower Freedom House Rankings. It is crucial to bear in mind that Freedom House rankings are reversed such that lower numbers correspond to higher levels of freedom.

The Freedom House metric is derived from scores assessed relative to checklists of questions about fair elections, freely elected representatives, independent media, free businesses, corruption, etc., and objective and subjective assessments. At the end of each year, Freedom House reports a rating from 1 to 7 for every country, from the greatest freedom to the least, respectively; this scale is then inverted and normalized to 100.

The strong clustering of data points indicates a trend line that represents the strength of the relationship between interconnectivity and democracy. If one believes the contention that democracies are more conducive to the protection of the human rights of their citizens, this analysis supports the further assertion that freedom of information on the Internet likely plays a vital role in strengthening human rights. New communications technologies, especially satellite TV, now seem to serve the same purpose in international politics as they do at the domestic level. Tyrannical behavior can be exposed, dissident opinions can be aired, and public opinion can be relayed back to governments.

Impact of ICTs on Democracy

The main impact of ICTs [and the internet] on democratic life concerns [their] ability to strengthen the public sphere by expanding the information resources, channels of electronic communication, and the networking capacity for many organized interest groups, social movements, NGOs, transnational policy networks, and political parties with the technical know-how and organizational flexibility to adapt to the new medium. For those who are convinced that the ideological role of communications systems is vital to the shaping, structuring or 'framing' of domestic and international relations , examining the role of communication technologies must precede any analysis of democracy and good governance.

Indeed, rights associated with communication have often been viewed as among the primary gauges of democracies (such as 'freedom of communication' or the 'right to communicate'), amidst some broader criteria like individual civil rights, stability, and free elections with opposition parties. Further confirming the integral role of ICTs in international relations is the proposition that the democracies they help to facilitate do not war with each other; this is very nearly considered empirical law in international relations.

While ICTs are indeed touted as the tools of bottom-up empowerment and democratization that actively thwart the ability of highly centralized dictatorial governments to take form, it is important to bear in mind the contradictory danger of facilitating a "tyranny of the majority." That ICTs help to lower the 'barriers to entry' to the political marketplace is not enough of a benefit to posit an assumption that equality of representation is the default outcome.

In countries - particularly in the developing world - where the tendency toward political factionalism is high, this can provide reinforcement for a political dynamic that is not conducive to development goals and human rights agendas. Indeed, such "weak states are one of the main impediments to effective governance today, at national and international levels alike." Moreover, the capacity for ICTs to mobilize mass segments of a population and to empower all the various players of civil society should not predispose one from recognizing that the pendulum does not always swing towards democracy as a model of governance.

Nevertheless, there has been a marked increase in the emergence of democracies over the past 20 years, supported by the Commission on Human Rights' articulation of a number of elements for their promotion and consolidation - including fair and periodic elections, an independent judiciary, a transparent government and a vibrant civil society. According to Freedom House, there are more democracies in the world today, and the highest proportion of democratic states, than ever before in history.

Since 1989, the UN has received over 140 requests for electoral assistance from Member States on the legal, technical, administrative and human rights aspects of conducting democratic elections. Occasionally, as in the cases of Kosovo and East Timor, the mandate has expanded to the provision of transitional administration, with supervision of an entire political process designed to promote human rights and democratic participation.

The nature of political interaction between representatives and their constituents is particularly interesting as it changes through the empowerment of citizens with access to information at ever-decreasing costs. Increasingly, electronic communications and networks are playing an important role in facilitating information sharing.

Reduction of the opportunity costs of participation is a potential ray of hope for the concomitant reduction of the negative political implications of geographical urban-rural divides. As the number of people with the capacity to have their voices 'heard' gradually increases despite the 'digital divide', so too does the range of considerations for their representatives, who must to a certain extent re-cast themselves and find balance between their jobs as decision-makers, and their role as active proxies for public opinion.

In some ways, representatives in a democratic system risk being marginalized at the hand of new technologies, as the information for which they are 'middlemen' now easily bypasses their filters and in a sense, undermines their position as focal point for their constituencies. Many hope that the Internet can strengthen the institutions of representative democracy including parliaments and political parties, as well as providing a platform for opposition parties, protest groups, and minorities seeking to challenge authoritarian regimes.

Although the Internet does bring an added component of asymmetrical interactivity unmatched by unidirectional radio and television predecessors, assumptions of its impact on political participation must be measured carefully. Basic literacy is naturally a prerequisite for the effective usage of these technologies in the forms envisaged by theorists. Many theorists have attempted to find a working model that explains the intuitive - albeit mysterious - relationship between democracy and technology. Some have attempted to build a case for the parallel linkage between democracy and interconnectivity in Africa, attempting to prove through statistical analysis a positive and causal relationship between the two.

In 1993 in 141 countries found a strong correlation between democratization and interconnectivity, even controlling for economic development. However conclusive empirical findings supporting the claim that electronic media have contributed to democracy in Africa are undermined by the lack of good aggregated data on the subject, by stagnant literacy rates, and by the fact that private radio and television have only recently been allowed to exist in most places. Lag time may be necessary for the effects of such technologies to be manifested. In other words, the extent to which the 'liberating potential' of ICTs is unleashed is contingent upon the way governments can influence/control the content, direction and nature of information flows.

E-Government - and specifically the enhanced ability to collect and share information is revolutionizing the way we look at traditional concepts of political legitimacy, representation and ministerial accountability. According to the OECD, the key issues include the necessity of addressing the needs of the polity as a whole, of facilitating the use of e-channels by disadvantaged groups early in the implementation process, and of building trust and confidence in e-services.

While ICTs provide obvious access to information about various topics (including justice and human rights), they also touch upon crucial interfaces vis-à-vis the direct participation of voters, thereby contributing to significant changes in electoral systems digital advocacy and lobbying, and online consultation are all part and parcel of the transformations of governance shaped by ICTs.

That said, however, it is important to note that these observations are themselves not yet established facts.

An OECD study of e-governance, based on a series of interviews with information specialists, public officials and the policymaking community in eight post-industrial societies in 1996-7, presented evidence that the overall impact of the Internet has failed to increase access to policymakers, to improve the transparency of government decision-making, or to facilitate public participation in policymaking.

The digital technologies have had greater impact in the dissemination of information to senior decision-makers and policy elites. A key problem is the fact that opportunities for 'bottom up' interactivity in communicating with official government departments are far fewer than the opportunities to read 'top down' information. Government websites rarely facilitate un-moderated public feedback, for example few published public reactions to policy proposals, or used discussion forums, listservs and bulletin boards, although there have been occasional experiments with interactive formats.

There are two camps in the arena of e-governance: cyber-optimists and cyber-pessimists. Cyber-optimists are hopeful that the development of interactive services, new channels of communication, and efficiency gains from digital technologies will contribute towards the revitalization of the role of government executives in representative democracies, facilitating communications between citizen and the state.

In contrast, cyber-pessimists express doubts about the capacity of governments to adapt to the new environment effectively and with positive result insofar as the questions of access and digital divide have repercussions for political participation. Some countries have already started to draw up principles or adapt existing guidelines for discussion in the online environment, and most have started to digitize information relevant to the citizenry.

The basis of e-democracy, and thus of online public consultations, involves giving the public the chance to consult government information electronically. It is not enough to give formal permission for information to be accessed, which is why a distinction is made between access and accessibility. The former refers to the real possibility of consulting or acquiring government information electronically, while the latter refers to the ease with which one can actually make use of the possibility of consulting government information online. E-governance is taking rapid hold around the world.

Affluent postindustrial societies characteristically have the widest access to multiple forms of communication technologies, and it makes sense that such an environment is most conducive to the spread of e-governance. The United Kingdom is a good example of a country that has been very active in bringing government online. Amidst changing public perceptions and expectations of the British Parliament, and authoritative evidence indicating a decline of public participation in the political process, efforts are being made in the U.K. to leverage ICTs in order to influence public perceptions, help meet public expectations, and facilitate the inevitable transition that Members of Parliament are bound to face as new technologies proliferate amongst their constituencies.

According to a biannually released survey conducted by the American Society for Public

Administration (ASPA) and the United Nations Division for Public Economics and Public Administration (UNDPEPA), the US was ranked first for its e-government initiatives ahead of Australia, New Zealand, Singapore and Norway. In all, sixty-one member state countries scored above the mean global index of 1.62; geographically by region, North America, Europe, South America and the Middle East all registered an index above the global mean, while Asia, the Caribbean, Central America and Africa fell below the index.

Of the 190 UN member states, 169 were providing some degree of information online in 2001, although for over 25% of these countries, the content of the websites was deemed to consist of insufficient information less geared toward public participation than to pure public relations. The capacity to conduct transaction of any kind online at the national government level was available in just 17 member states in 2001.

Milton argued that free and independent press within each nation can play a fundamental role in the process of democratization by contributing towards the right of freedom of expression, thought and conscience, strengthening the sensitivity of governments to all citizens, and providing a pluralist platform of political expression for a array of groups. According to Amartya Sen's premises, such political freedoms have an intrinsic link with economic and human development, particularly in low-income countries.

The monopoly of or interference in ICTs and media for the purpose of controlling information can be a core obstacle to the realization of the needs of a democratic society, and can be perpetrated by private and state entities alike. In this regard, it lies in the obligation of states "... to guarantee or promote a climate of open and plural public debate, and to correct a situation in which these characteristics are absent or distorted." This obligation has been articulated in the international arena, confirming the right of the public to be informed and to free expression: It has been encapsulated as a basic human right in the Universal Declaration of Human Rights adopted by the UN in 1948, the European Convention on Human Rights, and the African Charter on Human and Peoples' Rights.

The European Commission of Human Rights, for example, has officially affirmed the duty of the state to protect against excessive concentration of the press, while the Committee of Ministers of the Council of Europe declared in 1982 that "states have the duty to prevent infractions against freedom of expression and information and should adopt policies designed to promote... a variety of media and pluralism in the sources of information..."

The United Nations Human Rights Committee has stated similarly that, with the development of modern mass communications media, effective measures are needed to prevent the control of these media that interfere with the right of all to express themselves freely, contrary to the guarantees contained in the International Covenant in Article 19. In many ways, the impact of ICTs in the human rights context is tempered by the same factors that determine the extent to which a free press is able to manoeuvre in those countries where abuses are prevalent.

The ability of the media to function unfettered by government fosters the creation of strong social networks, while engaging citizens in public affairs. Arguably, the extent to which there is a functioning free press is indicative of the likelihood that human rights are going to be effectively impacted through ICTs.

Out of the top sixty countries with the most 'free press' violation alerts this past year according to the International Freedom of Expression Exchange, twenty-one of them- according to Reporters Sans Frontières, have been in active violation of the human rights of journalists - indicating major challenges to be faced particularly in Asia and Africa. These are listed on the 'Impunity Blacklist', comprised of those countries in which murderers, abductors and torturers of journalists are being granted full or partial impunity by their government.

Information technology is driving nation-states toward cooperation with each other. It has created a new world monetary standard, an 'information standard', which has replaced the gold standard and the Bretton Woods agreements. There is no way for any nation to opt out of the Information Standard." The electronic global market has produced what amounts to a giant vote-counting machine that conducts a running tally on what the world thinks of a government's diplomatic, fiscal, and monetary policies. That opinion is immediately reflected in the value the market places on a country's currency.

As ICTs propagate, the power to influence is more increasingly widely distributed, and hence the tasks of governance - on both national and international levels - become progressively more complex and challenging. A wide variety of modern trends are affecting the state-centric system of governance from all angles: these include international organizations like the UN and the E.U., nationalist separatist movements, international terrorist organizations like al-Qaeda, multinational organizations like General Motors, and international NGOs like Amnesty International.

The majority of these fall squarely within the confines of the 'realist' paradigm - in part because they are statist in orientation, or because they seek the control of power in the form of land and resources. In 1988, espousing 'critical social movements'- women's movements, environmental movements, antinuclear movements, and movements struggling for human rights. These types of entities are unique because they are geared toward the "... general transformation of public consciousness, which in turn affects the parameters of legitimacy within which traditional institutions must operate."

The information revolution is profoundly threatening to existing power structures in the international system because the nature and powers of the sovereign state are being challenged in fundamental ways. The constitutions of national governments and their treaties have been challenged by the demands of increasingly well-defined ethnic and other subgroups, confrontations to traditional borders created by new information technologies, and the globalization of economies.

On the other hand, the nation state retains its power in the modern era and the main trend has been towards the growth of regional blocs, where nation-states remain the primary actors, not the emergence of a new world order that transcends states. In any case, the more information is disseminated in the direction of those who have not been privy to it in the past, the more of a challenge there will be to political 'incumbents';

escalating pressures on governments for attention to freedom and human rights causes are a case in point.

According to the U.S. State Department, some of the most successful transnational networks are those that partner with, respond to, or support government initiatives on behalf of democracy and human rights. While there is no international consensus on how best to address the questions of past human rights violations, particularly in the context of complex democratic transitions, a great deal of concrete progress has nonetheless occurred, including the establishment of International Criminal Tribunals.

Legitimacy is a cornerstone of good governance, and to a very large extent, civil society representatives like NGOs and the tools they use to heighten global awareness and public sensitivities are indispensable to the solid construction of that legitimacy. The role of violence has indeed been considered central in state-centric politics, and in the process of state formation and evolution of the state system. States are in fact the main perpetrators of human rights abuses within their own borders - with examples of genocide and ethnic extermination rife even in the last fifty years.

Since the earliest emergence of new ICTs like radio, proselytizers of all kinds, since the era of the telegraph, have evoked images of the 'welding of humanity into one composite whole..." , and the "...[revitalization] of citizen-based democracy" ; as it has turned out, radio did not eliminate the inequalities of the world, and the capacity of the Internet or other new technologies to do the same is equally dubious. While indeed the Internet does create a new digital 'public sphere' due to its disintermediated nature, whether or not it can be actually free from the control of dominant political and economic powers is a tenuous point.

Theorists like Habermas believed that the existence of such a sphere would be a stepping-stone toward a higher quality of public participation in governance provided it was characterized by equality, inclusion, rationality and transparency. Yet, can "informed interactive debate... flower independent of government or commercial control" , and actually make a difference to the predicament of those who suffer human rights abuses? Some like Leggewie simply point to the under-utilization of multi-directional communication in cyberspace in refutation of the above notion of 'informed debate', citing instead an increasing trend of centralization that renders ICTs unable to fulfill their potential to bring about true "digital participatory democracy... and tele-democracy" .

According to optimists, however, the Internet serves multiple functions for organizations fighting for human rights and democracy, including email lobbying of elected representatives, public officials, and policy elites; networking with related associations and organizations; mobilizing organizers, activists and members using action alerts, newsletters and emails; raising funds and recruiting supporters; and communicating their message to the public via the traditional news media.

The Internet is most useful for transnational advocacy networks, exemplified by diverse campaigns such as the movement against the production and sale of land mines, demonstrators critical of the WTO meeting in Seattle, environmentalists in opposition of genetically modified foods, and anti-sweatshop campaigners. Indeed, see information technologies as the "backbone of

NGO collaboration." Conducting research in this area yields a great deal of information vis-à-vis online initiatives created by aforementioned civil society stakeholders, that espouse international human rights protection and target the general development goals encapsulated in the Millennium Declaration through the application of ICTs.

ICTs have been applied in a wide variety of cases and contexts, many of which have positively contributed to the protection of human rights in a given country by raising international awareness and mobilizing public opinion accordingly. The cases of South Africa and East Timor are most notable in this context. New technologies have been instrumental in the development of networking between all kinds of inter-communal and inter-ethnic groups, who have as a result of their coordinated activities, succeeded in having a real impact on all manner of government initiatives and projects.

Positive examples abound in India, Brazil, Canada, etc. On the other hand, there have also been many cases in which these same technologies have been used to provoke violence and promote hatred amidst the struggle of various entities to maintain power in their various locales. The most authoritarian regimes pass laws, monitor and censor with the greatest fervour. And yet, nothing reconfirms the potency of ICTs better than the formalized actions taken by governments in attempt to repress them; Cases A-H reflect positive applications of ICTs in the human rights sphere, Cases J and K are examples of banning/prohibition of new technologies for the purpose of retaining control, while Case I illustrates how ICTs can actually have an extremely detrimental roles in places where democracy, governance and rule of law are not intact.

Many NGO groups, through the use of websites, camcorders, and email, convey their uncensored messages to the world in order to activate and motivate. For example, the success of many international grassroots campaigns have been contingent upon usage of the web and the collaboration of a variety of international citizens' groups as they coordinate their positions, exchange information, and alert politicians. The WTO meeting in Seattle in late November 1999 is a good example of this phenomena, bringing together an alliance between labor and environmental activists - the Turtle Teamster partnership - along with a network of consumer advocates, anti-capitalists, and grassroots movements that attracted a media 'feeding frenzy'. Groups integrated the Internet into their strategies, for example the International Civil Society website, which provided hourly updates about the major demonstrations in Seattle to a network of almost 700 NGOs in some 80 countries, including groups of human rights organizations, environmentalists, students, religious groups, and others. Other well-known examples include the anti land-mine campaign in the mid to late-1990s, the anti-globalization protests against the World Bank and IMF in Prague, against the EU meetings in Gothenberg, and the G8 in Genoa, and the widespread anti-fuel tax protests that disrupted European politics in October 2000.

A global Internet campaign was launched in London, New York and other capitals last year to amplify the cause of children's rights. The goal was to leverage the power of the Internet to gain millions of individual pledges supporting the Convention on the Rights of the Child, with pledges gathered online and offline to be delivered to world leaders.

The Bangladesh Human Rights Portal will actively promote human rights reforms within Bangladesh and across geographical, social and political boundaries, supporting marginalized communities, women and children.

Bangladesh also happens to be home to one of the key global success stories of cellular telephony access provision (GrameenPhone) to the rural poor, leveraging Bangladesh-based Grameen Bank's networks to bring ICTs to village-based micro-enterprises.

Probidad promotes democratization efforts through diverse and integrated anti-corruption initiatives, most of which rely on the use of ICTs and an extensive network of contacts. The activities are designed to monitor corruption and control mechanisms, mobilize awareness about the complexities and costs of corruption and increased interest and participation in curbing it, enhance the anti-corruption capacity of other civil society organizations, media, government, business, and researchers in our region; and contribute to more informed local and context-specific measures that undermine corruption and promote good governance.

Armenia's National Academy of Sciences has launched a new website with support from UNDP to harness information and communications technology to promote democracy. The website helps to increase public participation in governance, create new opportunities to broaden public awareness about democratic issues and establish new opportunities for interaction.

"Your Lawyer", a new CD-ROM, is making Vietnam's laws and information on citizens' rights readily accessible, spelling out in simple language how to start a business, protect land rights and get a divorce. As a first step, the Office of the National Assembly (ONA) is distributing copies of the CD-ROM to offices of delegates to the National Assembly in all 61 provinces, offices of provincial People's Councils, and media organizations.

The NGO Network Alliance Project (NNAP) aims to strengthen the use of email and Internet strategies in Zimbabwean NGOs and civil society organizations. The NNAP will make human rights and civic education information accessible to the general public from a centralized, electronic source.

Idasa's Political Information and Monitoring Service (PIMS) aims to support democracy and promote good ethical governance in South Africa through the building of government and civic capacity for democracy, in particular through training and related activities. The Monitor aims to help audience engage with democracy, intervene in the legislative process and make submissions to parliament. The PIMS Monitor also offers comprehensive, plain-language summaries of complicated documents.

"Potentially radio is a very democratic medium, which, when used in a decentralized manner may give local people and communities an opportunity to express their grievances in representative discussions. This however presupposes the establishment of decentralized structures and local and community radio stations as well as radio stations representing the views of organizations in civil society such as trade unions."

The use of ICTs in a manner exceptionally detrimental to the protection of human rights is best exemplified in the case of Country C, wherein NGO human rights organizations and UN officials asserted publicly that radio transmissions were used to incite ethnic tension and murder on a mass scale. This took place in a country wherein the inadequacies of basic information infrastructure provided a stark contrast to the highly systematic and synchronized manner in which ethnic extermination was perpetrated.

Extremists from the military, the government, and business communities were responsible in this case for the widespread use of broadcasted communications to achieve their political aims. In many ways, this case became a hallmark example of the dilemma posed to the international community vis-à-vis the rights of sovereign states under international law and justifications for radio jamming.

The networks apparently allow main authorities an unprecedented ability to conduct surveillance and to monitor the activities of human rights and democracy advocates. With more than 20 million Internet users already, this country trains brigades of police officers to fight a war against anti-governmental articles published on the Web, and passes highly repressive laws: cyber-crime is punishable by the death penalty.

Democratic Governance in Africa

In UN Conference, France and US support, democracy, human rights, and good governance as cornerstones of their policies toward Africa. Both countries have moved to orient their programs toward, and condition their aid on, concern for democracy and good governance. In addition, the French government has reorganized its Foreign Affairs Ministry to better incorporate Africa into French global policy on a par with other regions of the world. Mutual understanding of these shifts in policy would itself have provided good reason for holding the conference, but the work of private and semi-private organizations had also gone unexamined, and the efforts of a vast number of nongovernmental organizations (NGOs) were not well understood in France and the United States.

Virtually no public dialogue had occurred in the United States, for instance, to compare and assess the two countries' respective programs, nor had there been an effort to elicit in a systematic way comparative African perspectives on such programs. It was for this reason that NED sought to convene practitioners from France, the United States, and Africa, as well as representatives of NGOs working on democracy and human rights programs, for a day-and-a-half of presentations and discussion.

UN conference served to highlight general areas of interest to the French and American governments and the African, French, and American practitioners in the field of human rights and democratic governance. Broadly speaking, these broke down into two categories: The issue of U.S./French bilateral cooperation and the status of international support for human rights protection and democratization in Africa. Concerning U.S./French cooperation, participants in the conference at the governmental policy level agreed that there was a need for greater cooperation and that the two governments should work towards "a new multinational partnership." It was accepted that French and U.S. policy makers had not always seen "eye-to-eye," but that they now need to redouble their efforts to coordinate policy and actions in the areas of human rights and democracy. Some from

Africa, while welcoming heightened international interest in and support to Africa, reminded listeners that in their view American and French interests have not always been benevolent and that any new involvement must "leave behind the horse-and-rider partnership" of the past.

A concern was also expressed about post-Cold War French and U.S. rivalries being played out in trade and investment competitions without the big powers having appropriate concern for the human rights and democracy credentials of the African countries in which they are interested. One official participant involved in negotiations in the Great Lakes Region cited the recent private visit of controversial Burundi President Pierre Buyoya to Paris as an example of the negative impact these perceptions can have. He said that some African observers had assumed the visit implied French support for Buyoya even though the participant knew that the visit was private. In response to doubts about French motives in Africa in connection with these newly expressed desires for partnerships, a French official stated that "partnership" within Africa has taken on a new meaning in recent months. "Partnership may mean something today," he said, "that it could not yesterday."

Africans are now full partners in their own destiny, with incumbent responsibility as well as expectations of a full contribution to their countries' stability and development. On France's behalf, the official stated that France will not intervene in African politics and that establishing new special security relations were no longer the basis of French policy. He also cautioned that French policy will, in the future, be more closely linked to European Union cooperation policy, which will have a political rationale, character, and objective that is European.

The franc of the African Financial Community (CFA) will be linked to the Euro, which will further stabilize currency in Francophone, CFA zone countries. On the U.S. side, questions about policy on Nigeria under the brutal Abacha regime prompted a response from the U.S. government spokesperson, who said that "the process of transition in Nigeria is seriously flawed and going off the rails." Prior to any normalization of relations, the U.S. insists that all political parties must nominate their own candidates; freedom of the press must be insured; political prisoners must be released; and there must be a "level playing field" for all nongovernmental organizations (NGOs).

Although an embargo was not currently in place, the U.S. has sanctions, to include no air traffic rights, restrictions on travel, no military sales, and a decertification of Nigeria as an aid recipient. The U.S. official stated that the U.S. will increase the existing sanctions if the Nigerian government does not meet the above criteria for a democratic transition.

One of the central aspects of the UN conference, the differences in U.S. and French approaches to human rights and democracy assistance in Africa. In terms of style, several participants stated that the U.S. government tends to work through NGOs to implement assistance, whereas the French tend to work more directly with African governments and state institutions. In response, French participants stated that the main focus of organizations like the Agence de la Francophonie, which is a multigovernmental structure, is to work with NGOs and non-executive institutions like parliaments and judiciaries.

These multilateral programs include supplying publications, helping to publish newspapers and journals, and providing computers. A French Senator expressed a strong opinion that French and U.S. interests are not at the same level. The French, he said, have very important historical and personal linkages to Africa and Africans in a way that Americans normally do not, particularly through French legislators and government officials, many of whom have lived and worked for years in Africa.

This reflects, he felt, the French policy of decentralization, where village-to-village and person-to-person relations are encouraged and a history of cross cultural contact is built up. The connection, he said, was "human, not colonial." It was also pointed out that political party foundations and non-partisan private-sector foundations like NED did not exist, for the most part, in France, with the exception of the Jean-Jaures Foundation, as they do in the U.S., Great Britain, and Germany.

Participants agreed that cooperation between France and the United States and coordination with African parties, both governmental and nongovernmental, should be strengthened in the arena of human rights, democracy, and governance promotion. Participants agreed that a primary focus on human rights, democracy, and good governance is essential to the final attainment of stable societies in Africa capable of sustaining development. No hope exists for a conducive environment for trade, investment, and growth unless people feel secure.

Despite the fact that democracy is by no means guaranteed nor is yet considered a national or individual right in many African countries, participants shared a sense that democratization is "irreversible" and that the public demand for democratic rights will continue to grow. The linkage of democratization and development was also recognized. There was one point of departure among participants concerning the nature of "democratic culture" in Africa and how that has impacted on current democratization tendencies. While all agreed that an understanding of democracy was not yet ingrained or anchored in the governance of the continent as a whole, there were differing opinions as to whether this was inherent in African societies or only a product of the destructive years of colonial rule and Cold War rivalries that dissipated the continent's resources and underpinned non-democratic regimes.

While one participant argued that democratization must be a slow process due to the lack of democratic culture in Africa, others pointed out that democracy, particularly at local and village levels, far predated colonialism and had been undercut by colonial and autocratic post-colonial governments. Even illiteracy, an issue that everyone agreed posed a challenge to civic education and understanding of democratic responsibilities, was arguably a result of colonialism and the denial of full human and civil rights. There also was wide agreement that all international assistance provided for the promotion of human rights and democracy should be effected through indigenous institutions.

Capacity building and the instilling of democratic culture were marshaled as examples in support of this view. Both French and American government representatives as well as NGO and donor spokepersons agreed that Africans and African leadership had to be at the center of all donor strategies.

One widely held proposition was that the large countries, like Nigeria, have such an immense regional impact due to their economic and political hegemony that instability due to conflict or human rights violations within them tends to destabilize the entire region. Thus, for instance, democracy in Benin, according to this argument, will always be tenuous as long as Nigeria is non-democratic.

The same situation would prevail in the nine countries bordering the Democratic Republic of the Congo. Therefore, according to this view, international donor strategies should focus on the big countries first. A counter argument was made that the world should not neglect the small countries struggling in the shadows of their regional giants in their search for democratic governance.

Examples of success, no matter how small, become role models for those individuals and organizations mirroring the struggle within those brutal and autocratic giants. Those who argued for a focus on the "big" countries also believed that the big, non-democratic regimes presented major obstacles because of the need to deal with such intransigent governments. This leads to a moral dilemma as well as the wasting of resources.

The long French colonial history and the involvement of the United States in the slave trade, along with both of their roles throughout the Cold War years to support ideologically palatable regimes, led many Africans to doubt their motives and look for hidden agendas when talk of human rights support ensued.

While both U.S. and French officials responded with reference to a "new day" in African policy, discussion concerning Western commitment to African human rights and democratic governance continued. "Ambiguity" was one modifier that frequently arose in describing U.S. and French policy. Comparisons were drawn between the Western reactions to the emergence of "democratic forces" in the former Soviet states in Eastern and Central Europe and those that arose in Africa.

The African perspective was that the West does not take seriously African efforts at democracy, often citing the lack of independent media, jailed opposition leaders, or boycotted elections as proof. These leaders and media are the very ones that need assistance. The political stability that the West often seems to want as a precursor to assistance is really only the status quo in African eyes. The issue of race also arose with respect to Western commitment and democracy assistance.

The U.S. and Europe reacted slowly to human rights crises or threats to democratization efforts when the people at risk were of color. Mention was made of the woefully inadequate response to the genocide in Rwanda in 1994. Both French and American presenters, public- and private- sector, admitted mistakes but, with humility, it was believed that a new way forward must be sought in which the overall objective of democracy does not become the victim of race or economic politics.

Concerning motives, there was some criticism of the ends that were being sought by Western donors. People who promote human rights and democracy goals in Africa. Both U.S. and French officials assured the conference that this was not the case, aside from a shared interest in seeing democratic transitions succeed in Africa.

In the face of the African caution about the Westernizing effects upon their institutions, participants from the U.S. and France spoke to the universality of democratic values. Nevertheless, everyone agreed that neither systems nor methodology should be imposed from the outside. Whatever was of value from the Western experience should and would be absorbed by African democrats, but African leadership, initiative, and experience is the key to a democratic future for the continent. At least three other issues were touched upon concerning donor strategies for assisting human rights and democratization in Africa.

The first emerged in the form of a critique, both of donors and recipient African-based organizations. It came from an African participant who said that the relationships between the nongovernmental groups receiving outside support tended to be more often "vertical" than "horizontal." In other words, their ties tended to be to the international donor community and not to sister organizations doing similar work within their country or region. Whereas the outside connection was imperative, the focus should be on inter- and intra-African cooperation to have maximum impact and to create sustainable capacity in human rights and democracy arenas.

Specifically, civic education, training, elections, and infrastructural support for indigenous groups of civil society were identified as important areas. Whether such support should be given government-to-government or should flow to or through NGOs. Obviously, there was a difference in practice between the U.S. and French governments on this issue. A U.S. government spokesperson stated that 40 percent of the $85 million committed annually to Africa for democracy and governance work goes to state institutions. The remainder, presumably, is given to NGOs or "civil society." The rationale offered was that the state is necessary for development and the question is how the African state can reform itself to promote democracy.

French NGO representatives, in fact, while verifying that institutions of state were the common target of democracy assistance, believed strongly that the rule of law, to include the strengthening of judiciaries and legislatures, particularly through the Agence de la Francophonie, is essential to attaining the shared goal of democratic governance. This view met with wide agreement among American and African participants.

The following were other targets agreed upon by the UN conference for international support:

— *Civic education:* While issues such as the depth of democratic culture were debated and some objections were raised to Western models, there was universal agreement on the need for civic education.

— *Training*: There was similar agreement on the need for training to build the capacity of Africans to address their own challenges, whether through the conduct of elections, the management of nongovernmental organizations, or the restructuring of judicial codes and constitutional law.

— *Elections*: There was some difference of opinion, rather passionate on both sides, concerning the importance of elections. Some African participants considered elections of secondary importance, believing that they are often rigged and seldom reflect the popular will. They view them as too often being rubber stamps for the status quo, a reflection of autocratic regimes attempting to legitimize themselves through the election process. Criticism also focused on the use of international funding for election monitoring that seldom leads to any international response.

— *Infrastructural support*: Specific mention was made of the need to strengthen the organizations of civil society that are on the front line of human rights and democracy work in Africa. Resources are key, and these must continue to flow. Technical assistance is also very important, as is organizational development, including administration, management, accountability, expanding membership bases, fundraising, media and public relations, and the development of democratic leadership and internal decision-making. This capacity building should be the first priority of international intervention.

— *Decentralization*: Decentralization was a major theme for several participants who viewed it as possibly the best approach for encouraging African states to be responsive to the needs of citizens. A U.S. government spokesperson said decentralization had been a focus of U.S. assistance for decades. Even in the most advanced democracy, national-level government seems abstract and removed from the everyday lives of most citizens.

— *Corruption*: The growing problem of corruption as one in which the international donor community should take greater interest. The reason is twofold. First, the economic costs of the continued diversion of public funds to personal use can be serious, undermining a country's stability, much as Mobutu had done in Zaire to the point where democratization became impossible. Second, corruption undermines the legitimacy and integrity of newly democratized systems and impedes the progress of countries in transition. Public faith is lost. Unfortunately, corrupt practices are easy. African governments are highly centralized and opportunity is plentiful. There are weak institutional safeguards and ineffective legal systems.

— *Conflict Prevention/Role of the Military*: The need for peace and stability in society is essential for a democratic culture to grow and for human rights adherence to be assured. Therefore, conference participants repeatedly came back to the issue of conflict prevention and mediation as additional dimensions of democratization on which international donors should work closely with their African partners.

2

Promotion of Human Rights

The promotion of human rights and democracy has become an extremely well integrated element of European Union (EU) external relations policy, with multiple references to it at various institutional levels. The Treaties of Maastricht, Amsterdam and Nice, agreed and signed at bi-annual European Council summit meetings, have successively built on each other. Most recently, the Nice Treaty extends the objective of promoting human rights and fundamental freedoms from development co-operation to all forms of co-operation with third countries , thus covering trade and association agreements. Additionally, the EU Charter of Fundamental Rights, also officially proclaimed at the Nice European Council summit in December 2000, aims at promoting coherence between internal and external policy. The Council of Ministers and European Commission have been similarly active in this area.

The Council of Ministers' landmark Resolution of November 1991, at which the promotion of human rights and democracy was made both an objective and condition of development co-operation, has been progressively followed-up over the past decade by the introduction of human rights and democracy elements into the Council Regulations that govern the array of regional co-operation agreements that the EU retains, for example with Asia and Latin America. The new Cotonou Agreement with the now 77 African, Caribbean and Pacific (ACP) countries, the successor to the Lome Convention, includes 'good governance' as a 'fundamental and positive element', in addition to respect for human rights, democratic principles and the rule of law as essential elements of the Agreement (Art. 9). The latter essential elements were established in Lome IV (revised), but the inclusion of good governance in the Cotonou agreement was one of the most controversial aspects of the negotiations between the ACP states and the EU. The ACP objected to good governance as an 'essential element', subject to a non-execution or suspension clause.

The resultant compromise of good governance as a 'fundamental and positive element' entails linguistic contortions, with good governance becoming the subject of regular dialogue and an area for positive support, but not subject to a non-execution clause, except in 'serious cases of corruption' where significant funds provided by the Community are involved (Art. 97). A 'Joint Statement on EC Development Policy' by the Council of Ministers and the European Commission in November 2000 incorporated the promotion of human rights, democracy, the rule of law and good governance as an integral part of development co-operation, signalling an intent to concentrate resources on this sector. It was subsequently declared that this policy statement represents a "new framework for the European Commission's activities in support of human rights and democratisation". Numerous European Commission communications on development co-operation, both of a general nature and region or country specific, have incorporated discussion of the political dimension. For instance, Commission proposals for reviews of regional development co-operation agreements invariably involve an upgrading of the human rights and democracy dimension, as is evident in the case of both Latin America and Mediterranean countries, with a Communication on relations with Asia forthcoming in late 2001.

A significant element of policy implementation has been the inclusion since 1992 of human rights and democracy clauses as essential elements in agreements with 'third countries', standardised from May 1995. Such clauses are essentially a conditionality mechanism, enabling suspension of agreement in the event of perceived violations of human rights and democratic principles. The EU annual report on human rights for 2000, the second such report published by the Council, congratulates itself for the insertion of such clauses in agreements with "more than 120 countries", though 77 of these are covered by the Lome (now Cotonou) Convention. However, that a human rights and democracy clause remains outstanding in the agreement with ASEAN (the Association of Southeast Asian Nations), nor the manipulation involved by the Council and Commission in avoiding a new agreement that would require the approval of the European Parliament, with ratification unlikely precisely due to the lack of such a clause.

The forthcoming Communication on relations with Asia will be interesting in this respect. At the general level, a new policy document was released in May 2001 on 'The European Union's Role in Promoting Human rights and Democratisation in Third Countries'. Focusing on the role of Commission-managed external assistance programmes in this field, the document emphasises the current prioritisation of human rights and democracy strategies and aims "to ensure that these issues permeate all Community policies. It identifies three areas for greater effectiveness of activity:

— Promoting coherent and consistent policies both within European Community activities, and between those and other EU actions, especially the CFSP, as well as Member State activities;

— Placing a higher priority on human rights and democratisation in relations with third countries and taking a more pro-active approach , using opportunities offered by political dialogue, trade and external assistance;

— Developing a more strategic approach to the European Initiative on Democracy and Human Rights;

The Commission explicitly states that it "wants to be judged on its performance in meeting the EU's policy goals" in the area of human rights and democracy promotion.

Evaluation of democracy in European Union

There are four evaluation studies have been conducted on European Commission assistance to democracy and human rights, each evaluation restricted to a particular budget line(s) or regional programme. An initial report on positive measures to support human rights and democracy in developing countries was undertaken by the German Development Institute and published in 1995, followed by three studies concentrating on different regions. An evaluation of the PHARE and TACIS Democracy Programmes in Central and Eastern Europe was undertaken by ISA Consult and the European Institute, University of Sussex. An evaluation of the MEDA Democracy Programme (MDP) from 1996 to1998 was undertaken for the European Commission by Nadim Karkutli and Dirk Butzler. Most recently, an evaluation of 'positive actions in the field of human rights and democracy' (1995-99) in the ACP) nations was undertaken by Franklin Advisory Services.

The latter three regional evaluations are examined here, undertaking a comparative analysis that focuses on evaluation objectives, methodological approaches, and findings. Additionally, the shortcomings and limitations of the studies are identified.

Methodological approaches likewise vary, partly reflecting the differing objectives, though with some similarities, particularly between the MDP and ACP studies. The PTDP study adopts a two-stage approach to macro-level impact evaluation. The first stage involves a democracy assessment of the strengths and weaknesses of the nine countries, using a methodology developed previously by Kaldor and Vejvoda. The second stage entails an examination of programmes to assess their contribution to democratisation in each country, that is, investigating to what extent they have contributed to the strengths and addressed the weaknesses. Eight evaluation criteria were invoked, fairly traditional in character:

relevance, consistency, adequacy of procedures, cost-effectiveness, impact (both intended and unintended), sustainability, replicability, visibility. A combination of quantitative and qualitative methods was used, with statistical analysis complemented by qualitative background studies and fieldwork interviews and roundtable discussions. The methodology of the MDP study was divided into two aspects, corresponding to the two distinct objectives.

— Background studies of the six country cases were completed and priority issues of democratisation ascertained for each country, pertinent to the evaluation of the intervention strategy.

— Project evaluation was based on the logical framework approach (LFA), with each programmes logframe used to assess the relevance, efficiency, effectiveness, impact and sustainability at project level.

Fieldwork methods included questionnaires, interviews and roundtable discussions. Interestingly, reservations were expressed as to the appropriateness of the logical framework approach. It was emphasised that such political programmes have "many 'soft' components with regard to programme results, objectives and impact... very difficult to measure in terms of the logical framework". Notwithstanding the terms of reference, the study intriguingly cites support from the Commission itself, quoting the statement that 'human rights, are quite different from infrastructure construction programmes, and the evaluation and selection criteria should therefore be based on a different approach". It would appear, however, that little progress has been made in developing such an approach. In contrast, the ACP study enthusiastically adopted the logical framework "as the cornerstone of its methodology", describing it as "the most widely accepted planning tool" and a "useful quality assessment tool".

A programme logframe was also constructed in order to evaluate the positive measures as a single programme, thus enabling general conclusions to be made without relying on an aggregation of "variable individual programme results". Somewhat bewilderingly, two programme logframes were then drawn up. One is described as the 'de facto' or 'restored' framework, based on existing Regulations and other Commission documents. While the other is labelled as the 'optimal' or 'recommended' framework, "as defined by the evaluation findings".

Additionally, the role played by the country case studies in the report and what research methods were used are not clearly elucidated. One aspect common to all three studies is the relative lack of participatory methods. Participation by stakeholders and beneficiaries of assistance is not completely absent, but limited and instrumental, used more as a means of gathering information, than valued as a essential and dynamic feature of evaluation in itself. The PTDP and MDP studies both use roundtables in the country studies as a method by which to ascertain opinions, while the ACP report uses stakeholder interviews for general validation purposes. The findings of the PTDP and the MDP studies are generally positive, while the ACP evaluation is more mixed in its overall findings. The most critical comments in each report are reserved for management and procedural issues.

The overall finding is that "the PTDP has been of considerable value for the development of democracy and civil society in Central and Eastern Europe". The most significant impact is judged as its contribution to the growth of a lively NGO sector in all nine countries examined, regarded in turn as crucial to the democratisation process. It is noted that it is difficult to distinguish the impact of the PTDP from other Western democracy assistance, and that democracy assistance itself is a "comparatively minor instrument in assisting the process of democratisation". Nevertheless, it is held that such assistance has been important financially, psychologically and politically to non-governmental groups. It is believed that foreign funds have helped create "a moral community" essential to the construction of a democratic political culture.

Findings on management of the programme were more mixed, noting delays in financial disbursements and the potential adverse effect on impact. Programme management up to the selection is deemed relatively satisfactory, contracted out to the European Human Rights Foundation, but subsequent procedures for issuing contracts and making payments, in the hands of the Commission, are severely criticised for serious delays, undermining and damaging the reputation of the programme. One interesting recommendation pertains to the formalising of a participatory dimension to programme planning. It is noted that NGOs in recipient countries have helped shape priorities informally, sometimes through their Western partners, alerting the EU to new issues. It is recommended that discussion of priorities for democratisation in each country should be formalised through regular round tables, like those organised for the study, involving recipients, EU delegations and outside experts. If implemented, two outstanding issues would concern the relative weight of internal and external personnel and the question of who participates from the recipient side.

The finding concerning the intervention strategy was basically that there wasn't one: "there has been no official formulation of a particular strategy". In other words, programme selection had been reactive and application-led, thus relatively ad hoc. Yet, rather than being critical of the lack of country-based strategies, the evaluators attempt to turn this into a positive. Such a 'reactive strategy' (as generously described) is "not to be seen as being negative" as "it guarantees a bottom-up approach" and "usually the human rights and democracy organisations on the ground have the best judgement on priorities for their country".

The strengthening of civil society is again highlighted as the main positive contribution of the programme, unsurprising given that 96 percent of NGOs. Such concentration of assistance is not only noted satisfactorily, but also the 'continuation and expansion of the support to local civil society' is recommended, perceived as playing 'a crucial role' in the 'long and hard road to democratisation in the Arab World'.

Whilst the significance of civil society to democratisation is not questioned here, an almost exclusive focus on channelling support to NGOs contains an inherent danger. It disregards the importance of democratising government institutions, of supporting pro-reform elements within government, and of strengthening government-related organisations that perform 'watchdog' and accountability functions, for instance, parliament, a human rights ombudsman, the auditor general. Impact at micro level was perceived as mainly good, though variable between different types of programmes.

One exception to the positive picture, however, was the negative findings with regard to the adequacy of procedures and management. Substantial delays were common due to understaffing and overextensive procedures, viewed as not only having adverse effects on the efficiency, effectiveness and impact of programmes but also on the credibility of the EU as a donor.

Such difficulties are not presented separately but integrated into the overall conclusions on the five stated criteria, as follows. Relevance of measures is generally very good, though with qualifications that a longer-term strategy is needed to replace short-term preoccupations and that some areas are relatively neglected, for example, governance, conflict, economic, social and cultural rights.

As regards programme impact, the country studies generally note positive contributions, but it is recognised that impact is difficult to ascertain due to the attributional problems associated with single programmes as triggering a particular change, as well as the lack of specific and realistic objectives by which to assess impact. Coherence, understood as the quality of the linkages between results achieved and objectives, is perceived as particularly problematic, due to:

— Weaknesses in the logical framework, focusing again on poorly defined specific objectives, often insufficiently related to the particular country context or a particular aspect of the EU's programme, resulting in a "problematic gap between the stated immediate objectives of the programmes, and the general objectives".

— Weaknesses in programme management, with the Commission's ability to set abstract goals not matched by its ability to put these goals in practice. The authors find that poor management affects all stages of the programme cycle, from programme selection and planning, to monitoring and evaluation. It is noteworthy that, unlike the PTDP, the Commission dealt with all aspects of programme management with ACP countries, with no contracting out of parts of the programme cycle. Importantly, the study also found evidence of good programme management on the ground, underlining that problems lay principally in Brussels. This leads to recommendations for greater involvement of EU Delegations in the identification of programmes and in programming generally. Whether this would lead to greater participation by domestic actors in the development of country strategies remains an open question, apparently not one addressed in the evaluation programme. Efficiency and effectiveness are found to be difficult to assess due to the lack of specific programme objectives, as referred to above.

Again, the harshest critique is reserved for poor management at the Commission level. Management is relatively good at country level, the process of internal reform in Commission structures has led to a shift of emphasis in programming away from Delegations to specialised units in Brussels, contrary to the report's recommendations. The report concludes that this trend has led in fact to a decrease in the effectiveness and efficiency of individual programmes since late 1998. In summary, especially compared with the other two regional studies, the authors of the ACP study identify considerable problems with EC interventions in the field of democracy and human rights. Predominantly, however, these pertain to design (logframe approach) and management issues (Commission structures and division of labour), rather than more major questions such as the development of coherent democratisation strategies at country level and the respective roles of internal and external actors in this task.

Political Analysis

The importance of background studies for country evaluations, analysing the political context with regard to changes towards (or away from) democratisation, is recognised to some extent by the PTDP and MDP evaluations. The former places most emphasis on this as an essential part of its methodology for determining the extent to which programmes have contributed to democratisation in each country. However, greater use could be made of the background studies, with their function limited to evaluating one criterion out of the eight listed. The MDP study only uses the background studies for its assessment of intervention strategy, not for impact evaluation.

The most evaluations either focus on measurable programmes outputs or seek evidence of impact in terms of the contribution of donors to macro-level political change". In the reports examined here, the PTDP study attempts impact evaluation at micro and macro levels, while the MDP and ACP studies investigate impact at the micro, programme level only. Micro level evaluations are perceived by Schmitter and Brouwer as generally limited, examining "only short-term visible and intended effects, while ignoring long-term processes as well as unintended effects". Additionally, the gulf between micro level and macro level programmes political change means that lines of causality are often intangible, with Schmitter and Brouwer noting a tendency "to assume rather than to prove the impact of individual programmes on the entire process of democratisation, even in the absence of any clear causal relationship between the two", and in fact cite the PTDP evaluation as an example. Additionally, although timely evaluation is desirable, impact evaluation of programmes and programmes that have only recently been completed may be more an act of faith than certainty, especially given that democratic change is a long-term process. This applies in particular to the MDP study, where some programmes remained relatively new and ongoing.

External intervention involves a dynamic, interactive process and can have unintended side effects, with an intensification of ethnic divisions one of the greatest concerns. Less dramatically, a distorting effect on the nature of civil society can occur as some NGOs "adapt to the discourse of the donors" in order to "enjoy funding, visibility and a certain influence", developing upward linkages and accountability to donors, with downward linkages and accountability to members detrimentally affected. Of the three studies examined here, the PTDP study does fleetingly acknowledge the issue of unintended impact, yet with no evidence that such effects were seriously looked for in the country cases.

Although criticisms are made of the management of democracy and human rights assistance, ones that are common to all Commission development programmes, the findings of all three studies are generally positive in relation to the substantive issues of democracy promotion, with limited critical analysis. This would seem to be a function of evaluation studies that are contracted by donor agencies, to whom various key actors may exist in a behoven relationship. Donors determine the terms of reference and thus limit the framework of study.

Consultants may be independent in theory, but dependent on ongoing donor contracts in practice. Similarly, beneficiaries of assistance are unlikely to 'bite the hand that feeds them'. Such scenarios can contribute to a lack of critical analysis and the failure to learn more fundamental lessons about the inadequacies of democracy assistance and how it could be improved. Again, a participatory approach is posed as a more critical alternative. Thus, in sum, the consequences of such limitations are that the judgements made concerning the value of EU human rights and democracy assistance are themselves undermined by the shortcomings of the evaluation studies themselves. They have not provided reliable and adequate assessments of the performance of EU efforts in meeting its stated policy goal of promoting human rights and democracy. Thus, an alternative approach to evaluation is proposed.

Evaluating Democracy and Human Rights

In developing an alternative approach to evaluation in this field, aims are two-fold. One is to contribute to resolving the methodological difficulties and therefore provide a more accurate assessment of democracy assistance activities. The other is to learn lessons from past efforts more effectively and thus to improve future strategy, notably at country level. The methodology aims to evaluate the impact of external actors' contribution to the democratisation process in individual countries, including at the meso level, that is the thematic or partial regime level. Meso level evaluation could also contribute to comparative thematic studies, with analysis from a number of country case-studies examining different aspects of democracy promotion, for example, legislative strengthening or support for independent media. There are three main elements to the proposed methodology:

— *Political context studies:* i.e. background political analysis of the particular country context and the trends towards (or regression from) democratisation.

— A three-fold linkage between micro, meso and macro levels as an appropriate means for achieving impact evaluation.

— *A participatory approach to evaluation:* This latter proposition is the most central to the proposed methodology. Each of these three components is examined below.

Political context studies would concentrate on general democratisation trends, in both progressive and regressive directions, at the regime and partial regime levels. Partial regimes are the various sectors, as well as linkages between them, that make up the political regime as a whole. Instances of partial regimes include: electoral systems, the division of power between the executive, legislature and judiciary, civil-military relations the NGO environment and so forth.

Political context studies would also focus on the opportunities for and challenges to democratisation. Such studies would be undertaken by local academic specialists and could make use of democratic audit methodology, as well as surveys of academic literature and other sources. Political context studies are invaluable not only as essential background to the assessment of the contribution of external actors to democratic reform processes, but also for future strategic planning, indicating priority themes and emerging issues.

The impact of a programme can be assessed at three distinct levels: micro, meso and macro.

— Micro is the impact of the programme at the local level, i.e. the impact on single organisations and institutions (e.g. a specific NGO or legislature strengthened), often corresponding to the fulfilment of programme objectives, at times as stated in the programmes logical framework.

— Meso is the impact at sectoral or thematic level, e.g. the impact on civil society (rather than on a specific NGO); on the legal system (rather than on the judiciary or police); on democratic decentralisation; on women's role in politics, and so forth. The meso level is sometimes referred to as the partial regime level.

— Macro is the impact at the national level in terms of the overall political regime and its progress towards (or regression from) democratisation.

The benefits of a meso perspective are its recognition that 'even if donors provide assistance to a single NGO, this affects a large part or even the entire NGO community and the relationship between the community and the state/government'. Meso level analysis goes beyond the impact of a single examines changes that have occurred to a specific and limited set of organisations and institutions, while avoiding the more speculative leaps of faith regarding the influence of external assistance on national processes of democratisation.

Thus, given the wide gap between analysis at micro and macro levels, the meso level can act as an important linkage, enabling a more reliable assessment of the impact of external interventions generally. Evidence of micro-level outcomes and impact can contribute to pictures of meso level impact. In turn, macro level analysis can be based more credibly on impact analyses of a variety of partial regimes.

Participatory evaluation

Participatory evaluation (PE) is not a new concept, however, and its own history can be traced back at least twenty years to discussion by contributors in the volume edited by Fernandes and Tandon of participatory research and evaluation in India. More recently, UNDP have provided a useful definition and summary of PE. It "involves the stakeholders and beneficiaries of a programme in the collective examination and assessment of that programme. It is people-centred: stakeholders and beneficiaries are the key actors of the evaluation process and not the mere objects of the evaluation." Its key characteristics include:

- — drawing on local resources and capacities;
- — recognising the innate wisdom and knowledge of end-users;
- — demonstrating that end-users are creative and knowledgeable about their environment;

— ensuring that stakeholders are part of the decision-making process;

— using facilitators who act as catalysts and who assist stakeholders in asking key questions.

Although PE is not new, it has not been applied in the field of democracy and governance assistance by the European Commission or by other international donor agencies. A recent study of evaluation reports in this area found that only two reports out of sixty could be regarded as participatory. This finding is confirmed in Estrella and Gaventa's review of participatory monitoring and evaluation (PM&E). Their selection of 20 case examples to illustrate the types of programme using PM&E did not include a single one from the political aid sector. Nevertheless, it is asserted here that a participatory approach to evaluation is appropriate and beneficial in evaluating democracy and governance assistance for the following reasons:

— PE addresses some of the shortcomings of evaluations in this area;

— The process of PE is akin to the process of democratisation itself;

— The principles of PE relate closely to the principles of democracy .

These perceived advantages are examined in more detail in turn. Challenges in evaluating democracy and human rights assistance A number of problematic issues can be outlined, including some identified in the studies examined here:

— How to determine the main opportunities for and obstacles to democratic development and to assess the relevance of external actors' efforts?

— How to untangle the multiplicity of actors and factors involved in democratisation trends and to single out the contribution of external assistance?

— How to assess the impact of donor activities at micro and meso levels and to construct the linkages in order to evaluate impact at the macro level of regime change?

— How to disentangle external—internal relations and to ascertain the extent to which perceived donor success is dependent on local support, or, conversely, the extent to which donor efforts are undermined by countervailing.

— How to determine whether there have been unintended, negative effects on the democratisation process through external activities?

It is proposed here that these difficult questions can be most satisfactorily addressed and answered by the reflections and analysis of well-informed national actors, engaged in a collective process of dialogue and negotiation. The process of PE is akin to the process of democratisation itself.

There is general consensus that democratisation is essentially an internal or autochthonous process. From an actor-oriented theoretical perspective in particular, democracy is constructed and crafted (and resisted and undermined) by various coalitions of domestic actors and interest groups, inclusive of elite groups. Frequently, it is local knowledge of rapidly changing regime circumstances and the alliances between national, pro-democratic actors that are central to processes of democratic transition and consolidation. Despite the contemporary phenomena of democracy promotion from outside, there is agreement that internal actors and activities are key to democratisation, and that the contribution of external actors, while frequently not insignificant, remains marginal. Nevertheless, one problem identified with the democracy and governance assistance activities of agencies such as the European Commission is the limited involvement of recipient organisations, both government and non-government, in the design and implementation of programmes.

At worst, this can be perceived as the notion that 'donors know best'. Such ideas are underlined by the application of a standard model of democratisation and menu of democracy assistance activities, with little consideration of the particular country context. Evaluation provides an opportunity for reflection on and analysis of democracy promotion activities, as well as consideration of issues such as the degree of recipient involvement. If evaluation studies are themselves donor-focused and conducted by external consultants, then this can become an opportunity lost as the moment for critical thinking descends into mere corroboration and affirmation of donor efforts, as mainly found here. In contrast, PE not only provides that essential input of local knowledge and critical analysis, but also the very process of a participatory evaluation is akin to the process of democratisation itself.

PE entails a group of well-informed representatives of local groups who discuss the strengths and limitations of donor activities in the context of the prospects for and constraints upon sustained democratisation in the particular country context. The anticipated outcome of such negotiation and consensus-seeking is a learning process for both participants and donor organisations: past and current efforts are examined and reflected upon, objectives are revisited and future strategies determined. Knowledge is enhanced, as is the capacity to take appropriate action in pursuit of democratic change, both by internal and external actors.

EU promotion of democracy and human rights through development co-operation is high on rhetoric but low on achievement. The European Commission has stated it 'wants to be judged on its performance'. Yet, evaluation studies thus far have been limited in both the degree of critical analysis achieved and in their engagement with the methodological difficulties in this field. In order to address such shortcomings, an alternative methodology is proposed here for undertaking impact evaluations of country programmes, comprised of three main elements. Political context studies, undertaken by national academic experts, provide the background picture of movement along the democratisation continuum, both at the national regime level and at the partial regime or thematic levels, highlighting both opportunities for and constraints upon sustained democratic reform.

The addition of meso level analysis provides the 'missing link' between micro and macro level analyses, enabling more grounded and credible impact evaluations. Finally, a participatory approach entails control of the evaluation process being placed in the hands of well-informed, national actors, representative of a range of pro-democratic groups and organisations. Advantages are claimed as two-fold, with both intended to re-assert domestic control over EU assistance.

— External activities are subject to a more rigorous critique, in which the perceptions of knowledgeable domestic actors are regarded as essential to judgements on the relevance, effectiveness and impact of external activities.

— Lessons learned are based on detailed knowledge of a country's political context and the overall prospects for and constraints on democratisation. In turn, the European Commission can integrate such lessons into revised programmes, guided by internal forces and in which domestic authorship is maximised (in contrast to 'ownership' of external schemes), as appropriate to processes of democratisation.

Progress of Human Development

Human development is about people, about expanding their choices to lead lives they value. Economic growth, increased international trade and investment, technological advance all are very important. But they are means, not ends. Whether they contribute to human development in the 21st century will depend on whether they expand people's choices, whether they help create an environment for people to develop their full potential and lead productive, creative lives. Fundamental to enlarging human choices is building human capabilities: the range of things that people can do or be. The most basic capabilities for human development are leading a long and healthy life, being educated, having access to the resources needed for a decent standard of living and being able to participate in the life of one's community. A poor man who cannot afford to send his children to school, but must send them to work in the fields, is lacking in human development. So is a wealthy educated woman whose gender excludes her from voting in elections.

The share of the world's people living in extreme poverty is slowly but steadily declining, from 29% in 1990 to 23% in 1999. Primary school enrolments have risen worldwide, from 80% in 1990 to 84% in 1998. Since 1990, 800 million people have gained access to improved water supplies, and 750 million to improved sanitation. There have also been great improvements in political and civil rights: since 1980, 81 countries have taken significant steps in democratization, with 33 military regimes replaced by civilian governments. But in a globalizing world the increasing interconnectedness of nations and peoples has made the differences between them more glaring. And the richest 5% of the world's people have incomes 114 times those of the poorest 5%. Every day more than 30,000 children around the world die of preventable diseases, and nearly 14,000 people are infected with HIV/AIDS.

In Sub-Saharan Africa human development has actually regressed in recent years, and the lives of its very poor people are getting worse. The share of people living on $1 a day was about the same at the end of the 1990s -47%/as at the start. Thus, because of population growth, the number of poor people in the region has increased. And while most of the world has increased the share of children who are immunized against the leading diseases, since 1990 immunization rates in Sub-Saharan Africa have fallen below 50%. Global progress on political freedoms has also been uneven. The spread of democratization appears to have stalled, with many countries failing to consolidate and deepen the first steps towards democracy and several slipping back into authoritarianism. Some 73 countries with 42% of the world's people still do not hold free and fair elections, and 106 governments still restrict many civil and political freedoms.

In addition, conflict continues to blight the lives of millions: since 1990, 3.6 million people have died in civil wars and ethnic violence, more than 16 times the number killed in wars between states. There is growing recognition that all countries pay a price for these global injustices. And there is greater acceptance of the need for action to narrow the gap between global potential and reality and to advance global human development in its deepest sense. It then considers the Millennium Development Goals, set by the global community to monitor development along a number of dimensions. It assesses progress towards the goals, showing that many countries are on track but that many others are lagging and unlikely to achieve the goals.

Political participation and freedom are fundamental parts of human development. The world has more democratic countries and more political participation than ever, with 140 countries holding multiparty elections. Of 147 countries with data, 121 with 68% of the world's people had some or all of the elements of formal democracy in 2000. This compares with only 54 countries, with 46% of the world's people, in 1980. Since then 81 countries have taken significant steps in democratization, while 6 have regressed. Scores of authoritarian regimes have been replaced by governments more accountable to the people a real achievement for human development. But true democratization means more than elections. It requires the consolidation of democratic institutions and the strengthening of democratic practices, with democratic values and norms embedded in all parts of society.

The last two decades of the 20th century have been dubbed the 'third wave' of democratization, as dictatorial regimes fell in scores of countries. Like history's other movements for liberation, these democratic revolutions were propelled by people. In the 1980s growing pressures against the excesses of military dictatorships in Latin America caused them to topple one after another, starting with Ecuador and Peru. In Central and Eastern Europe and what is now the Commonwealth of Independent States (CIS), the fall of the Berlin Wall in 1989 was the turning point. For some countries the transition has been less dramatic, as with the move to civilian rule in the Republic of Korea and Thailand and the introduction of elections in Nepal. Perhaps most striking was the advent of full democracy in South Africa in 1994 the result of long negotiations.

Democratic reforms have been relatively modest in the Arab States, with a few cases of democratic ferment. But monarchies such as Jordan and Morocco have increased space for people's participation in the political life of the community, and Tunisia has taken steps to expand political participation. Still, the region has been slower to democratize than other parts of the world, and only 4 of 7 countries have multiparty electoral systems.

The global shift from authoritarian to democratic regimes shows up in various indicators of governance. The number of authoritarian countries fell from almost 70 in 1980 to fewer than 30 in 2000. Over the same period the number of democratic regimes doubled, from 41 to 82. The breakup of the Soviet Union contributed to the jump in country coverage. Overall, the former Soviet Union and the rest of Eastern Europe have become more democratic. General indicators do not capture the complexity of political transitions. Most attempts at democratization are fragmented, involving small steps and large, forward and back. Take Peru. In 1980, after 12 years of military rule, it shifted to a democratic regime.

Many others do not seem to be in transition to anything or have lapsed back into authoritarianism or conflict, as in the Democratic Republic of Congo, Sierra Leone and others. This has been especially common in Sub-Saharan Africa and Central Asia. In Belarus, Cameroon, Togo, Uzbekistan and elsewhere, one-party states have allowed elections but ended up permitting only limited opening for political competition. Most of these 'limited' democracies suffer from shallow political participation, where citizens have little trust in their governments and are disaffected from politics, or the countries are dominated by a single powerful party or group despite formal elections.

Measures of Participation and Political Freedom

Democratic political participation requires more than elections for governments truly democratic politics requires civil and political rights to provide the space for effective participation. Illustrating the greater importance attached to human rights worldwide, the number of countries ratifying the six main human rights conventions and covenants has increased dramatically since 1990. Upholding human rights is crucial for guaranteeing people's well-being and securing a humane and non-discriminatory society and for enabling an active and engaged citizenry. Freedoms of association and assembly, of expression and conscience, as laid out in the International Covenant on Civil and Political Rights, are fundamental to political participation. A free and active press is particularly important for the creation and consolidation of democracy. Freedom House's Freedom of the Press Index indicates levels and trends worldwide, showing that press freedom has also been increasing. In addition to civil and political rights, equitable opportunities for participation are crucial to democratic politics. But around the world, women are seriously underrepresented in domestic politics, accounting for only 14% of national parliamentarians. There is little difference between industrial and developing countries.

The stalling of democratic transitions highlights the fragility of democracies. The proliferation of conflicts, particularly internal conflicts, highlights the fragility of states. Internal conflicts today vastly outnumber wars between states. Since 1990 an estimated 220,000 people have died in wars between states compared with nearly 3.6 million in wars within states. Particularly tragic is the fact that civilians, not soldiers, are increasingly the victims of conflicts.

Civilians have accounted for more than 90% of the casualties either injured or killed in postcold war conflicts. Moreover, internal conflicts are usually fought with small weapons, and combatants use strategies that have the strongest impact on the vulnerable. Children account for half of all civilian casualties in wars, and worldwide there are an estimated 300,000 child soldiers in Sierra Leone, Sudan and elsewhere. Civil wars also have grave effects on economic growth and food production, as revealed by such human development indicators as infant mortality rates and school enrolments. Seven of the ten countries with the lowest human development indices have recently suffered major civil wars.

During Mozambique's 16-year civil war more than 40% of schools were destroyed or forced to close, and more than 40% of health centres were destroyed. Industries were so damaged that postwar production was only 20-40% of prewar capacity, with economic losses estimated at $15 billion several times Mozambique's prewar GDP. Fighting between and within states also causes massive refugee flows and displaced populations. At the end of 2000 more than 12 million people were refugees, 6 million were internally displaced and nearly 4 million were returning refugees, asylum-seekers or people otherwise of concern to the UN High Commissioner for Refugees 30 in all, 50% more than in 1990. The increase in refugees and displaced populations indicates that today's armed conflicts are more intense.

Millennium Development Goals

At the UN General Assembly in 2000, heads of state and government took stock of the gross inequalities in human development worldwide and recognized their collective responsibility to uphold the principles of human dignity, equality and equity at the global level. In addition to declaring their support for freedom, democracy and human rights, they set eight goals for development and poverty eradication, to be achieved by 2015:

— Eradicate extreme poverty and hunger.
— Achieve universal primary education.

— Achieve gender equality and empower women.
— Reduce child mortality.
— Improve maternal health.
— Combat HIV/AIDS, malaria and other diseases.
— Ensure environmental sustainability.
— Develop a global partnership for development.

Most of the Millennium Development Goals have quantifiable, monitorable targets to measure progress against standards set by the international community. How likely countries are to achieve the goals by 2015 if recent trends continue, classifying them as achieved, on track, lagging, far behind or slipping back. The analysis assumes that trends over the next decade will be the same as over the past decade. Whether countries fall behind or surpass this expectation will depend on their actions and those of the global community between now and 2015. Many countries have made progress. But much of the world, generally the poorest countries, seems unlikely to achieve the goals. Although 55 countries, with 23% of the world's people, are on track to achieve at least three-quarters of the goals, 33 countries with 26% of the world's people are failing on more than half.

Especially extraordinary efforts will be needed in Sub-Saharan Africa, where 23 countries are failing and 11 others do not have enough data to be assessed a possible indication that they are even further behind. That leaves just 10 Sub-Saharan countries on track to meet at least half of the goals. Lack of data makes it difficult to assess progress on the goal of halving income poverty. But slow growth in average incomes indicates that many countries will have to struggle to achieve the goal.

Optimistic estimates suggest that 3.7% annual growth in per capita GDP will be needed, yet in the 1990s only 24 countries achieved such growth. China and India, the most populous countries, are in this group. But incomes in nearly 130 countries, with 40% of the world's people, are not growing fast enough including 52 countries that actually had negative growth in the 1990s. Again, progress is most elusive in the poorest countries: 40 of 44 Sub-Saharan countries, with 93% of the region's people, grew too slowly. Half of those 40 countries, with more than half of the region's people, are poorer now than in 1990. These include 11 of the world's 20 poorest countries. Countries have come closer to some goals than others. Many developing countries have already achieved or are on track to achieve universal primary education and gender equity in education. Given the importance of education to so many other areas of development, this bodes well for accelerating progress towards the other goals.

Most developing countries have also achieved or are on track to achieve the targets for eradicating hunger and improving water supplies (part of the environmental goal). But more than 40 countries, with 28% of the world's people, are not on track to halve hunger by 2015. And 25 countries, with 32% of the world's people, may not halve the share of people lacking access to an improved water source. Most pressing, however, is child mortality: 85 countries with more than 60% of the world's people are not on track to achieve the goal. A goal that cannot be monitored cannot be met or missed and one of the most startling conclusions is the lack of data. The targets for poverty, HIV/AIDS and maternal mortality cannot be monitored directly with current international data. Even targets that can be monitored have many gaps in the data. Complicating matters, countries lacking data may have the worst performance, giving an inflated impression of the proportion of countries that are progressing.

Goal -1: Eradicating Extreme Poverty and Hunger

During the 1990s the number of extremely poor people dropped only slightly. But because of population growth, the share of the world's people living in extreme poverty fell from 29% in 1990 to 23% in 1999. The declining share of people in extreme poverty is hopeful, but the level remains disturbingly high. And the failure to reduce poverty in Sub-Saharan Africa, the world's poorest region, is a grave concern.

Per capita income: A country's income poverty rate is determined by its per capita income and by the distribution of that income. Though there is no guarantee that poor people will benefit from an increase in their country's average per capita income, aggregate growth typically does increase their incomes. Since the mid-1970s growth in per capita income has varied dramatically across regions.

East Asia and the Pacific's impressive poverty reduction is primarily due to a quadrupling in its per capita GDP between 1975 and 2000. But Sub-Saharan Africa ended the millennium 5% poorer than in 1990. Central and Eastern Europe and the CIS was the only other region to suffer a decline in per capita income during the 1990s. Growth in the region is picking up, and a few countries have done quite well. But in many countries incomes remain far lower than in the past.

Income inequality within countries: The amount of growth required to reduce poverty depends on a country's level of inequality the more unequal is the distribution of income, the fewer are the benefits of growth to poor people. Studies of inequality trends within countries suffer from a lack of reliable, comparable data. The limited available evidence indicates that worldwide, within-country income inequality has been increasing for the past 30 years. Among the 73 countries with data, 48 have seen inequality increase since the 1950s, 16 have experienced no change and only 9 with just 4% of the world's people have seen inequality fall. The increase in inequality has impeded poverty reduction. Given current inequality levels, most countries are not growing fast enough to meet the poverty target. Thus efforts must focus on making growth more pro-poor.

Inequalities beyond income: The human development index (HDI), when calculated for regions and for groups within countries, can provide summary information on inequalities in several aspects of human development within countries. This information can spotlight stark contrasts that in many countries have fuelled national debates and helped policy-makers assess differences in human development between regions, between rural and urban areas and between ethnic and income groups.

In South Africa in 1996 the HDI for the Northern Province was just 0.531, compared with 0.712 for Gauteng. In Guatemala in 1998 the rural HDI, at 0.536, was well below the urban HDI, at 0.672. In 1996 the HDI for 'untouchables' in Nepal, at 0.239, was almost half that for Brahmins, at 0.439.

Another way to look at the distribution of human development achievements within countries is to estimate the human poverty index (HPI). The United Republic of Tanzania and Uganda, for example, have similar HDI rankings (151 and 150), but Uganda has higher human poverty. Poverty is not just an issue for developing countries. The HPI-2, calculated for certain countries that belong to the Organisation for Economic Co-operation and Development (OECD), can be particularly revealing. Its focus on deprivations differentiates industrial countries more clearly, using such indicators as poverty rates, functional literacy and long-term unemployment. Estimated for 17 OECD countries with nearly identical HDIs the HPI-2s range from 6.8% in Sweden to 15.8% in the United States.

In 50 countries with almost 80% of the world's people, more than one-fifth of children under the age of five are underweight. That 17 of those countries are in the medium human development category underscores hunger's pervasiveness. Still, the problem is worst among the world's poorest countries.

In Sub-Saharan Africa only South Africa has less than a 10% incidence of child malnourishment. In six Sub-Saharan countries that figure is more than 40%. A rough indication of how countries are moving towards halving hunger by 2015 comes from changes in the number of malnourished people a less precise indicator of hunger than child malnutrition rates, based on national food availability and estimated distribution. In 1997-99 an estimated 815 million people were undernourished: 777 million in developing countries, 27 million in transition economies and 11 million in industrial countries.

There are some reasons for optimism. Fifty-seven countries, with half of the world's people, have halved hunger or are on track to do so by 2015. But progress is far from universal. Twenty-four countries are far behind in achieving the target. And in 15 more 6 from Sub-Saharan Africa the situation worsened in the 1990s. While the proportion of hungry people has been declining, the world's booming population means that the number of malnourished people has not been falling fast enough. During the 1990s it declined by just 6 million people a year. At this rate it would take more than 130 years to rid the world of hunger.

Goal-2: Achieving Universal Primary Education

Education is important in its own right and has strong spillover benefits to mortality rates, income and even social cohesion. Worldwide, primary enrollments have been improving, rising from 80% in 1990 to 84% in 1998. But that still means that of the 680 million children of primary school age, 113 million are not in school -97% of them in developing countries. Many countries have good prospects for achieving universal primary education. But there is little middle ground: most of those not on track to achieve the goal are far behind or have worsening primary enrollments.

Sub-Saharan Africa fares worst of the 21 countries with data, 14 are far behind the target or have deteriorating enrollments. Furthermore, 93 countries with 39% of the world's people do not have sufficient data to make a judgement. Enrolling children in primary school is only half the battle, because it is meaningful only if they complete it which requires that they and their families be able to resist the pressures of forgone income and work in the home. Of the few countries with data on primary school completion, most seem to be on track. But again the news is worse for Sub-Saharan Africa, where 6 countries are on track and 5 are far behind or slipping back and the 33 countries without data are likely to be among the poor performers.

Literacy: One of the most important outcomes of primary education is literacy. And literacy rates are slow to change, reflecting the education of previous generations of children and the history of school enrolment. Since 1975 literacy rates have increased substantially in all developing regions.

East Asia and the Pacific and Latin America and the Caribbean seem to be converging, with close to 90% adult literacy. But Sub-Saharan Africa, South Asia and Arab States, despite significant progress, are much further behind, with adult literacy rates of about 60%. In the past 25 years literacy rates in low human development countries have doubled though only to 50%.

Among OECD countries, literacy rates are often assumed to be close to 100%. But the truth is very different. The concept of functional illiteracy describes the inability to understand and use common channels of communication and information in an everyday context, from newspapers and books to pamphlets and instructions on medicine bottles. Based on this measure, in most OECD countries an incredible 10 -20% of people are functionally illiterate, with Sweden and Norway doing relatively well at 8% and 9% while Ireland, the United Kingdom and the United States have levels over 20%.

Goal 3-Achieving Gender Equality and Empowering Women

Eliminate gender disparities in primary and secondary education, preferably by 2005, and in all levels of education by 2015 : The Millennium Development Goal for gender equality in education responds to dramatic gender disparities in many parts of the world, particularly South Asia and West, Central and North Africa. In India the enrolment ratio of boys aged 6 -14 is 17 percentage points higher than that of girls the same age, in Benin 21 percentage points. Yet in many developing countries, mostly in Latin America, girls have no disadvantage or even a small advantage. Still, of the world's estimated 854 million illiterate adults, 544 million are women and of the 113 million children not in primary school, 60% are girls. The world is still a long way from achieving equal rights and opportunities between females and males. The gaps are closing in primary and, to a lesser extent, secondary enrollments: 90 countries, with more than 60% of the world's people, have achieved or are on track to achieving gender equality in primary education by 2015 and more than 80 in secondary education. Perhaps most surprising is the performance of Arab States countries generally associated with high gender inequality. All but one of those with data are on track to meet the target for primary enrollments. Again, Sub-Saharan Africa is making the least progress, but even there most countries have achieved or are on track to achieve gender equality in primary enrolment.

Education is just one aspect of human development in which there is discrimination between the sexes. Around the world, women still earn only around 75% as much as men. Domestic violence against women is common in many societies. And around the world there are an estimated 100 million 'missing' women— 50 million in India alone who would be alive but for infanticide, neglect or sex-selective abortions.

A survey in India found 10,000 cases of female infanticide a year, and a study of a clinic in Bombay found that 7,999 of 8,000 aborted foetuses were female. The gender-related development index (GDI) adjusts the HDI for inequalities in the achievements of men and women. With gender equality in human development, the GDI and the HDI would be the same. But for all countries the GDI is lower than the HDI, indicating gender inequality everywhere.

Worse outcomes for women in many aspects of human development result from the fact that their voices have less impact than men's in the decisions that shape their lives. This inequality in empowerment is partly captured by the gender empowerment measure (GEM), introduced in Human Development Report 1995 to help assess gender inequality in economic and political opportunities. This year the GEM has been estimated for 66 countries. Some observations:

— GEM values range from less than 0.300 to more than 0.800 -indicating enormous variation around the world in empowering women.

— Only 5 of the 66 countries -Denmark, Finland, Iceland, Norway and Sweden -have a GEM above 0.800, while 22 have a GEM below 0.500.

— Some developing countries outperform much richer industrial countries.

The Bahamas and Trinidad and Tobago are ahead of Italy and Japan. Barbados 's GEM is 25% higher than Greece's.

The message: high income is not a prerequisite to creating opportunities for women. Inequalities beyond gender. The Millennium Development Goals consider gender inequality in education but this is only one aspect of unfair access to schooling.

While gender gaps in education are large in some countries and nonexistent in others, wealth gaps exist the world over. Extreme examples include Senegal, where the enrolment ratio for 6 -14-year-olds from the poorest households is 52 percentage points lower than for those from the richest households, and Zambia, with a 36 point difference. Such wealth gaps perpetuate the cycle of poverty: those born poor are likely to die poor. Furthermore, in some countries (Egypt, India, Morocco, Niger, Pakistan) the gender gap in education is much larger for poor households. In India the gender gap in enrolment is only 3 percentage points in the richest households, but 34 points in the poorest.

One cause of such gaps is that in many countries, public spending on education is skewed towards the rich. In Ecuador the poorest 20% of households receive only 11% of public education spending, while the richest 20% receive 26%- more than twice as much. Even when public spending is distributed more equitably, rich parents can buy a far better education for their children at private schools. In Chile, Peru, the Philippines and Thailand private spending accounts for more than 40% of education spending. Education inequality is also a serious problem in some industrial countries. In the United States race is a significant factor: minorities have lower schooling levels and less access to high-quality schooling. Controlling for parental education and immigrant status, young African Americans perform worse in functional literacy tests than do young white Americans on average, by the equivalent of four to five years of schooling. The gap for Hispanic Americans is one and a half to two years.

Goal-4: Reducing Child Mortality

Reduce infant and under five mortality rates by two-thirds. Every year about 11 million children die of preventable causes, often for want of simple and easily provided improvements in nutrition, sanitation and maternal health and education. Some developing regions have made rapid improvements in this area -especially Arab States, where 6% of children die before age five, down from 20% in 1970. Although Latin America and the Caribbean is doing well as a whole, eight countries are far from achieving the infant mortality target. In East Asia and the Pacific 13 countries are on track but 3, including China, are far behind and in Cambodia under five mortality rates are increasing. Central and Eastern Europe and the CIS, doing badly as a whole, combines good performance from the European countries and worse performance from the more populous CIS countries. In Sub-Saharan Africa 34 of 44 countries are far behind or slipping back. Immunizations against leading diseases are a vital element in improving child survival. After soaring in the 1980s, immunizations in developing countries levelled off at about 75% in the 1990s. And in recent years the proportion of children immunized in Sub-Saharan Africa has fallen below 50%.

Child mortality has a dramatic effect on a country's life expectancy, which is part of the HDI and is an excellent indicator of a country's overall health. Between

1975 and 2000 East Asia and the Pacific increased life expectancy by about 8 years, to almost 70. South Asia, Latin America and the Caribbean and Arab States also achieved consistent increases. But high-income OECD countries are still head and shoulders above the rest, with a life expectancy of 77 years -7 years more than the next-highest region. Sub-Saharan Africa, ravaged by HIV/AIDS and conflict, saw life expectancy reverse in the 1990s from already tragically low levels. Eastern Europe and the CIS also suffered a decline, and is the only other region where life expectancy is lower now than in 1990.

Goal-5 : Improving Material Health

Reduce maternal mortality ratios by three-quarters: Every year more than 500,000 women die as a result of pregnancy and childbirth, with huge regional disparities. The situation is worst in Sub-Saharan Africa, where a woman has a 1 in 13 chance of dying in pregnancy or childbirth. Increasing the number of births attended by skilled health personnel is key to reducing maternal mortality ratios, and again there is wide variation with as few as 29% of births attended by skilled personnel in South Asia and 37% in Sub-Saharan Africa. There are not enough data on maternal mortality or births attended by skilled health personnel to assess how countries are progressing towards this important goal, indicating an urgent need for more complete, comparable data on this vital issue.

Goal -6 : Combating HIV/AIDS Malaria and other diseases

By the end of 2000 almost 22 million people had died

from AIDS, 13 million children had lost their mother or both parents to the disease and more than 40 million people were living with the HIV virus -90 % of them in developing countries, 75% in Sub-Saharan Africa. In Botswana, the most affected country, more than a third of adults have HIV/AIDS and a child born today can expect to live only 36 years about half as long as if the disease did not exist. In Burkina Faso, the 20th most affected country, 330,000 adults are living with HIV/AIDS, and life expectancy has fallen by 8 years. The toll on life expectancy is only the beginning. In Thailand one-third of AIDS affected rural families saw their incomes fall by half because the time of farmers, and those caring for them, was taken from the fields. At the same time, medical expenses shoot up.

The effect on poor households, with little or no savings to cope with such shocks, is devastating. HIV/AIDS is also a concern in the Caribbean, the region with the second highest infection rate. In Latin America 1.3 million people have HIV/AIDS. Central and Eastern Europe and the CIS has fastrising infection rates 240,000 people are now infected in Ukraine. And there are warnings that Asia is on the verge of an epidemic. In Ho Chi Minh City, Vietnam, one sex worker in five is HIV positive, up from almost none in the mid-1990s. And nearly 4 million people are now infected in India, second only to South Africa.

Without strong preventative measures, as in Thailand, the epidemic could rage out of control. There are no comparable trend data for assessing how well countries are fighting the disease. But it is clear that policies can make a difference and that contraceptive prevalence and reproductive rights for women are vital. Through preventive measures, Uganda reduced HIV rates from 14% in the early 1990s to around 8% by the end of the 1990s.

Also vital is providing treatment and care to those already affected. But at a cost of $300 per year per patient well over half the GDP per capita of Sub-Saharan Africa antiretroviral drugs that can prolong life expectancy are out of reach for the average African HIV patient.

As homes to the leading pharmaceutical companies, some industrial countries have pressured developing countries not to manufacture generic alternatives of these patented drugs. But in November 2001 the World Trade Organization ministerial conference in Doha, Qatar, adopted the Declaration on Trade-Related Intellectual Property Rights and Public Health, affirming the sovereign right of governments to protect public health. The legal status of this declaration is not yet clear, but it indicates that rulings on disputes may now favour public health.

One issue that remains uncertain is whether countries can override patents and produce generic drugs for export to other developing countries a crucial question for all developing countries with no pharmaceutical industry of their own. Goal 8, developing a global partnership for development, includes the aspiration of resolving this problem with the help of pharmaceutical companies. Whether this proves to be possible, in the wake of the Doha declaration it is clear that international law must put global public health first.

Every year there are more than 300 million cases of malaria, 90% of them in Sub-Saharan Africa. And every year 60 million people are infected with tuberculosis. Current medical technologies can prevent these diseases from being fatal, but lack of access means that tuberculosis kills 2 million people a year 66 and malaria 1 million. The poorest people typically suffer most. Without much more effective control, by 2020 nearly 1 billion people will be infected and 35 million will die from tuberculosis. In addition to its human costs, disease takes a heavy economic toll: for instance, high malaria prevalence can lower economic growth by 1% or more a year.

Work is under way to strengthen national health systems and increase international support, and there are some encouraging signs: the World Health Organization, for example, has struck a deal with the Swiss firm Novartis on the drug Coartem, an extremely effective malaria treatment. The price of this drug, which can reduce infection and fatality rates by 75%, has fallen to less than $2.50 a treatment. But this is still far more than many people can afford -and only the beginning of efforts to overcome these diseases.

Goal 7—: Ensuring Environmental Sustainability

The diversity of environmental issues across countries and regions makes it extremely difficult to set global targets, so this goal sets out general principles for achieving sustainability and reducing the human costs of environmental degradation. Integrate the principles of sustainable development into country policies and programmes and reverse the loss of environmental resources. Global warming is a universal concern and carbon dioxide emissions are one of its main causes. Such emissions have increased dramatically, to more than 6.6 billion tons in 1998, up from 5.3 billion in 1980. High-income countries generate a far higher proportion than their share of the world's population. Around the world, goods production has generally become more energy-efficient in the past few decades. But the increased volume of global production means that such improvements are far from sufficient to reduce world carbon dioxide emissions.

The ratification of international treaties can be a useful means of measuring a country's formal commitment to key environmental issues that are not globally monitorable. Deforestation, risks to endangered species and the state of the world's fisheries are broadly covered by the 1992 Convention on Biological Diversity, ratified by 168 countries. But such treaties are no guarantee of action. What is needed is detailed understanding of the situation in each country, with plans to ensure that people's enjoyment of the Earth is not at the expense of others today or in the future.

More than 250 million people living off the land are directly affected by desertification. In addition, the livelihoods of 1 billion people in more than a hundred countries are at risk. These include many of the world's poorest, most marginalized and politically powerless people. The United Nations Convention to Combat Desertification ratified by 115 countries aims to combat desertification and mitigate the effects of drought, particularly in Africa. This requires long-term integrated strategies that focus on increasing the productivity of land and on rehabilitating, conserving and sustainably managing land and water resources.

Traditional hazards such as lack of safe drinking water, sanitation and waste disposal lead to major outbreaks of diarrhoea, malaria and cholera. Modern hazards such as urban and indoor air pollution can lead to respiratory infections, while exposure to agroindustrial chemicals and waste also causes harm. The Millennium Declaration separates the goals for safe water and sanitation, using sanitation as an indicator of improving the lives of slum dwellers. In 2000,1.1 billion people lacked access to safe water, and 2.4 billion did not have access to any form of improved sanitation services. The health consequences are significant. About 4 billion cases of diarrhoea occur each year, leading to 2.2 million deaths, predominantly among children representing 15% of child deaths in developing countries. Other concerns include intestinal worms, which infect about 10% of people in the developing world, and trachoma, which has left 6 million people blind and another 500 million at risk.

Human dignity is also at stake. A survey in the Philippines found that among the reasons given for wanting latrines, rural households cited the desire for privacy, cleaner surroundings, lack of flies and lack of embarrassment ahead of health benefits. There was progress in the 1990s: 800 million more people now have access to improved water than in 1990, and 750 million more to improved sanitation. Most countries with data are on track to halving the proportion of people without access to improved water sources. But the challenge remains enormous, with 27% of the world's people living in countries that are far behind the target.

Goal 8: Developing A Global Partnership for Development

Calculating an overall estimate of the cost of achieving all the goals using less direct means is tricky because it must take into account the positive side effects of achieving success in different areas. Some consensus is being reached on a figure that takes these synergies into account -giving a rough total of $40 -60 billion a year in addition to the current $56 billion. While approximate, these numbers give an idea of what is required. When compared with current official development assistance from industrial countries, around $56 billion a year, it is clear that aid needs to double. That would amount to about 0.5% of GNP of the countries on the Development Assistance Committee (DAC) of the Organisation for Economic Co-operation and Development -substantially less than the 0.7% agreed at the UN General Assembly in 1970. The Millennium Declaration set no specific targets for aid, but if it had most OECD countries would be performing badly.

Aid has fallen substantially in recent years, but announcements in March 2002 at the UN's International Conference on Financing for Development suggest that this trend may be reversing. The Bush administration proposed increasing aid over the next three fiscal years so that from the third year onwards the United States would give an additional $5 billion a year over the current level representing a 50% increase, to about 0.15% of GNP. EU heads of state and government announced a new target of 0.39% of GNP, to be achieved by 2006, representing an additional $7 billion a year. Though short of doubling aid, and the 0.5% of GNP needed, the proposed increases are a step in the right direction. Some countries, generally smaller, have bucked the recent trend of diminishing aid. During the 1990s Ireland doubled its aid from 0.16% of GNP to 0.30%, and Luxembourg tripled its from 0.21% to 0.71%. Alternative forms of financing have become more important but fall far short of substituting for increased official aid. Though small relative to official development assistance, resources generated by non-governmental organizations (NGOs) are substantial.

The most recent move to reduce debt is the Havily Indebted Poor Countries (HIPC) initiative, launched by the World Bank and the International Monetary Fund (IMF) in 1996 to provide comprehensive debt relief to the world's poorest, most heavily indebted countries. For low human development countries, 28 of them part of the initiative, debt service fell from 5.1% of GDP in 1990 to 3.6% in 2000. But there have been calls, led by Jubilee 2000, that the relief is not enough and that too many countries desperately in need are not included. Recent new commitments by the World Bank and the IMF to deepen and broaden debt relief are positive developments.

3

Human Rights Governance in Ethnic Diversity

National democracies have classically presumed a certain degree of cultural homogeneity. Increased cultural diversity, however, is calling for new types of democratic policies, which recognize particularistic identity claims and, at the same time, strengthen social integration in the national polity. Such policies are mainly discussed under the label of "multiculturalism".

Multiculturalism is the analysis of linguistic diversity, because it challenges a core assumption of classical theories of democracy. Conceiving of rational discourse as constitutive for political legitimization in democratic societies, these theories presuppose that one language fulfils a function of social integration at the societal level. However, the assumption of linguistically mediated integration, that is of the existence of a sphere of "public discourse" or of a "community of communication", cannot easily be warranted in multilingual societies.

Language policies instructed by general principles of democratic governance have therefore to respond to the questions of how the identity of linguistic groups can be respected and how, at the same time, equal participation of each linguistic group in a shared public sphere can be guaranteed.

Multicultural language policies are most likely to succeed in the double task of respecting particular identity claims and maintaining social integration in a shared public sphere.

The most important international conventions and declarations setting standards for the protection of linguistic rights are analyzed in their capacity to provide a normative basis for the formulation of multicultural language policies. In both parts, the major argument is illustrated by an analysis of language conflicts and language policy development in the Kyrgyz Republic, a society explicitly committed to democracy, yet affected by the problematic role of linguistic diversity in the process of post-Soviet state-formation and nation-building.

A Democracy Training Project", which was launched in 1997 on the request of the Kyrgyz Government, and is organized in co-operation with the Swiss Government and the Commission for Democracy through Law of the Council of Europe.

Language and Social Integration

The conceptual and theoretical instruments available for analyzing the social consequences of linguistic diversity. An analysis of the function of language in social interaction and its role in the constitution of ethnicity, informed by the sociology of language and socio-linguistics, provides the basis for a structural explanation of language conflicts in the modern nation-state and their changing logic under conditions of globalization. The analysis of language conflicts in Kyrgyzstan serves as an example of how ethnic groups are politically mobilized along linguistic boundaries in processes of post-Soviet social transition.

In general, the social function of language is regarded as a mechanism of social integration. However, a closer analysis of language instructed by sociology of language and socio-linguistics gives a more differentiated account of the role of language in social interaction (a) and in the construction of "ethnicity"(b).

a) Sociological theories of language generally analyze language as a system of communication and as a system of representation. It is evident that social interaction between two individuals requires a shared system of communication. Analytically, it can be shown that without shared systems of communication, participants in social interaction would fail in cooperating, that is in co-ordinating their respective action plans. Although not the only one, language is the most fundamental of such systems of communication, both in an evolutionary and a psycho-developmental sense. It has been argued that the evolutionary emergence of human society is mediated by linguistic structures which allow the human organism to acquire the competence to understand the other through symbolic interaction. A similar learning process has been regarded as constitutive for the socialization and the identity-formation of individuals. Hence, the social process of reaching understanding, the co-ordination of action, and the socialization of individuals have been identified as core functions of language. It can be concluded, that it is by its *communicative function* that language contributes to social integration. The second social function of language is most prominently theorized in the sociology of knowledge. Here, language is analyzed not only as a system of communication on the level of social interaction but also as a system of representation providing a shared world-view on the level of society. Reality as it is perceived by members of a social group is considered to be the result of a social process of externalization, objectification and internalization which is mediated by systems of representations and, above all, by language. Speaking a language is to share a common reality with others. By providing a common world-view, language therefore plays a crucial role in the constitution of a group consciousness and the symbolization of collective identity. Hence, it is not only by its communicative but also by its symbolic function that language contributes to social integration. Differentiating these two functions is an important tool for analyzing the relation of language to ethnicity and its changing nature under conditions of modernization and globalization.

(b) The relation of language and ethnicity has been extensively debated in the discipline of socio-linguistics. Most generally said, language is a constitutive factor of ethnicity, in so far as it fulfils a communicative and a symbolic function at the same time. It is useful, however, to go beyond this general account by relating socio-linguistics to other theoretical approaches to "ethnicity", which have come to the fore of academic discourse in the context of post-colonial social science in the early 1970s.

There are mainly three theoretical approaches to the phenomenon of ethnicity: priomordialism, constructivism and instrumentalism. While it is only in its extreme forms that priomordialism sees ethnicity in socio-biological categories, it generally assumes social groups to be characterized by features such as territory, religion, culture, social organization or language which are considered to be objectively "given". It is true that this theory of ethnicity had a strong influence, especially in the Soviet school of ethnology. However, this approach is not tenable on methodological grounds, because it gives an ontological or essential status to collective entities, whereas social science needs to interpret and explain their emergence, their stabilization and their change over time by reconstructing ethnicity from the subjective perspective of the actor.

The constructivist approach was most prominently formulated by Fredrik Barth who views ethnic identity as the result of a complex social process in which symbolic boundaries are continuously constructed and reconstructed by the use of mythologies, an historical account of a common past or language. The instrumentalist approach to ethnicity pays more attention to the processes of political mobilization and manipulation by which social groups are constituted on the basis of ethnic attributes such as nationality, religion, race or language. Instead of regarding these two approaches as being mutually exclusive, they should be regarded as complementary; while the former focuses on the socio-*cultural* construction of ethnicity, the latter emphasizes socio-*political* (and economical) factors underlying the formation of ethnic groups. Now, both the constructivist and the instrumentalist approach to ethnicity can be related to certain strands of socio-linguistics.

In correspondence to the argument which explains ethnicity as the result of processes of symbolic boundary-making, many linguists see language as the most important symbolic vehicle for the construction of collective identity.

In empirical and applied socio-linguistics, patterns of language use in situations of linguistic diversity including mechanisms of language acquisition, causes of language maintenance, bilingualism and language shift among linguistic minorities have been studied in order to elucidate such a linguistic construction of ethnicity.

In more recent socio-linguistics, there have been attempts to focus rather on the political and, particularly, on the economic factors underlying patterns of language use and, hence, on the instrumental aspect of language. It could be shown, for instance, that deprived socio-economic status is correlated to minority language status and that this, in turn, affects individual language use.

Although these sociological and socio-linguistic approaches to ethnicity are useful in understanding the dynamics of group formation, they need to be complemented by a socio-historical analysis of the emergence of the modern nation-state. It has, in fact, only been in the context of modern state formation and nation building that ethnicity and language have become sources of political mobilization and political conflict.

Dynamics of language conflict in the modern nation-state

The specific patterns of integration in modernity can be explained by an increased functional differentiation of social subsystems. The emergence of a capitalist world system, the political system of nation-states and a universalistic legal system have been accompanied by the wider use of generalized symbolic media of communication such as money and power. As Habermas argues, this process has in many spheres of social interaction caused the substitution of language-mediated social integration by systemic integration. However, it is mainly by an analysis of changes in the pattern of social integration.

Problems of social integration in the modern nation-state have been the result of different, yet interrelated processes of social change, including the structural dynamics of bureaucratization, industrialization and legal rationalization as well as the construction of "imagined communities". The two main models for constructing modern nation-states, the civic and the ethnic model of the nation-state, have both supposed a strong degree of social cohesion on the societal level.

The political (or contractual) model of the nation-state, typically formulated in Republican political theory, assumed that in the modern nation, bonds of particularistic solidarity would be replaced by formal citizenship and a legal system founded on universalistic norms, especially on individual rights. It was supposed that social integration could be achieved by establishing a de-ethnicized public sphere in which social conflicts would be resolved democratically and by recourse to constitutional provisions. In contradistinction to this concept of a political constitution of the nation, the ethnic (or descent) model of the nation-state, related predominantly to German Romanticism, assumed that social integration in the modern nation-state was based on the shared identity of a *Volk*. State formation was therefore considered an instrument for the self-articulation of a pre-existent national community, characterized by common historical origin and destiny, shared culture, mentality and custom and, not least, a common language. The mobilizing force of this model of the nation-state is proven by the success of nationalist movements in the 19th and early 20th century.

There are several ways in which both models of the nation-state have been interwoven with the ideal of *monolinguism*. In general, monolinguism can be regarded as a component of those policies of cultural homogenization, which were caused by the states' attempts to meet functional requirements of industrialization and bureaucratization. In so far as the political promotion of a single language was aimed at guaranteeing the efficiency of public communication in a complex and differentiated society, language in the modern nation state has become reduced to its instrumental, communicative function.

At the same time, however, the construction of modern nation-states, assuming the congruency of cultural nation and political state, has also emphasized the symbolic function of language. In the *political* (or contractual) model of the nation-state, in which language was supposedly disconnected from any representation of collective identity, the inclusion of all citizens in a common polity was perceived to have as its precondition a certain linguistic unity. Thus, in the French Republic the ideal of strict monolinguism was implemented through various homogenizing policies, e.g. through administrative centralization and a uniform education, and has rendered the French language a symbol for Republican identity. The existence of regional linguistic minorities in the French territory has, therefore, deliberately been ignored.

The exclusionary impact of the ideal of monolinguism is even more obvious in the *ethnic* (or descent) model of the nation-state, since the assumption of a common cultural and linguistic heritage is one of its organizing principles.

It can be concluded that nation-building has been based on large-scale policies of homogenizing culturally and linguistically diverse populations. To assess the potential of linguistic diversity to cause ethnic conflicts, it is therefore imperative to analyze the effects of the two models of the nation-state, and their common ideal of monolinguism, on the formation of ethnic and linguistic minorities.

The dynamics of the modern nation-state have had a double effect on linguistic minority groups. On the one hand, the (re-)ethnicization of language in the ethnic model of the nation-state as well as the general ideal of national monolinguism have caused discrimination against non-dominant linguistic groups.

National governments have typically responded to the presence of linguistic minorities on their territory by language policies aimed at extinguishing the respective minority languages, be they regional languages, immigrant languages or indigenous languages. The most important instruments of such policies can be analyzed by distinguishing between "status planning" and "corpus planning".

Monolingual policies of status planning are mainly aimed at the legal establishment of an official language in the areas of media, education and political communication, whereas monolingual policies of corpus planning intend to modernize and standardize the use of the official language by codifying phonetic, semantic and grammatical aspects of the language.

On the other hand, however, the successive establishment of a legal system based on the recognition of individual rights and supportive of a de-ethnicized understanding of language has highlighted the illegitimacy of discriminating against minorities on grounds of their respective language and has provided linguistic minorities with resources for claiming legal and political recognition. As shown by historical research on language groups in Europe in the 19th and the 20th century, it is precisely this double dynamics of modern nation-building that accounts for the reconstruction of linguistic minorities as ethnic groups affirming their particular identity and claiming their recognition in the political sphere.

A socio-historical analysis of identity-construction of linguistic minorities, therefore, proves what can be generally said about any construction of ethnicity, be it founded on race, on religion, on nationality or on language: it is an inherently modern phenomenon related to structural problems of social integration in the modern nation-state. It follows that ethnic or language conflicts are not caused by the symbolic resources for identity-construction *per se* but are related to complex processes of political mobilization. As will be shown below, these dynamics are reinforced by more recent processes of globalization.

Globalization and the Reconstruction of Ethnic Identities

In the last decade, "globalization" has become a core concept in the social sciences as well as in other discourses. Referring to the experience of an increasing compression of time and space and, thus, drawing attention to large-scale social and cultural transformations, it challenges the national focus of classical social sciences. Thus, functional differentiation does not primarily occur on the level of modernizing national societies but on the level of modern world society, in which autonomous social subsystems cross national boundaries. However, it is again crucial to focus precisely on the effects of globalization for patterns of social integration and cohesion in the modern nation-state (a), in order to grasp the logic of contemporary ethnic and linguistic conflict (b).

On the one hand, it has been argued that globalization is to some extent undermining the sovereignty of the nation-state as regards its capacity to control economic, cultural and social systems.

The international flux of financial markets, the autonomous acting of transnational corporations, the world-wide dissemination of information by electronic media and increases in international migration are, in fact, seriously reducing the autonomy of the nation-state. On the other hand, however, it has been pointed out that globalization by no means diminishes the dominant structural role of the nation-state and national governments within the global political system. That the nation-state is indeed highly institutionalized in the political system is shown by the proliferation of post-colonial nation-states after World War II and the formation of successor states after the break-down of the Soviet Union.

Correspondingly, both the civic-political model of the nation-state, with its emphasis on the constitutional guarantee of individual rights and citizenship, and the ethno-cultural model of the nation-state are shaping modes of political organization and mobilization on a global scale. It seems that both trends, the institutionalization of the nation-state as dominant structural feature of the global political system and the reduction of its scope of action, account for the proliferation of ethnic groups articulating claims for recognition in the political arena. Of particular importance in this respect is that international law is increasingly imposing universalistic legal frameworks on emerging nation-states. Indigenous people, regional minorities and immigrants, formerly subjected to homogenizing policies, discrimination or genocide, have gained more autonomy over the nation-state by means of international standards which were absent during European state-formation.

In addition, the cultural dimension of globalization, that is the relativization of traditional identities, seems to provoke the reassertion and reconstruction of particular identities. The major result has been the emergence of ethno-political movements drawing on nationalism, religious or sectarian belonging, race and language as resources for the construction of particular identities and for their political mobilization. It can be concluded that globalization intensifies the above-mentioned dynamics of ethnic mobilization and eventually exacerbates the conflict between different ethnic groups over political power.

There are various forms in which globalization intensifies the construction and political articulation of ethnic identities. With regard to language groups, globalization is producing linguistic diversity on the national level by the following mechanisms. Increases in international migration have diversified the population of "old", monolingual nation-states. While the USA, Canada and Australia have had long experiences with immigrants of different linguistic backgrounds, European and East Asian states have equally become confronted with large-scale immigration induced by refugee movements, asylum seekers, permanent emigration and market-driven labor migration.

Furthermore, in the processes of post-colonial state-formation, for instance in Africa, India and the Pacific Rim, national borders were drawn without taking into account the presence or absence of social cohesion in the respective territory. It should be obvious, that each attempt at monolingual language policies in these states, which are characterized by a complex arrangement of mother tongues, languages of inter-ethnic communication and international languages, would produce conflict between linguistic groups.

One of the regions, in which the structural constraints put on social cohesion on the national level by the processes of modernization and globalization are most obvious, is Central Asia. State-formation in the newly independent Republics, which was induced by the disintegration of the Soviet Union, has been accompanied by national and ethnic revivals which are threatening the transition to democracy. It is in this context that the dynamics of ethnic conflict and its causes in nationalist monolingual language planning under conditions of linguistic diversity, such as in Kyrgyzstan, have to be understood.

As in many other post-Soviet states, language controversies have been an important dimension of political conflict in Kyrgyzstan after 1990. On the basis of the theoretical framework developed above, this section analyzes linguistic change under Soviet rule (a), in order to explain the politicization of ethnic identities in the process of post-Soviet state-formation (b). The inclusion of the Central Asian region into the Soviet Empire dramatically transformed social structures in Kyrgyzstan.

— The introduction of Soviet administrative and economical structures forced Kyrgyz nomadic tribes to change their patterns of social organization by settling in Soviet *kolkhoz* and adopting new forms of agricultural production.

— The Soviet policy of relocating entire populations was particularly effective in Kyrgyzstan, which eventually became the Soviet Republic with the highest percentage of Russians (in 1989 32% of the population) and a considerable number of Uzbeks (in 1989 13% of the population).

— The process of modernization in Kyrgyzstan was accompanied by the emergence of ethnic stratification, with the Russian fraction of the population being the politically dominant ethnic group. In addition to their political dominance, the level of education and vocational training was highest among Russians, who also participated more actively in the industrial and in the administrative sector.

— While the Kyrgyz population did not remain unaffected by rapid urbanization, it is significant that in the 1950s the majority of the urban population was Russian

The unequal inclusion of Russians and Kyrgyz in the processes of industrialization and urbanization was reflected in the language situation. To be sure, Soviet language policy did not simply impose the Russian language on the non-Russian populations. On the contrary, the Leninist ideology of "language building" was explicitly aimed at modernizing and standardizing the national and minority languages of the multi-ethnic Soviet Empire.

In the case of the Kyrgyz language, for instance, a member of the Turkic language group written in Arabic script since the islamization of the Kyrgyz tribes in the 18th century, Soviet language policy adopted several measures of corpus planning, such as the introduction first of Latin, then of Cyrillic as the standard script, the codification of the language through dictionaries and textbooks and the translation of modern Soviet vocabulary into the titular language (korenizatsiya).

But despite this concept of "language building", the Russian language eventually became dominant in Kyrgyzstan. Besides a stronger political emphasis on the dissemination of Russian as vernacular language after the Second World War and its ideological legitimization by the "Soviet people" doctrine in the 1980s, the major factor for this development was the dominance of Russian in the modernizing sectors of society. In the educational system, for instance, the use of Kyrgyz as language of instruction correlated negatively with the level of education. Figures of 1990 show, that the percentage of students receiving education in Kyrgyz was 23.4% in higher education (76.3% in Russian) and 18.0% in special secondary schools (81.1% in Russian), while it was relatively high on the level of vocational schools (49.2%) and in secondary schools (55.6%) and quite common in primary schools on the countryside.

Similarly, Kyrgyz was hardly used in the public domain, as is shown by the near absence of books, newspapers, radio and television channels in that language in the late 1980s. The dominance of the Russian language not only increased the number of bilingual speakers, it sometimes even induced an entire language shift from Kyrgyz to Russian, especially among the urban Kyrgyz intelligentsia. As a consequence of these socio-structural and linguistic developments, Russian became the vernacular language in the economic, administrative, and educational system and the major instrument of inter-ethnic communication in Kyrgyzstan

It should be emphasised that the spread of Russian in the Soviet Republics, although a concomitant to the totalitarian imposition of modern social structures, was less the result of nationalist identity politics drawing on the symbolic function of language than the effect of structural changes favoring the use of Russian as the language of wider communication. It was only during post-Soviet processes of state-formation and nation-building that the symbolic function of language has come to the fore of public debate.

Although most post-Soviet nationalist movements have their roots in the 1980s, it was primarily after the disintegration of the Soviet Union that the ethnic model of the nation-state became the dominant political ideology in many of the former Soviet Republics. Since liberation from the totalitarian system of the Soviet Union was often regarded as identical with independence from Russian domination, hostility against the Russian population was a typical feature of post-Soviet nationalism. Nationalism has, however, also caused inner-ethnic conflict among the Kyrgyz, in so far as the urban Kyrgyz, who had switched to Russian as vernacular language and lost linguistic competence in the Kyrgyz language, were denounced as traitors (*mankurts*) of Kyrgyz ethnic identity.

In both inter- and intra-ethnic conflict, language has therefore functioned as an important symbol in the construction of ethno-national identity. The re-emergence of an ethno-national Kyrgyz identity was instrumentalized by political elites in the early process of post-Soviet state-formation.

The nationalism underlying the process of state-formation in Kyrgyzstan has, in particular, been operative in language policies guided by the ideal of monolinguism and aimed at excluding the Russian population. While language legislation in the 1980s provided for official bilingualism, the 1990 Language Law nullified the official status previously given to Russian and laid out a successive transition to the exclusive use of Kyrgyz as official language. Similarly, it was agreed, in 1993, to reintroduce the Latin script, in order to restore a non-Russian national identity.

As an effect of the emergence of ethno-national movements and their instrumentalization in the process of post-Soviet state-formation, there has been a considerable emigration of Russians and other nationalities towards Europe and Russia, especially among the skilled labour force.

From 1989 to 1990, for instance, the rate of urban Russian out-migration increased by almost 40%, reaching a peak in 1993. This increase of out-migration of highly educated Russians, along with discrimination in the labour market against those who stayed, has had damaging effects on the Kyrgyz economic system.

It is less clear, however, to what extent the rise of ethno-nationalism based on the reconstruction of linguistic identity has actually induced language shifts to Kyrgyz, or whether it has solely functioned as rhetoric for the legitimisation of social exclusion in the economic and political sector.

Empirical social research on linguistic revival movements in some post-Soviet societies has shown that such inverse language shifts in the context of ethno-nationalism are conditioned by a complicated set of factors, such as the perceived prestige of the respective languages, inter-generational linguistic change and patterns of language use in the public sector. Within the analytical framework outlined above and illustrated by the Kyrgyz situation, one can highlight the core dilemma of contemporary language policies in democratic states.

On the one hand, public policies are called to respond democratically to increases in linguistic diversity and to the political claims of ethnic identity groups. On the other hand, they have to promote the institutional structures of a common public sphere in a situation in which the vacuum left by the de-legitimization of a nationalist conception of the state is threatening social integration and eventually causing ethnic conflict. It is this dilemma to which democratic governance in multilingual societies has to respond.

Policies of Multiculturalism

Social science analysis to a normative, yet context-sensitive reflection on problems of linguistic diversity, aimed at the formulation of policy-recommendations. It will be argued that adopting multiculturalism provides a democratic response to the structural dilemma of language policies outlined above. While the discussion of multiculturalism has been dominated by philosophical arguments pertaining to the balance of individual rights and collective identity, the following discussion attempts to formulate an institutional-normative justification for the adoption of multicultural language policies on the basis of international human rights standards pertaining to linguistic rights. As in the first part, the main argument is highlighted by an exemplary analysis of language policies in the Kyrgyz Republic.

Linguistic rights in international law : Early provisions concerning the status of linguistic minorities can be found in some international treaties in the 19th century and, at the end of the First World War, in the framework of the so-called minorities treaties overseen by the League of Nations and aimed at protecting national minorities in Europe.

Granting persons belonging to minorities the right to equal treatment and non-discrimination, the right to citizenship and the right to establish schools and other institutions in order to preserve their national peculiarities, these treaties obliged the state to respect and, in some cases, even to support the use of minority languages in private and public. However, it was only after the Second World War, that linguistic rights have explicitly been understood as a component of universal human rights, especially under the United Nations. Hence, there are a number of international legal standards of linguistic rights which are related predominantly to human rights principles such as equality and non-discrimination. Although the question of minority rights was originally not explicitly addressed in setting human rights standards, the UN General Assembly asked the Sub-Commission on the Prevention of Discrimination and Protection of Minorities of the Commission on Human Rights to elaborate more specific provisions on the rights of members of minorities as early as in 1948. As a result of four decades of debate, the UN General Assembly has adopted the Declaration on the Rights of Persons Belonging to National or Ethnic, Religious and Linguistic Minorities (UN Declaration) on 18 December 1992. In the following, a brief overview of major conventions and declarations pertaining to linguistic rights, especially to the rights of member of linguistic minorities will be given:

a) in order to examine in some more detail the provisions set fourth in the UN Declaration

b) Finally, the legal and political implications of such linguistic rights will be related to the social science analysis of language conflict outlined above (c).

   a) The International Bill of Human Rights, consisting of the Universal Declaration of Human Rights (UDHR), adopted and proclaimed by the UN General Assembly in Resolution 217A (III) on 10 December 1948, the International Covenant on

Economic, Social and Cultural Rights (CESCR), and the International Covenant on Civil and Political Rights (ICCPR), both adopted by the UN General Assembly on 19 December 1966, (16) commits the member states to the basic principles of equality and non-discrimination which are also prescribed in the UN Charter (Articles 1 and 55).

Whereas some other human rights, such as the freedom of expression (Article 19 UDHR and Article 19 ICCPR) and the right to an interpreter in criminal proceedings when an accused does not understand the language used in court (Article 14(3.) ICCPR), have indirect implications for linguistic rights, the rights to non-discrimination and to equal treatment directly affect the individual's linguistic rights, since they regulate state activities involving linguistic preference. The general prohibition of discrimination and unequal treatment is stated, above, all, in Paragraph 2(1.) of the UDHR which reads:

> Everyone is entitled to all the rights and freedoms set forth in this Declaration, without distinctions of any kind, such as race, colour, sex, language, religion, political or other opinion, national or social origin, property, birth or other status (General Assembly Resolution 217 A III).

This principle is restated in Articles 2(1.) and 26 of the ICCPR. Now, the right to non-discrimination and equal treatment has particular implications for members of linguistic minorities, because, given a sufficiently high number of minority language speakers, the state may legitimately be obliged to provide special institutions and mechanisms to implement the principle of non-discrimination. Thus, the UNESCO Convention Against Discrimination, adopted on 14 December 1960, recalling the principle of non-discrimination (Article 1) stipulates in Article 5(1.):

> The States Parties to this Convention agree that: [...] It is essential to recognize the right of members of national minorities to carry on their own educational activities, including the maintenance of schools and, depending on the educational policy of each State, the use of the teaching of their own language, provided however: That this right is not exercised in a manner which prevents the members of these minorities from understanding the culture and language of the community as a whole and from participating in its activities, or which prejudices national sovereignty [...] (UNTS, vol. 429: 93).

By formulating provisions of how to implement the principle of non-discrimination in the educational system, the UNESCO Convention is, in fact, the first international convention addressing expressis verbis one of the rights of members of minorities. Similarly, the International Convention on the Elimination of All Forms of Racial Discrimination, adopted by the UN General Assembly on 7 March 1966, on the basis of a broad definition of "racial discrimination" confirms the principle of non-discrimination of minorities (UNTS, vol. 660: 195). Aimed at specifying the implications of the principle of non-discrimination, these two conventions have in fact paved the way for a more refined understanding of the rights of members of minorities.

There are some early international provisions granting specific rights to members of linguistic minorities in the areas of education, media and political participation. The International Labour Organization Convention (No.107) Concerning the Protection and Integration of Indigenous and other Tribal and Semi-

Tribal Populations in Independent Countries (1957) urges in Article 23 to provide, if practicable, for education in the mother tongue and eventually for progressive transition to the national language (UNTS, vol. 328: 247). Besides the non-discrimination articles in the UNESCO Convention and in the anti-discrimination convention mentioned above, the most important article referring to minority rights has been Article 27 of the ICCPR. This article has been incorporated, with small alterations, in other international legal instruments such as in Article 30 of the Convention on the Rights of the Child, adopted by the UN General Assembly on 20 November 1989, and in several Council of Europe and CSCE documents. It reads:

> In those states in which ethnic, religious or linguistic minorities exist, persons belonging to such minorities shall not be denied the right, in community with other members of their group, to enjoy their own culture, to profess and practice their own religion, or to use their own language.

A close analysis of this article shows that it implies two requirements. Firstly, it presupposes the prohibition of discrimination on the basis of language, as covered by the international legal conventions and declarations mentioned above; secondly, it additionally obliges the state not to interfere in the affairs of linguistic minorities. The requirement that persons belonging to minorities shall not be denied the right to use their own language is, however, more ambiguous than it seems. In fact, Article 27 is neither clear on whether the state shall not only permit the private and public use of minority languages but shall also use the minority language in the conduct of its own affairs, nor on whether the state is obliged to take positive action and to promote the minority identity in order to implement this right. Most legal scholars agree, in fact, that Article 27 does not impose any requirements on the state to use a minority language in the conduct of its own affairs and that it does not oblige the state to provide facilities for the promotion of minority identities. On these grounds, it has been criticized by Skutnabb-Kangas for promoting "covert assimilation-oriented toleration" of linguistic minorities.

Both the private-public issue and the question of protection through promotion are resolved in later provisions which pay more attention to the right to cultural identity. As human rights scholar Stavenhagen has argued, notwithstanding the principles of non-discrimination and equality, the right to cultural identity requires an extension of the individualist understanding of human rights and calls for recognizing the necessity to develop more effective means of protecting the identity of minorities, since the right to cultural identity can only be enjoyed in community with others. The first comprehensive and universal standard setting international declaration acknowledging the necessity to promote minority identities and explicating the rights of members of minorities is the UN Declaration on the Rights of Persons Belonging to National or Ethnic, Religious and Linguistic Minorities.

b) The UN Declaration is based on the principles of Article 27 ICCPR, the prohibition of discrimination of minorities and the obligation to non-interference, which it reformulates in Article 2(1.) and 2(5.). (17) However, it goes beyond the principles of non-discrimination and equality by obliging the state to pro-actively protect and promote the identity of minorities. As a programmatic provision, the UN Declaration states in Article 1(1.):

> States shall protect the existence and the national or ethnic, cultural, religious and linguistic identity of minorities within their respective territories, and shall encourage conditions for the promotion of that identity (UN General Assembly Resolution 47/135).

The formulation of this provision is sufficiently broad to allow for context-specific specifications regarding the implementation of the obligation to promote the identity of minorities. As suggested by Article 4(2.), the programmatic provision rests on the conviction that it is through the promotion of the collective identity of minorities that the principles of non-discrimination and equality of individuals are safeguarded.

States shall take measures to create favourable conditions to enable persons belonging to minorities to express their characteristics and to develop their culture, language, religion, traditions and customs, except where specific practices are in violation of national law and contrary to international standards.

This provision would, for instance, oblige the State to prohibit acts of intolerance demeaning a minority language and its speakers as well as to enforce this prohibition by legislation. As suggested in de Varennes' legal analysis, the UN Declaration implies obligations and recommendations for both private and public language use of a minority language.

The UN Declaration unambiguously obliges the State to allow private language use in private, in public and in collective action. It is obvious that it would violate the principle of non-discrimination to prohibit the use of a minority language in private, such as for example in the private choice of names and their script.

Moreover, the State must not prevent the prohibit use of a minority language in situations where the public is affected, especially in private media including books, newspapers, radio or television. Finally, the State, while not obliged to financial support, must not prevent the use of a minority language in collective action, such as maintaining associations and establishing private schools where the minority language is the language of instruction. The UN Declaration also refers to public use of a minority language. With regard to education, for instance, it provides in Article 4(3.) and 4(4.):

> (3.) States should take appropriate measures so that, wherever possible, persons belonging to minorities have adequate opportunities to learn their mother tongue or to have instruction in their mother tongue.
> (4.) States should, where appropriate, take measures in the field of education, in order to encourage the knowledge of the history, traditions, language and culture of the minorities existing within their territory. Persons belonging to minorities should have adequate opportunities to gain knowledge of the society as a whole.

Although formulated as less binding than the other articles, these provisions are aimed at promoting the identity of linguistic minorities through education and at furthering mutual understanding of majority and minorities. The desirability of support for minority language education and for inter-culturalism in education, as formulated in the UN Declaration, confirms that an inclusive approach to the presence of minorities in States has been adopted in international law.

The concern for the promotion of the identity of minorities as expressed in the UN Declaration is reformulated in other recent international human rights provisions, such as paragraph 19 of the Vienna Declaration and Programme of Action, adopted by the World Conference on Human Rights on 25 June 1993, in which it is stressed that through the provisions as set fourth in the UN Declaration, the fundamental principles of non-discrimination and equality are to be implemented (UN Doc. A/CONF.157/24). On the European level, a similar understanding of linguistic rights has emerged during the past decades. Thus, the Council of Europe has adopted the European Charter for Regional or Minority Languages on 2 December 1992 which, among other objectives, stresses the values of interculturalism and multilingualism and calls for the protection and promotion of regional or minority languages (Article 7). It commits the member states to eliminate discrimination in the areas of jurisdiction, public services, economic and life. It specifies that states should make available pre-school, primary, secondary, vocational, university and continuing education in the regional or minority language within their respective territories (Article 8), and that they should facilitate the creation and maintenance of media in the minority language (Article 11). Similarly, the Document of the Copenhagen Meeting on the Human Dimension of the Conference for Security and Cooperation in Europe, adopted 29 June 1990, urges the member States to both protect and promote the linguistic identity of minorities on their respective territory on the basis of the principles of non-discrimination and equality, and it specifies a variety of mechanisms to attain this goal (Articles 31, 32, 33, 34, 35).

c) Analyzing the progression of linguistic rights provisions from assimilation-oriented toleration to explicit promotion of linguistic minorities finally calls for addressing the question, how preservation and promotion of the identity of linguistic minorities is co-ordinated with the functioning of the public sphere. At the outset, it should be emphasized that most legal scholars agree on an individualistic understanding of linguistic rights. The protection and promotion of linguistic minorities are seen as an instrument of implementing the individual rights to non-discrimination, equality and cultural identity. This interpretation is supported by the very definition of "minorities" in international law which sees auto-categorization and the subjective intention to safeguard a particular identity, besides the numerical factor, as constitutive factors of a "minority". This definition of a "minority" is well in line with the social science approach to "ethnicity" emphasizing the subjective perspective of the actor. Now, conceptual co-ordination of the promotion of minority identities with the functioning of the shared public sphere can be achieved by using the distinction between different domains of society as developed by human rights scholar Asbjørn Eide. While the promotion of minority identities can be located in what Eide has called "separate domain", there is a necessity to ensure social integration in a "common domain", although the principles of non-discrimination and equality have to be acknowledged therein. It would be the task of constitutional provisions and public policies on the national level to find context-sensitive ways of combining these two domains by multilevel mechanisms of power-sharing, in order to achieve "pluralism in togetherness".

At this point, the analysis of international human rights standards converges with the social science analysis which has shown that in the "common domain", that is in the economic and the political sector, symbols of collective identity are increasingly de-ethnicized and substituted by generalized media of communication, while they are proliferating in the "separate domain", that is in the sphere of particular identity groups.

While in the former, language is reduced to its instrumental function, it maintains a symbolic function in the latter. Both analyses therefore suggest that complex models of power-sharing and political participation are best-equipped to maintain peace and stability among ethnic groups and thus to respond democratically to the dilemma of social integration under conditions of globalization. The most prominent of such models is multiculturalism.

Multiculturalism: Democratic Language Policies

The term "multiculturalism", as it is used in public debate, comprises mainly three different meanings. In its demographic-descriptive meaning it refers to the fact of cultural or ethnic diversity, in its ideological-normative sense it applies to philosophical arguments underlining the legitimacy of claims to the recognition of particular identity groups, and in its programmatic-political sense it pertains to policies designed to respond to the problems posed by diversity. In the following, multiculturalism is understood in its third meaning, that is as a set of programs and policy initiatives addressing ethnic and, in particular, linguistic diversity (a). As a policy strategy, multiculturalism can and should be subjected to an empirical evaluation regarding its success in managing ethnic conflict. Hence, some examples of multicultural policies, their potential and their problems will be given (b).

a) Adopting multiculturalism as a policy strategy is an integral part of developing new forms of democratic governance which respond to the structural dilemma of integration in the nation-state. The concept of "governance" has come to the fore of political debate in the international community since the late 1980s and has been used by representatives of different ideological convictions for a variety of purposes. It is generally associated with the shift of power from the public to the private sector, with the strengthening of civil society, and with institutional reforms within the public sector. It has particularly attracted the interest of policy-makers involved in the management of social reconstruction in post-communist states. If used in the context of theories of financial and economic restructuring, the concept of governance often supports trends of marketization and privatization which in fact diminish democratic representation and participation in a common polity. In contradistinction to those ideologies of mere economic liberalization, recent political theory has emphasized that democracy presupposes the existence of civil society as an autonomous sector, separate from both the administrative and the economic system, and characterized by a pluralism of actors, voluntary civic associations, and interest groups. The functioning of civil society, in turn, requires a pluralistic public sphere in which citizens are actively involved, and it also implies the commitment of all individuals and groups to shared principles of the constitution. Although it does imply a certain shrinking of the administrative state, democratic governance does therefore not imply a shrinking of the public domain. As regards the

> problem of ethnic and cultural diversity, multiculturalism can be inscribed into the framework of democratic governance, in so far as it recognizes the claims of ethnic or cultural identity groups in a pluralistic civil society, promotes intercultural communication and therefore provides a model of social integration on the basis of a collectively acknowledged constitution.

The characteristics of multiculturalism in the area of language planning can be highlighted by contrasting it with other models of language policy. Drawing on typologies developed in legal and policy analysis, one can roughly discern three ideal types of language policies: assimilationist, differentialist and multicultural language policy models. The assimilationist model of language policy is guided by the ideal of monolinguism, as described above, and is aimed at the linguistic homogenization of society.

Although linguistic minorities might be tolerated and members of linguistic minorities be granted the right to equal treatment, assimilation-oriented policy strategies discourage the maintenance of the non-official minority language, for instance by educational policies fostering monolingual instruction in public schools in the official language. Whilst the differentialist (or exclusionist) model of language policies is equally guided by the ideal of monolinguism, it systematically excludes linguistic minorities. In some moderate cases, it allows linguistic minorities to build parallel institutions, such as schools, private media, associations in their own language.

By marginalizing the parallel institutions of linguistic minorities, however, the differentialist model intends to restrict the participation of persons belonging to those minorities in mainstream institutions of society. The multicultural (or pluralist) model of language policies aimed at political power-sharing and an equal participation of linguistic minorities in the public sphere, has two subtypes. The regional variant of multiculturalism, mainly instructed by Lijphart's concept of consociational democracy, intends to achieve non-discrimination, to guarantee equality treatment and to promote the identity of linguistic minorities by territorial subdivision, federalism and multilevel arrangements of political representation.

The socio-cultural variant of multiculturalism protects and promotes the identity of linguistic minorities allowing and encouraging the creation of parallel institutions (schools, media, civic associations), which are granted equal status in the public sphere. To provide for a functioning communication in the public sphere, it particularly promotes bi- or multilingualism in education and media. Both, the regional and the socio-cultural variant of multiculturalism are principally well-equipped to implement the human rights principles of non-discrimination and equal treatment as well to promote the identities of linguistic minorities.

b) In addition to the normative justification of multicultural language policies by human rights standards, the preferential option for such policies also requires an assessment of their empirical impact. Such an empirical analysis of existing multicultural language policies in Australia, Canada and the European Union demonstrates that, although historical traditions and local conditions might call for a combination of different types of language policies, the socio-cultural variant of multiculturalism

> has the greatest potential for a peaceful management of ethnic conflict rooted in linguistic diversity. However, it equally shows that ignoring the instrumental relevance of link languages or languages of wider communication actually disadvantages minority groups, most notably in the economic and political sector but also in civil society.

The regional variant of multicultural language policies has a long tradition in Switzerland and Belgium, countries which have often been considered ideal models of consociational democracy. The Swiss constitution, for instance, declaring French, German and Italian as both national and official languages and Rheto-Romansh as national language, has established a regime of cantonal sovereignty, according to which each linguistic group has control over public schools, public media and so forth in their respective cantons, while non-discrimination clauses accommodate for the respect of individual linguistic rights within the canton.

On the national level, institutional arrangements are provided to ensure equal representation and participation of the main linguistic groups in legislation, jurisdiction and administration. However, the empirical limitations of the Swiss model of power-sharing between linguistic groups have not gone without notice. Legally, the regional model with its focus on the principle of territoriality does not resolve the problem of reconciling individual linguistic rights with the promotion of the identity of linguistic minorities.

Moreover, this model often reinforces economic and political inequality, because it does not take into account the inferior status of minority languages such as Italian in Switzerland. Finally, it aggravates mutual ignorance between linguistic groups, because it lacks mechanisms such as multilingual education which would strengthen social cohesion on the national level. In Belgium, where a similar model of regional power-sharing has evolved, the public discussion of these limitations has resulted in a constitutional reform, in which the principle of territoriality has been complemented by the principle of linguistic self-determination. Hence, both the three Regions and the three Communities enjoy autonomous status and are co-ordinated by a highly complex institutional arrangement. The controversies over the Swiss and the Belgium model of consociationalism show that urbanization, increased mobility and economic interdependency seriously limit the empirical effectiveness of the regional variant of multicultural language policies to implement linguistic rights.

Similar limitations of multicultural language policies adopting a regional approach can be discerned in the process of European integration. Within the framework of the EC and the EU, the preservation of linguistic diversity has mainly been understood as a political goal on the supra-national level, leaving unaffected the ideal of national monolinguism.

Since the early 1990s, however, accelerated European integration has given rise to a new concern for regional or linguistic minorities, to sharp criticism of the ideal of national monolinguism, and to the promotion of multicultural language policies on the national and sub-national level. This has, for instance, led to the adoption of the European Charter for Regional or Minority Languages by the Council of Europe. Based on the principle of territoriality, however, the Charter only supports the regional variant of multicultural language policies, while it explicitly excludes the linguistic rights of immigrants. The exclusion of immigrant languages from this policy strategy, however, is at odds with their increasing relevance in European societies—there are, for instance, about two million Turkish or Arab speaking immigrants in Europe.

Although there have been attempts, for instance in the European Committee on Migration, to foster integration and equal opportunities policies towards immigrants, language policies have mainly followed the assimilationist or differentialist model. While it is true that public debate in several countries, especially in Belgium, Germany and the Netherlands, is increasingly becoming aware of the cultural, legal and economic importance of maintaining the linguistic identity of immigrants, for instance through "immigrant minority language instruction" (IMLI), educational policies in most European countries have been reluctant in shifting to a socio-cultural model of multicultural language policies which would include the protection and promotion of immigrant minority languages.

Since the socio-cultural model of multicultural language policies overtly supports the linguistic identity of both regional and immigrant minorities and includes strategies such as IMLI, it is not surprising that it was first adopted by countries facing large-scale immigration, especially by Canada and Australia. In Canada, increases in immigration have resulted in attacks on the policy of anglo- or franco-conformity and in the eventual adoption of the "policy of multiculturalism within a bilingual framework" in 1971, confirmed by the 1988 Multiculturalism Act.

In the area of education, fluency in both the mother tongue and one of the two national languages has been the primary objective of multicultural language policies, and it has been implemented by supplementing national language(s) instruction by IMLI and bilingual education. While social integration of immigrants coming from diverse linguistic backgrounds has been generally strengthened by multicultural language policies in Canada, the case of Quebec illustrates some problems of multicultural language policies within a bilingual framework. The adoption of multicultural language policies in the 1970s tended to weaken the status of French and to favor the use of English as high-status language of upward mobility among immigrant and ethnocultural communities in Quebec. As a reaction, Quebecois language policies have shifted to preferential treatment of French in order to affirm the identity of a "distinct francophone society" - although with limited success.

In Australia, the adoption of multiculturalism meant the shift from a strictly monolingual and assimilationist policy to the recognition of linguistic rights of both Aboriginals and immigrants from diverse linguistic backgrounds. The motivating factor for this change in public policy being the valuing of Asian languages as important tool for international trade, it was only in the 80s that public policy regarded the recognition of identity claims of linguistic groups and the promotion of internal cultural and linguistic diversity as the foundation of social integration in Australia.

The strategies of multicultural language policies, codified in the National Policy on Languages program, are aimed at facilitating education in both English and immigrant languages (IMLI) and instruction on cultural diversity, at establishing multilingual media, such as the Special Broadcasting Program which disseminates information in up to 63 languages, and at providing public services for non-English speakers, such as the Translating and Interpreting Service. As early as the mid-1980s, however, it was observed that since the national language was still functioning as the main instrument of communication, the "ethnic option", that is the mere promotion of minority identities, ran the risk of reinforcing existing power differentials in the economic and political sector.

As a consequence, public policy in Australia has moved to more complex models of multicultural language policies promoting the use of minority languages while, at the same time, furthering linguistic competence in a language of wider communication.

It can be concluded that multicultural language policies not only confirm with international human rights standards pertaining to linguistic rights, but also seem to be empirically more effective in reducing ethnic conflict than the assimilationist and the differentialist policy strategy, if they succeed in balancing the legitimacy of particular linguistic identities and the linguistic requirements of a functioning economic and political system.

Respecting the differentiation between a "separate domain" and a "common domain", therefore, constitutes an effective democratic response to the structural dilemma of social integration in contemporary nation-states. The following explores in some more detail the development of language policies in the Kyrgyz Republic, in order to assess the potential of multicultural language policies to manage ethnic conflict under conditions of post-Soviet state formation.

Developing Multicultural Language Policies

Formulating multicultural language policies in post-Soviet societies, therefore, presupposes a critical analysis of existing ethnic policies. Post-Soviet language policies have been strongly affected by the ethno-cultural model of the nation-state and the ideal of monolinguism, the result being a moderate form of differentialist language policies. Thus, Article 5 of the Kyrgyz constitution states:

> The official language of the Kyrgyz Republic shall be the Kyrgyz language. The Kyrgyz Republic shall guarantee preservation, equal and free development and functioning of the Russian language and all other languages which are used by the population of the Republic. Infringements of the citizens' rights on the ground of absence of knowledge and command of the official language shall not be allowed.

While certain basic linguistic rights seem to be acknowledged in this provision, the political instrumentalization of the Kyrgyz ethno-linguistic identity in the process of state formation and nation building has, as mentioned above, caused ethnic conflict along linguistic lines and has resulted in considerable Russian emigration. In addition to its potential of generating ethnic conflict, such a moderate differentialist language policy violates the rights of members of linguistic minorities. It is true that language policies in the Kyrgyz Republic need to respect the specific demands of the formerly dominated Kyrgyz fraction of the population. To the extent that ethnic identity is symbolically expressed through language, public recognition of the identity claims of the Kyrgyz people indeed implies the preferential treatment of the Kyrgyz language in education, media and public services. But the promotion of the Kyrgyz language must not be carried through at the expense of the linguistic rights of Russian and other minority speakers in the Kyrgyz Republic. Moreover, special status seems to be appropriate for the Russian language, which has operated as primary language in the educational system, as language of inter-ethnic communication and as an important link language for economic and political integration in the Central Asian region. Therefore, the adoption of multicultural language policies, for instance by establishing bilingual education and multilingual media system in the framework of a pluralistic political system, seems to be a context-sensitive and more democratic strategy of promoting social integration in the new Kyrgyz Republic.

The ethno-national thrust of the constitutional and legal provisions regulating language use in Kyrgyzstan has in fact been an issue of many public controversies. The protest not only of Russians but also of urbanized and highly educated Kyrgyz against the subordination of the Russian language and the growing awareness of the negative repercussions of monolingual language policies, such as increased ethnic conflict, emigration and disintegration in the region, have eventually resulted in far-reaching modifications of the monolingual doctrine.

After a series of jurisdictional and legislative activities, in which, for example, the legislature voted to accord the Russian language equal status in the Constitution by an amendment to Article 5 in May 1993, Russians and Germans were granted dual citizenship and a decree was passed to make Russian an official language in those regions where the majority of the population spoke Russian, and the Lower House of the Parliament approved Russian as an official language in March 1996 and passed a revision of Article 5 of the Constitution which states:

> "In the Kyrgyz Republic, the Russian language can be used as an official language".

Similarly, the President of the Republic has recognized the importance of Russian as the language of inter-ethnic communication and has therefore supported the adoption of official bilingualism in Kyrgyzstan. All these developments suggest that there has been a successive evolution from strict monolingualism to more pluralist language policies, combining the regional with the socio-cultural variant of multiculturalism. This, however, has by no means precluded the strengthening of the Kyrgyz language in the areas of education and public media.

On 16 January 1998, for instance, the President signed a decree which promotes the idea of corpus planning of the Kyrgyz language and establishes a special council responsible for co-ordinating and controlling the use of Kyrgyz as a state language.

However, these attempts have to be regarded in the framework of an evolving pluralistic language policy. The support of the Kyrgyz language in the educational system, for instance, has been complemented by the establishment of institutions with non-titular languages of instruction, such as the Kyrgyz-Russian-University, the Kyrgyz-Uzbek University, the Kyrgyz-American Faculty and the Kyrgyz-Turkish University. Also, the strengthening of Kyrgyz media has not hindered the proliferation of various Russian and Uzbek newspapers, radio and television channels and has therefore strengthened a pluralistic civil society.

The last two decades of the 20th century saw a historic shift in the global spread of democracy. Some 81 countries 29 in Sub-Saharan Africa, 23 in Europe, 14 in Latin America, 10 in Asia and 5 in the Arab states took steps towards democratization. Often this meant the overthrow of an authoritarian one-party regime, the introduction of multiparty elections or both a major advance. But the recent mixed experience with democracy in these countries and around the world shows that the process of deepening democracy and making it work for people has barely begun. Why is there less optimism about democracy today than in the euphoric period just after the cold war? One reason is that many countries that embraced democracy have suffered reversals, while many others have limited political competition and continuing abuse of political and civil rights.

Today 47 of the 81 countries are considered functioning democracies. Then there's the disturbing spread of 'illiberal' democracies, as in Kyrgyzstan and Zimbabwe, where elected governments act the same as their authoritarian predecessors, depriving citizens of human rights and ignoring constitutional limits on power. So, why call them 'transitional'? They do not seem to be transitioning anywhere. Even where democracy is more firmly established, people are disappointed by the economic and social results. Many fought for and won democracy in the hope of greater social justice, broader political participation and peaceful resolution of violent conflicts. Rightly or wrongly, they expected democracy to bring more effective development. Just since 2000 in Latin America alone, presidents have been pressured to resign in Argentina (twice), Ecuador, Peru and Venezuela. Now, 10 to 20 years later, democracy has not produced dividends in the lives of ordinary people in too many countries.

Income inequality and poverty have risen sharply in Eastern Europe and the former Soviet Union, sometimes at unprecedented rates. Poverty has continued to increase in a more democratic Sub-Saharan Africa. And many newly democratic regimes in Latin America seem no better equipped to tackle the region's high poverty and inequality than their authoritarian predecessors. Political instability and violence have also marred democratic transitions in Indonesia, Nigeria, the former Yugoslavia and elsewhere. Perhaps most serious, people around the world seem to have lost confidence in the effectiveness of their governments and often seem to be losing faith in democracy. More than 70% of survey respondents in Latin America complain of increasing poverty, crime, corruption and drug trafficking and addiction. Nor is reduced faith in governments and politics limited to new democracies. The links between democracy and human development can be strong but they are not automatic. And in almost every country those links need to be strengthened.

Public Accountability of Democratic Institutions

If democracies are not always responsive to the needs and concerns of ordinary people, how can they be made to work better? The answer turns on whether people can go beyond simply expressing their views and preferences to check the power of rulers and influence decisions. Accountability is about power about people having not just a say in official decisions but also the right to hold their rulers to account. They can demand answers to questions about decisions and actions. And they can sanction public officials or bodies that do not live up to their responsibilities. Today the insistence that public officials be held accountable is extending to corporations, multinational organizations and others who have more power in public decision-making. Because of their influence over the lives of people and communities, they are holders of the public trust and so answerable for their actions to national legislatures and to the public. Accountability means different things in different contexts.

In democracies, people can demand accountability in two ways: through action by civil society and through structures of representation and delegation. But apart from elections, most formal mechanisms of accountability are delegated. The most important are the checks and balances between the judiciary, legislature and executive and specialized and independent oversight entities such as human rights commissions, electoral commissions, public service commissions, ombuds persons, auditors general and anticorruption bodies. The problem is, democratic institutions in many countries especially newer democracies are overburdened and lack the means to do their jobs. Political parties are disorganized. Representatives cannot keep in close contact with their constituents. Oversight and regulatory agencies lack well-trained staff. And bureaucrats are underpaid, overworked or both.

Many countries that held multiparty presidential elections for the first time in the 1980s and 1990s did so with political parties created just months before. Resource constraints are not the only institutional weakness. Sometimes national institutions are ineffective because real power lies elsewhere. In a more integrated world, weak and indebted states face vast areas of policy-making over which they share control with international actors if they share it at all. Decisions at the global level can bind states, and national elections and checks and balances lack the reach to hold powerful global actors to account. Or states may have little real authority because subversive groups have taken over: guerrilla movements, international drug traffickers and crime syndicates, powerful rural landowners, slum-land gangs. Even where arrangements for accountability exist, they do not function well in many democracies. They do not promote the interests of most people. And they do an even poorer job of protecting the interests of minorities, women and poor people. There are two main reasons:

— Democratic institutions are subverted by corruption and elite capture.

— Democratic institutions have inadequate reach, and there are gaps in democratic practice.

Corruption, abuses of power, intimidations by criminal elements all weaken democratic accountability. Oversight and regulatory agencies may also fail to act when they have been captured by political or special interests. For example, in the late 1990s South-East Asia suffered from a persistent atmospheric haze-creating. Accountability power having official the rulers serious health hazards because plantation owners bribed Indonesian officials to turn a blind eye to illegal forest fires. Burning land was much cheaper than clearing it manually. Pay-offs flowed into all levels of the administrative hierarchy, almost guaranteeing that supervisors would not penalize junior officers for failing to enforce regulations. Subordinates returned the favour by not blowing the whistle on those higher up.

Only when the haze from the fires began spreading over Malaysia and Singapore in 1997 did international embarrassment catalyse a crackdown. Transparency International Bangladesh, in a 2000 study of the nation's banking industry, found that people getting credit from the formal banking sector had to pay a direct bribe equal to 2 -90 % of the loan value. The higher percentages were extorted from uneducated rural applicants, partly because the bribes were being shared with government officials reviewing the loans. Worse, borrowers often paid up to half of a loan's value to secure a promise from branch managers that the loan would not have to be repaid, a promise often breached. When the supposed beneficiaries are left with little choice but to collude in bribery, it undermines their willingness to protest and corruption becomes harder to expose. Judicial proceedings can also be undermined, providing little protection to ordinary people, especially poor people. Judicial systems are often inaccessible. They use official language that many people cannot speak or write. And too often they are open to bribes. Where victims have no judicial recourse, their abusers often go unpunished especially when they are members of the police. Studies in Latin America have shown that minorities, poor people and other marginalized groups (such as homosexuals and street children) are disproportionately the victims of physical abuse and other mistreatment by the police. Gender bias in judicial proceedings is another problem. Male-dominated village councils systematically fail to uphold the rights of women, as in land disputes in Uganda.

Numerous elections have been contested by opposition candidates charging fraud and irregularities. In 1997 Cameroonian President Paul Biya was re-elected with 93% of the vote but the three main opposition parties had boycotted the election, and the government had dismissed demands for an independent electoral commission. Too many other recent elections have been similarly marred: among others, Haiti in 2000, Chad in 2001, Zimbabwe in 2002, Madagascar in 2002. Money in politics is especially serious because it can distort democratic institutions at every level. It can distort the election process and the extent to which elected leaders represent their constituents. And it can distort parliamentary politics and the functioning of the judiciary and the executive. This problem has recently reached the top of the political agenda in many countries, often as a result of scandals at the highest levels of government. In several countries politicians have been charged with accepting money from criminals, for their private benefit or for campaign purposes.

The down-fall of the Christian Democrats in Italy in the 1990s owed much to accusations that the party was "financially connected to the mafia ". And in Germany in the early 1980s the "Flick Affair " severely shook the nation as it uncovered illegal contributions from the Flick Company. Senior politicians from all the main political parties allegedly disregarded campaign financing laws. The scandal prompted the passage of campaign contribution laws meant to prevent political financing abuse. Yet in 1999 Helmut Kohl, the former chancellor, resigned as honorary chairman of his party after acknowledging having run a network of secret accounts and receiving clandestine donations equal to $6. 5 million. This scandal later ensnared other members of the Christian Democratic Union.

Electoral processes cannot operate without financing. But where money plays a decisive role in politics, it turns unequal economic power into unequal political advantage and undermines the principle of "one person, one vote ". The problem is not new. But the soaring cost of elections has almost certainly made the situation worse. In 1980 US presidential candidates spent $92 million -but that rose to $211 million in 1988 and $343 million in 2000. Including spending by political parties, the total cost in 2000 was more than $1 billion. Though a large campaign budget does not guarantee success, it is important in many contests: one study of US. campaigns in the 1970s showed that candidates challenging incumbent members of Congress won an extra 1 percentage point of votes for every $10, 000 spent. Such costs make for an uneven playing field in political contests because they make it almost impossible for an underfunded candidate to enter a race. These costs also increases politicians dependence on certain sources of financing, leaving the democratic system vulnerable to the undue influence of special interest groups particularly corporate interests.

Even well-functioning formal structures of participation and accountability are at best only blunt instruments. Elections and other formal checks enable citizens only to end the tenure of politicians who abuse their mandates. And joining political parties, seeking to influence their agendas and voting in elections have rarely been enough to safeguard the rights of women, minorities and poor people.

Nor do these mechanisms have the reach to tackle injustices that affect people's daily lives. For example, a recent World Bank review of the weak impact of Colombia's land reforms concluded that even repeated parliamentary questioning had not gone to the heart of the problem, which was that elites had captured the program and distorted it to their own ends. There was collusion between sellers and buyers to overstate land prices, divide the surplus and let the government foot the bill. One solution to such problems is to decentralize power to lower levels of government bringing it closer to the people. But local officials are no more immune to elite capture than officials in central government. Indeed, far from strengthening local democracy, decentralization can actually reinforce the power and influence of local elites. In these circumstances citizens may have more luck with officials who are farther away. A recent survey of 12 countries found that in only half was there any evidence some quite limited that decentralization empowers more people, reduces poverty, enhances social progress or mitigates spatial inequality. Decentralization helps poor people most when local politics are democratic, with strong structures and open participatory practices. Only if accompanied by strong support to community groups can decentralization empower ordinary people. Thus formal structures of accountability in democracy are strong in theory but are often undermined by self-perpetuating concentrations of power and influence.

In some countries the same prime ministers have alternated at the helm for decades, and dynastic politics continues. In Mexico the same party was in power for more than 70 years until the 2000 elections ended its rule. Despite democratic upheavals and some inroads into politics by underrepresented groups, elites hold on to state power, and unequal power structures prevail. Breaking such vicious circles will require strengthening democratic institutions and state capacities. But that is only part of the solution. Political pressure also has to come from outside formal structures, through the emergence of a more vibrant democratic politics.

Most of the 81 countries that recently took steps towards democratization have yet to shake off the legacies of authoritarian pasts, and democratic institutions and practices have yet to take root. Representative processes appear to be in crisis even in well-established democracies. In the United States the turnout of registered voters in presidential elections fell from 96% in 1960 to 51% in 2000, and in the United Kingdom from 78% in 1992 to 59% in 2001. Though these trends are not universal -voter turnout has been rising in some countries, especially in Latin America large drops have been seen in eight other OECD countries. In France, Italy, Norway and the United States party membership is half (or less) of what it was 20 years ago. According to recent surveys in Latin America and Central and Eastern Europe, far fewer people have confidence in political parties than in the church, the armed forces or television. Countries can start to restore public trust in representative structures and reduce the concentration of political power by:

— Developing stronger vehicles for formal political participation and representation through political parties and electoral systems.

— Strengthening checks on arbitrary power by separating powers among the executive, judiciary and legislature, and by creating effective independent entities.

— Decentralizing democratically: devolving power from the central government to provinces and villages, underpinned by stronger local democratic institutions and practices.

— Developing free and independent media.

A well-functioning democracy depends on well-functioning political parties responsive to people, but new democracies mean new parties. These parties are not yet able to fulfil their traditional functions of political education, mobilization and representation of diverse interests. In many African countries opposition parties disappear between elections, while ruling parties behave like they used to under single-party systems. A dearth of public funding and limits on fundraising leave parties dependent on a few wealthy individuals to finance their activities and campaigns. And with perks and patronage flowing from ruling parties, politicians are increasingly switching party affiliation "crossing the carpet "to join the winning party. This practice has become so common in West Africa that some governments, as in Benin and Niger, have made it illegal. Too often the organizational structure of parties is anything but participatory. Parties that are not open and transparent are unlikely to be democratic in their policy commitments. Without internal democracy, parties become individual fiefdoms. Charismatic leadership, more than party platform, often drives party loyalty. Creating a culture of democracy in political parties is thus vital. At the very least this should involve open, competitive elections for party leadership. Such a requirement would be useful to include in any agenda for political reform as in Panama's new electoral code, established in 1995.

Elections are complex processes requiring systematic organization. Improving voter registration and rolls and setting up independent electoral commissions are cornerstones of a free and fair system. The inclusion of parties and candidates as stakeholders, monitors and defenders of elections, and not just as contenders, can help ensure stability as in Mozambique in 1994, where party representatives were included in every aspect in the run-up to the elections. The media can also contribute to this effort -diffusing information, focusing public debate and increasing civic and voter education. So can civil society. In Indonesia non-governmental organizations (NGOs) played a central role in voter education, explaining to citizens their rights and duties to vote according to their free will and conscience, the value of voting in a democracy and the nature of new election laws. These campaigns also helped convince citizens of the fairness of the system, its new transparency and the new parties and personalities entering into the political life of the country.

Many countries are trying to strengthen systems of representation. Whether in established or new democracies, these efforts tend to have common elements:

— Improving governance in political parties, with ethical standards, training, discipline and better financial management. The Democrat Party of Thailand, for example, has embarked on a process to professionalize party management. The Labang Demokratikong Pilipino Party of the Philippines is working on the problem of patronage, establishing a research institute and conducting seminars and policy discussions.

— Promoting the participation of minorities and women. Political parties have been a major institutional factor behind the chronic underrepresentation of minorities and women. The situation is improving, but at a snail's pace. In 103 countries the proportion of women in parliament increased between 1995 and 2000, but around the world it still averages just 14%. Affirmative action is often needed to overcome entrenched obstacles. Quotas, either in legislatures or in parties, have been instrumental in raising representation. They have been used in the countries with the highest representation of women in parliament and are making changes in countries where female participation in politics has historically been lower, such as France and South Africa.

— Building electoral systems. Many countries, both long-established and new democracies, are reforming their electoral systems. The success of the 2000 Mexican elections largely rested on the 1996 reform of electoral and political frameworks, as well as the complete reform of the electoral commission, the Instituto Federal Electoral.

— Limiting the distorting influence of money in politics. Reform of political finance is under active debate in many countries, aiming to improve transparency, level the playing field (by setting limits on spending and contributions), encourage public subsidies and grassroots contributions and manage undue corporate and business influences on public policy. In the wake of allegations of political corruption a common response has been new laws already introduced in some countries such as France and the United States and hotly debated in others such as India. Elements of these initiatives include disclosure laws, spending limits, contribution limits, bans on certain types of donations, direct and indirect public subsidies for parties and candidates and subsidies for political broadcasting. But a study of 60 countries by

> the International Institute for Democracy and Electoral Assistance shows that stricter laws are only a first step -and that when political financing laws are accompanied by silence, indifference and lack of technical training, abuses are best able to flourish.

Democracies suffer reversals when elected governments are overturned. But many elected governments have turned authoritarian, increasingly behaving like their autocratic predecessors. The keys to preventing such abuses of power are strengthening the separation of powers and the independence of the legislature and judiciary -and professionalizing the bureaucracy and the military.

Whether the judiciary can maintain its independence is often the litmus test for whether democratically elected rule can avoid turning autocratic. The fierce independence of India's judiciary is a cornerstone of the country's democracy. Indeed, the tug of war between a judiciary fighting to stay autonomous and political parties and the executive is a continuing feature of Indian political life. From the efforts to eliminate judicial review of legislation in the 1970s to the judicial activism of the 1990s in taking up cases of political corruption, the judiciary has vigorously defended the separation of powers and ensured that checks and balances are a reality.

In Egypt the Constitutional Court played a key role in imposing judicial supervision of polling stations in the 1987 and 2001 elections. In 1997 Mali's Constitutional Court annulled the first round of legislative elections and ordered new balloting in response to a petition from opposition parties. And in 2001 Gabon's Constitutional Court quashed a presidential decree appointing all the members of the country's Economic and Social Council, saying that the decree violated a constitutional requirement that 85% of the council's members be elected by their peers from throughout the country.

During apartheid South Africa's government used the law and the courts to implement -and defend -its policies, causing the oppressed majority to view the judicial system as a tool of white oppression. But human rights lawyers and a few sympathetic judges kept the judicial process from losing all credibility, which proved crucial to the establishment of a democratic constitution. Today strong measures guarantee an independent judiciary, and the Constitutional Court ensures an appropriate separation of powers between the three branches of government. In addition, the Constitutional Court and the independent Judicial Services Commission have made courts more representative of 199 superior court judges, are black and 26 are women. In 1994, when apartheid ended, there were no more than one or two of either. In many new democracies, however, domination by the executive branch and excessive influence of security forces, especially the military remain stubborn legacies. Shifting to a more balanced system, with an independent judiciary and legislature, does not happen overnight.

The legislature often plays a limited role in policy-making for example, with budgets discussed only at their final stage in many parliaments. In South Africa parliamentarians have no power to amend budgets, only to approve what is presented or reject it outright. But rejection is not a realistic option, because it would immobilize the business of government. In other countries the controlling majority often amends constitutions without broad debate. As political pressure mounts to challenge their power, rulers may try to maintain their hold on it through, for example, constitutional amendments that reinforce the power of the executive. In Cameroon military tribunals can exercise jurisdiction over civilians in cases involving civil unrest. Establishing civilian control of the military and the police is an enormous challenge in many new democracies.

In many countries bureaucratic rule continues as well, often conflicting with democratic reforms even in long-established democracies such as Japan. Civil servants may not readily adjust to the role of holder of public trust. Jurisdictional conflicts between electoral commissions and ministries of the interior highlight the difficulties of overcoming bureaucratic rule. So does the reluctance of presidential appointees and auxiliaries to tolerate the emergence of political parties and civil society organizations. Often the legislature and the judiciary simply lack technical capacity, office space and access to information. A 1993 study of Argentina, Bolivia, Brazil, Chile and Honduras found that parliamentary committees lacked skilled staff.

Parliamentarians in El Salvador and Mexico are also bereft of professional assistance, staffed only by secretaries. Fewer than a dozen of Nepal's 205 members of parliament have any training in economics. Many countries are trying to confront these problems, with mixed success. In addition to providing parliaments and judiciaries with equipment, procedures and adequately trained professional staff, they are introducing innovations and structural reforms to reinforce checks on abuses of power, and they are strengthening parliamentary committees to foster more effective decision-making and to monitor the executive.

In 1983 Ireland established a committee system that conducts research for members of parliament. In Portugal, Romania and elsewhere, opposition leaders are appointed to lead powerful legislative committees, including the finance committee. And in Morocco the 1996 constitution introduced a bicameral legislature to promote more pluralistic representation. Another approach is to strengthen independent entities especially ombuds persons, electoral commissions and human rights commissions. All can promote and defend critical reforms and democratic practices in countries with imbalances of power between the executive and the other branches. Independent electoral commissions play a critical role in ensuring free and fair elections. An important condition for their independence is budgetary independence, best secured by legal arrangements -and with budgets not only for elections but also for preparatory processes, then audited.

Independent commissions have been critical to protecting and promoting human rights. By 1998, 40% of the world's parliaments had formal human rights bodies. South Africa's commission actively monitors the application of constitutionally guaranteed rights. It has tackled a wide range of issues, including the provision of social services, human rights in farming communities and racism in the media. The commission is making the vision of a nation founded on human rights a reality.

Decentralizing Democratically

In principle, decentralizing power from the centre to provinces, districts or villages enables people to participate in decision-making more directly. But in reality it can simply transfer power from one set of elites to another. Democratic decentralization truly giving voice to the people requires more than just decentralizing and devolving power. It also requires widening participation especially by people who are often marginalized, such as women, minorities and the poor and increasing the accountability of public officials at local levels.

India's panchayati raj illustrate this process. Despite democracy's success at the national and state levels, India's constitutionally mandated local governments -the panchayati rajused to be prone to capture by elites and to subversion by central political authority. The 1992 and 1993 constitutional amendments revitalized the panchayats by giving them constitutional status, providing for regular elections and reserving one-third of seats for women and proportional representation for marginalized social groups. In many parts of India this change dramatically increased the visibility and extent of popular participation. It also enabled marginalized groups to enter political debates infusing new political resources into the system, enhancing the legitimacy of state institutions and bringing a measure of uniformity to the institutional structure of local governments all over the country.

In Madhya Pradesh and Rajasthan, two states with low incomes and some of the country's worst schooling and literacy rates, literacy jumped 20 percentage points between 1991 and 2001. Community involvement in mapping households and identifying children out of school was a major factor in voicing need. Although 80, 000 schools had opened in the 50 years since independence, 30, 000 more were created within three years of the scheme's announcement in 1997. In addition, enrolments of girls and tribal children increased enormously.

Not all panchayati raj institutions have been affected the same way. Political authorities in several states - Kerala, Madhya Pradesh, Maharashtra, Rajasthan, West Bengal have supported decentralization through the panchayats and effectively decentralized decision-making to local levels. In some states progress has been slower in the absence of resource transfers. And in others, such as Bihar, the reform has exacerbated social divisions and violence, further weakening these institutions. The successes have been most pronounced in states where democratic principles permeate local political parties and other institutions and processes and are reflected in the strong trust people have in them. Where local hierarchies are more deeply entrenched, the reform has made less headway.

Bolivia provides another interesting example of democratic decentralization. Its 1994 Popular Participation Law broadened political participation and decentralized fiscal decision-making. The law created municipalities in rural areas with no previous state presence. It officially recognized local grass-roots organizations. It reduced inequality by redistributing fiscal resources based on population density. And it gave more power to local governments by decentralizing physical infrastructure for health care, education, local roads, irrigation systems and cultural activities. The grass-roots organizations play a key role: the law establishes procedures for them to make proposals to satisfy municipal needs and to oversee municipal government services and projects.

Bolivia's law led to very positive empowerment in some communities but not others. Some critics say that the local organizations are too heterogeneous and disorganized and that they undermine other civil society organizations, such as labour unions, that represent people's interests. Others say that elites can still hijack the process. They say that the impact of the law would have been greater had it been accompanied by measures to restructure local party politics and crack down on local corruption. They attribute the law's limited results to the continuing hold of patronage-based political systems and processes in which decisions are made without systematic consultation. Still, this innovative initiative brings civil society groups more clearly into local governance and deepens democratic practice.

Democratic decentralization is also spreading in industrial countries, with moves to devolve power to Scotland and Wales in the United Kingdom and to the regions in Italy and Spain. But perhaps one of the most interesting developments in decentralization over the past decade has been the expansion of people's participation and public officials accountability at the local level in China and Viet Nam.

In 1998 Viet Nam issued the Grass-roots Democracy Decree, partly in response to some farmers dissatisfaction with the lack of transparency in local budget allocations. The decree defines areas of policy where local people need to be kept informed, including administrative procedures and budget planning and spending. It also outlines areas where local people should discuss and comment on government decisions before they are made. Meanwhile, China has introduced elections in villages and in some townships.

Developing Free and Independent Media

Perhaps no reform can be as significant for making

democratic institutions work as reform of the media: building diverse and pluralistic media that are free and independent, that achieve mass access and diffusion, that present accurate and unbiased information. Informed debate is the lifeblood of democracies. Without it, citizens and decision-makers are disempowered, lacking the basic tools for informed participation and representation.

Free media play three crucial roles in promoting democratic governance:

— As a civic forum, giving voice to different parts of society and enabling debate from all viewpoints.

— As a mobilizing agent, facilitating civic engagement among all sectors of society and strengthening channels of public participation.

— As a watchdog, checking abuses of power, increasing government transparency and holding public officials accountable for their actions in the court of public opinion.

The past two decades have seen major advances in the spread of independent media. Economic and political reforms have loosened restrictions on the media including censorship and ownership controls and strengthened constitutional and legal guarantees of freedom of speech and information.

Many countries, from Indonesia to Qatar, have abolished restrictive press laws. And deregulation and privatization of media markets have made them more competitive and often more diverse and pluralistic - notably through the increased penetration of global and regional multimedia companies, such as CNN and Al-Jazeira, into national markets. Information technology and the Internet have also greatly broadened the scope for mass communications, making it possible for even small media organizations to reach large audiences. The Internet can also break the barriers of state control.

These changes have dramatically expanded the media's nature and scale. Between 1970 and 1996 the number of daily newspapers in developing countries more than doubled, from 29 to 60 copies per 1, 000 people. In many countries political, economic and technological forces are levelling the playing field in the market for ideas, enabling new voices and viewpoints to be heard. Most people have many more sources of information both in quantity and diversity than they did just 10 years ago. Widely available information is crucial to democratic governance because it helps challenge government authorities and provokes more balanced debate on problems and policies.

Freedom and diversity are reinforcing the media's roles as mobilizing agents and watchdogs. Still, many countries are a long way from having a genuinely free and independent media that can serve democratic purposes. State-owned media monopolies persist: for example, Lebanon is the only Arab state that allows private broadcasting. Few countries have freedom of information laws, and journalists often work under strict constraints. According to Freedom House, in only a handful of new democracies is press freedom comparable to that in most established democracies.

Making the list are most countries in Central and Eastern Europe and the Baltics, several in Latin America and the Caribbean (such as Costa Rica, Jamaica and Trinidad and Tobago) and a few in Africa (Mauritius, Senegal, South Africa) and Asia (Mongolia, the

Philippines, Thailand). Even where press freedoms are constitutionally guaranteed, governments have invented new ways to rein in the press. In many countries in Central and Eastern Europe and elsewhere, libel laws are used to silence critics. In Chile "contempt of authority" is a crime against state security, and despite the 2001 Press Law, restrictions on freedom of expression still pervade Chilean legislation where the defamation laws that Augusto Pinochet's regime used to great effect are still in force. In several countries the vague crime of 'dangerousness' has been used to curtail independent journalism. The Democratic Republic of Congo outlaws reporting that might 'demoralize' the public. In Zimbabwe, with a history of a vigorous and independent media, the president has forced through legislation that severely constrains press freedoms.

Journalism also remains a hazardous occupation. In 2001, 37 journalists died in the line of duty. Another 118 were imprisoned. Worldwide, more than 600 journalists or their news organizations were intimidated or physically attacked -mostly because some people did not agree with what they reported. In 1944 writer Albert Camus said, "The press is free when it does not depend on either the power of government or the power of money." To be free and independent and to produce factual, unbiased information, the media must be free not just from state control but also from corporate and political pressures.

With greater media pluralism comes an expectation of greater political pluralism in the media and greater potential for broader, better-informed debate. But commercial and political pressures still skew the market for ideas. Liberalization, privatization and new technology have taken the media out of government hands and into private hands. Most of the world's publishing media are privately owned, although the public sector still accounts for 60% of television station ownership worldwide. However, private ownership of the media is highly concentrated, often by families. In the United Kingdom four groups own 85% of the daily press (accounting for two-thirds of total circulation). In the United States six companies control most of the media: AOL Time Warner, General Electric, Viacom, Disney, Bertelsmann, News Corporation.

In Australia Rupert Murdoch's media empire controls 60% of the circulation of daily newspapers. In a few countries families of influential politicians are major owners of the media, the most well-known case is Silvio Berlusconi and his family in Italy. Mexico's Televisa and Brazil's Globo are two of the world's greatest media monopolies controlled by individuals and their families, encompassing all aspects of production and distribution of television, radio, film, video and much of the advertising industries in their countries.

In Venezuela two large family-owned companies dominate the market: Grupo Phelps and Grupo Cisneros. From Bolivia to France to the United States, citizens, politicians and journalists are engaging in lively debates about how the media's politicization and poor professional standards contribute to the deterioration of democratic life. The media can be subjected to overtly political aims, compromising basic professional ethics of providing unbiased, accurate information. Truth is the first casualty of war, but the media are usually the victims, not the aggressors. But not in Rwanda in 1994, when radio the country's most common media was used to incite genocide.

The journalists involved now face charges of crimes against humanity before the International Criminal Tribunal for Rwanda. Media companies are businesses and can be expected to behave as such. Hence the increasing trend towards "infotainment "-the merging of information and entertainment also viewed as a threat by many. Media companies also have a civic role as providers of news and information. The tensions between these two roles will never be eliminated -and the answer to excessive corporate influence over the news cannot be a return to excessive control by the state. Solutions must combine the need to hold the media accountable and responsible with the need to keep it free. The media can be free of both corporate and state control if it serves the public first and foremost and follows higher standards of professionalism and ethics. A range of mechanisms for promoting higher standards of professionalism and responsibility do not depend on restrictive state controls:

— *Independent media commissions:* Among the handful of independent media commissions is the Ghana Media Commission, which is authorized 'to take all appropriate measures to ensure the establishment and maintenance of the highest journalistic standards in the mass media'. Using a combination of moral suasion and professional goodwill, the commission has often ruled against the abuse of power by newspapers and directed them to issue apologies and retractions. So far it has taken on more than 50 cases, and has resolved 28 amicably.

— *Market sanctions voting with the pocket book:* The public can always withdraw its support for an offending newspaper or medium by refusing to buy or view it. Zimbabwe's state-owned newspaper. The Herald lost more than 40% of its readers, from 744, 000 in 2000 to

430, 000 in 2001, partly because people lost faith in its credibility. By contrast, the private Daily News saw its readership grow from 512, 000 in 2000 to 582, 000 in 2001.

— *Self-regulation:* Self-regulation includes professional standards and internal guidelines by newspapers and news agencies. Press councils that examine complaints about media performance are another key element. Ombudsper-sons, maintained by newspapers in Brazil, Canada, Japan, Spain and the United States, also belong to this category. There is greater attention to the need to raise professional standards through codes of ethics, training, education and a broader emphasis on quality. Many of the above elements come together in Claude Jean Bertrand's Media Accountability System, which emphasizes greater efforts by the media to develop ethical standards, especially through open debates with the public.

The system also makes clear that media responsibility does not derive solely from institutional efforts. It starts with the consciences of individual journalists and must be based on socially accepted norms and standards of fair conduct. In recent years there have been positive developments in this regard: the news media are more willing to publicly examine press ethics and performance, and journalism courses are addressing ethics more often.

Promoting Democratic Politics to Deepen Democratic Practice

Though strengthening democratic institutions is essential,

it is not enough to promote more effective participation by people and more responsive decision-making by those in power. An alert citizenry is what makes democratic institutions and processes work. Political pressure from below is usually the most effective trigger of change. Major advances in human development over the past two centuries the abolition of slavery, the recognition of equal rights of women, the advance of democracy itself would not have been granted from above. They had to be fought for.

While much has been written about the challenges of creating democratic institutions, there has been much less analysis of democratic politics: the struggles of poor and marginalized people to claim their rights and to overcome institutionalized obstacles. These struggles depend as much on strengthening civil liberties, civil society institutions and a free media as on strengthening political liberties and political institutions. "It is quite possible to have accountability in the high politics of the state, honest rulers and free elections, and yet profound injustice or irresponsibility in the deep politics of society, that is, the relations between rich and poor, powerful and weak. A trend of the past decade is the expansion of democratic politics, with a groundswell of civic activism around the world demanding greater accountability of government authorities and of private business and multilateral organizations. These civil society actors are using new and innovative approaches to get their messages heard, and expanding their role from watchdogs that monitor to active participants in setting agendas.

One of the more significant examples is the rise of participatory and accountable budgeting: civil society initiatives to scrutinize public spending and in some cases participate in the development of official budgets. Few government decisions mean as much for ordinary people as those made during the writing of public budgets -especially for poor people who rely on "public incomes " such as schooling, , health care, roads, water supply and electricity. Yet ordinary people typically have little say in budget formulation. In most countries the budget process is almost exclusively the prerogative of bureaucrats and the executive branch. Parliaments also participate, but often only at the end. And much of the process is usually shrouded in secrecy unmatched by any other part of government decision-making aside from national security.

But recent initiatives by citizen groups to examine local and central budgets are helping to open this process to the voices of ordinary people. Many of these initiatives start with social audits or impact evaluations -analyses that elicit concerns about spending priorities and the misuse of funds. These efforts sometimes help reverse official decisions. In Israel the government proposed deep cuts in social spending in 1998. The Adva Centre, a nonpartisan, action oriented policy analysis organization, assessed the potential impact of these cuts. As a result a wide coalition lobbied the government -and cuts in child care and pensions were withdrawn, universal health care was preserved and cutbacks in teaching hours and housing assistance were reduced.

In Rajasthan, India, a grass-roots organization called Mazdoor Kisan Shakti Sangathan launched a campaign in 1988 to secure minimum wages for government drought-relief workers. It soon became clear that corruption was at the root of low wages. The MKSS analysed government accounts and discovered that local authorities were billing the central and state governments for wage costs far above what workers were being paid. To combat this and other fraud including inflated estimates for public works projects and the use of shoddy materials the MKSS investigations catalysed state agencies to monitor spending and require all village accounts to be scrutinized at village meetings open to all.

These new types of popular participation are spreading across the globe as civil society groups go beyond whistle-blowing and protests to take on oversight functions that are normally the responsibility of state institutions. Moreover, the movement is forcing change through better enforcement of existing rules and regulations, institutional reform and enhanced transparency and monitoring. Such initiatives have led to participatory budgeting more systematic, institutionalized public participation in the preparation of budgets. In 1989 Porto Alegre, Brazil, introduced a process that enables citizens to participate in preparing municipal budgets. In its first seven years the process resulted in remarkable gains in human development spending for poor people: the share of households with access to water services rose from 80% to 98%, the portion of people with access to sewage facilities jumped from 46% to 85% and the number of children enrolled in public school doubled. 60 This approach has been replicated in about 100 other municipalities in Brazil. In addition, more than 40 countries have used participatory budgeting to promote gender-responsive public spending.

Participatory budgeting shows that even the veil of technical complexity that has protected budgets from open questioning can be lifted once citizen groups have time, skills and access to information. These new forms of people's participation from influencing agendas through protests to increasing collaboration in decision-making are reinforcing democratic institutions. E-governance is another emerging avenue for people's participation in politics, encouraging more direct citizen engagement with elected representatives.

Popular demands for greater accountability no longer stop at the state or at national boundaries. Global economic integration has reinforced the power and influence of global actors -intergovernmental organizations such as the World Bank, International Monetary Fund, World Trade Organization and global corporations. These global institutions and their rules govern important aspects of national economic policies and have enormous impacts on people's lives creating a global-national gap in democratic participation and accountability.

Global civil society networks are working to redress such gaps, with varying success. They are being aided in their efforts by the Internet, which makes it possible to create formal networks of non-governmental organizations (NGOs) as well as much looser networks of individuals and organizations that can quickly mobilize collective action. For example, a campaign by Rain Forest Action Network and Greenpeace led Home Depot, the world's largest lumber retailer, to stop buying timber from endangered forests and from suppliers that engaged in unsustainable harvesting. The key feature of this initiative was that it mobilized hundreds of environmental organizations and grass-roots groups. Many such actions abound. If not for the Internet, these organizations and grass-roots groups would have remained isolated, engaged in dispersed efforts. How such global public action has become a real force in global governance, providing checks and balances on corporations, governments and intergovernmental organizations and achieving important breakthroughs for human development.

These autonomous efforts offer enormous promise because they offer a more direct channel of accountability -defying conventional constraints on social action, which typically require going through established institutions of accountability. But that disregard for convention also raises difficult questions for accountability and democratic governance. In particular, the ability of these global networks to inflict large and immediate costs on the reputations of public and private actors tends to work against the notion of due process. Criteria for weighing information are usually vague and subject to change without notice, and the scope for malicious misinformation is enormous.

These and other concerns about the proper roles and responsibilities of civil society actors have created demand for these groups to be more publicly accountable for their activities: a demand that many are working to meet. Ethiopian NGOs have adopted codes of conduct for effective self-regulation. The codes emphasize the importance of transparency and accountability and the need to ensure that the NGOs are truly representative of the people whose lives they affect.

Expanding political and civic space for popular social engagement is critical for deepening democracy and building democratic governance. Responsibilities for expanding this space lie both with the state, which must protect civil and political freedoms, and with the members of society who engage in and invigorate this exercise. Over the past decade 68 countries signed the International Covenant on Civil and Political rights, nearly twice the number that signed in the preceding 25 years. But as of February 2002, 39 countries still had not. And while guaranteeing basic political and civil freedoms is a crucial first step, many countries restrict the activities of trade unions, professional organizations and NGOs. In some countries NGOs can be banned for having political aims. And as noted, in many countries the media are restricted from voicing dissent or have inadequate dissemination.

Civic activism cannot be said to have failed just because some actions do not lead to change. Some initiatives are bound to fail, just as all but one candidate will necessarily lose an election. What is important in democracies is the spread of democratic practice, where people can voice their views, influence decisions and monitor performance against commitments both national and international. Thailand's unique approach to drafting its constitution is an example of this kind of participatory democracy.

Deepening Democracy for Human Development

Strengthening accountability is central to a larger process of embedding democratic values, practices and principles in every aspect of society to build strong, durable and inclusive democracies more responsive and accountable to ordinary people. But the gap between democratic aspiration and practice is wide in long-standing democracies as well as new ones. The chronic underrepresentation of women, the neglect of minority interests and the unaccountable and untransparent military and civil service are common issues. Costa Rica's remarkable experiment in public consultations on the state of democracy illustrates this well.

Democratic deficits can mean hollow citizenship. People do not have fully equal rights and entitlements because constitutions fail to guarantee them or because administrative institutions fail to enforce them. And when there is a lag between norms and entitlements, rights are not respected as is often the case with discrimination against women.

Democratic realists say that this is to be expected of representative democracy, which above all is a system of political competition, not one intended exclusively to empower citizens, generate high or direct participation in government affairs or produce economic and social justice. And certainly, democratization does not guarantee social justice any more than it guarantees economic growth, social peace, administrative efficiency, political harmony, free markets or the end of ideology. But the institutions, practices and ideals of democracy have the capacity to challenge the concentration of political power and prevent the emergence of tyranny. Thus they play a crucial role in building governance that is by the people as well as for the people.

4

Towards Conflict Resolution

Achieving human development also depends on peace and personal security. The challenge of sustaining peace looms large in many other countries, including many that triumphantly embraced democracy in the 1980s and 1990s. Since 1989 national armies have intervened in the political affairs of 13 Sub-Saharan states: about one in four countries in the region.

In Pakistan in 1999, military leaders resumed control of democratic institutions under the banner of maintaining civil peace. People in these countries will never see enduring public peace and personal security until the police, military and other security forces are under firm democratic control.

That democratic countries seem to enjoy a permanent peace among themselves challenges the widely held view that nation-states are doomed to exist in a state of war. Yet history also shows that the early years of building a democratic state tend to be the most perilous: both for democracy and for civil peace. Between 1951 and 1999, 46 elected governments were forcibly overturned by authoritarian rule. And nearly all of today's most stable democracies -including the United States -suffered a civil war early in their history. Most took several generations to develop a professional army under democratic civil control. This should give pause to any who would argue that the goals of building democracy and securing public order are perfectly aligned. To achieve personal security and peace, are so hard even in well-established democracies.

Human development will be held back in any country where the military, police and other security-related institutions hold sway over democratic institutions or are not democratically accountable for much of their power or are fragmented and anarchic. Yet that is the situation in most developing countries today. In the second half of the 20th century 50 countries moved from authoritarian military rule to democratically elected governments.

In many other developing democracies the military continues to exert profound political and economic influence. Moreover, security forces are often largely responsible for formulating security policy in new and old democracies alike. In both democratic and non-democratic countries, parts of the security sector can become the tools of extremist politicians or parties. Or they may actually rest in private hands -with warlords, paramilitary groups or private security companies.

Moreover, legitimate security services are often unable to deal with rising crime, human rights violations or ethnic violence. In all these cases personal security and democratic governance are at risk, because the means for the legitimate use of force are not subject to democratic control.

Today, in many developing countries, authoritarian governments have resisted or overturned moves towards democracy -arguing that democracy is incompatible with public order and personal security. But the record suggests that the opposite is true: democratic civil control over state security forces, far from opposing personal security, is essential to it. Without that control the supposed guarantors of personal security can be its greatest threat. During the 20th century "deaths by government " or "democides "-through direct violence or gross negligence in major disasters -were estimated at 170 million people, far higher than the number of deaths in wars.

The democides include millions of deaths in China, Germany and the Soviet Union, and many more on a smaller scale. None of this would have been possible without the support and efforts of police, intelligence services, the military and official and unofficial paramilitary forces. Where governments rely on security for their power base, security forces are often the main cause of insecurity for their citizens and neighbouring states. Unchecked and unaccountable, security institutions often prey on the most vulnerable members of society, hampering daily struggles for survival and other basic freedoms.

Throughout much of Africa there is widespread torture, intimidation and harassment of civilians by police on behalf of ruling regimes. And worldwide, too many police forces are absent where needed, fail to respond to calls for help or arrive on the scene only when someone has been killed. Despite all this, people desperately need the police to provide basic physical security in their neighbourhoods.

Participatory poverty assessments often find that lack of physical security is one of poor people's main concerns. The irony is that those most in need of professional, well-functioning security forces -poor and socially excluded people are generally the most suspicious of the services these public institutions provide, and not without reason. They recognize that, all too often, security forces are behind the proliferation of civil conflict. Undemocratic governance of security forces can also distort security priorities.

In many countries a bias towards military security has led governments to militarize police forces or to seriously underfund them, undermining their capacity to guarantee people's safety and security. Especially in low-income countries, the police and other security forces have barely subsistence wages, limited or no training, corrupt management and high illiteracy levels.

So, economic and social inequalities translate into large inequalities in personal security. In response, poor communities feel that they must create local militias or even resort to less organized forms of delivering "justice ". Even in the United States poor people are much more likely than rich people to fall victim to violent crime. Moreover, in industrial countries businesses and individuals increasingly contribute to the $100 billion a year private global security industry -a direct consequence of weak public security.

Elected leaders in fledgling democracies often depend on security forces, including military units, to stay in office because those forces are the most powerful in society. For the same reason, leaders may actively resist greater accountability and openness for the military, because they depend on its power for their own ends. Another reason is the natural tendency towards secrecy and lack of transparency in security affairs.

Security policies -both internal and external -are at the centre of power relations within and among societies. Yet they are also usually the area where civil society, the government and its oversight institutions have the least say. The lack of transparency and accountability is particularly problematic in budgeting, where a select few individuals in the executive branch make decisions on security policies and resources.

Parliamentary bodies -which may even have oversight authority in the national constitution -and the media and civil society are routinely kept in the dark. Making matters worse in many countries is that the military has income sources outside the formal budget.

The Chinese People's Liberation Army had an extensive business empire. This began to be dismantled by the central government in 1998, causing the official defence budget to increase. Such extra-budgetary activities tend to be almost impossible to oversee and control, giving armed forces considerable leeway to run their affairs independently of any democratic control. And given the secrecy that often shrouds arms purchases, the procurement of expensive weapons by unaccountable military leaders is prone to corruption even when direct military rule has ended.

Procurement decisions are often based on foreign policy, not just technical criteria. That allows military decision-makers, and their civilian counterparts in the executive branch, to hide personal financial interests behind poorly defined claims of "national security ". Strict military hierarchies and a lack of parliamentary and auditing control in security matters further limit careful scrutiny of arms contracts. According to one U.S. government study, about half the known bribes since the mid-1990s were for defence contracts -and those are just the known bribes.

Arms dealers from both industrial and developing countries conduct their dealings in private and often route arms and payments through intermediate countries that do not cooperate in corruption cases. The global arms bazaar, underpinned by powerful economic interests, reinforces excessive secrecy and corruption in many countries ' security sectors. Governments and their security forces have an obligation to protect the security of their borders and their people. This perhaps justifies more confidentiality than applies to other parts of government.

But in democratic systems there should also be an obligation for policy-makers and security forces to be accountable to the public for their decisions and for their use of public resources. Minor adjustments can accommodate legitimate needs for confidentiality without violating the principles of sound public management. Effective accountability in security matters will never materialize if oversight institutions lack the capacity to assess security activities.

Without that capacity, a cycle of ignorance will persist. When legitimate civilian actors are denied participation or a monitoring role over security policy-making, they lack detailed knowledge of security issues.

This limited knowledge then enables security forces to argue that decision-making should rest with those with relevant knowledge -with the security forces. Core principles for democratic governance of the security sector can help governments balance the need for secrecy with the need for greater democratic control.

The democratic governance of security forces face three challenges:

— The first is establishing direct leadership of security forces by executive departments, fiscal oversight by parliament and specialized auditing bodies and monitoring by the media and civil society.

— The second challenge is developing a culture of professionalism and political neutrality within security forces.

— The third is clearly separating an effective police force from the military and encouraging community policing.

In many countries the military has a highly privileged position in the allocation of national resources. Similarly, spending on security forces does not compete on an equal footing with spending to meet the basic needs of all people, particularly the vulnerable.

Democratic governance requires that decisions about the size, structure and operations of security forces rest on solid legal foundations, exercised with political responsibility. Civil authorities need to be in control, but they also need to give clear guidance to security forces, working with them and respecting their expertise. The budget process is the main instrument for transparency and accountability. Budgets provide a detailed statement of plans to which people can hold parliament accountable, and to whose proper execution parliament can hold security forces accountable. Managing security spending has four related elements:

— Identifying the needs and key objectives of the security sector as a whole and the specific missions that different security forces will be asked to undertake.

— Determining what is affordable.

— Allocating resources based on priorities within and between different security agencies.

— Ensuring the efficient, effective use of resources.

Strengthening the capacity of civilians to manage and monitor the budgets of security forces is therefore a high priority, especially where military elites dominate decision-making because of unequal power and knowledge. All spending on different security forces - their personnel, operations and equipment -should be included in their budgets. Those budgets should also indicate how this spending is financed. Yet most security budgets meet neither condition. Intrabudgetary allocations are opaque, and total spending -which may include funds from a number of departments -remains unclear. In countries with extensive off-budget activities, governments themselves often lack accurate information.

The quality of leadership in the executive branch is critical in determining the extent to which legal and cultural norms for democratic governance find acceptance. Efforts to create a security force that follows democratic principles and sound public spending will succeed only if a country's political and administrative leadership is committed to creating effective, accountable institutions and ensuring that they function well. Mature democracies suggest that a wide range of formal oversight bodies can strengthen and enforce democratic civil control of the security sector, particularly by providing fiscal transparency. These include specialized parliamentary oversight committees and independent audit boards. But such bodies are effective only to the extent that they have the information and expertise needed to do their jobs.

Many legislatures are not equipped to play even a limited role in oversight, partly because of decades -and sometimes centuries -of executive supremacy and partly because of the culture of secrecy. Confidentiality should not be the rule -it should be the well-justified exception. A culture of secrecy and unaccountable authority can undermine civil oversight from day one. When security budgeting and other aspects of security policy move closer to the ideals of transparency, chances are they will also move closer to true democratic civil control. Increased transparency strengthens the hand of formal democratic institutions such as parliament and the judiciary. Citizens can help shape security policy even in the poorest countries.

In Sierra Leone in 1998, shortly after the restoration of the elected government that had been overthrown by the army and Revolutionary United Front rebels, the executive branch began developing plans for reconstituting the armed forces. In response, civil society organizations held multistakeholder consultations and offered the government a range of reform proposals - including widely circulating photographs of all recruits so that civilians could vet them for human rights abuses.

Popular participation promotes public trust and boosts the morale of security forces even as it helps hold security actors accountable. These efforts are leading to new thinking about democracy and security. Since the early 1990s many Central and Eastern European countries

-the Czech Republic, Estonia, Hungary, Latvia, Lithuania, Poland, Slovenia and to a lesser extent Bulgaria and Romania -have been democratizing civil-military relations. With few exceptions, there is little threat of direct military intervention in domestic politics.

New legal and institutional mechanisms for civilian oversight of military affairs have created opportunities for greater transparency and for participation in security policy by parliaments, media, academics and civil society organizations. In forging a more holistic approach to civil-military relations, these democratic reforms have buttressed steps in many countries to establish civilian mechanisms for making defence policy and managing the security sector. But when interior ministry troops, paramilitary police and intelligence services are drawn into domestic political struggles, efforts to improve democratic civil control are often jeopardized.

Efforts to transform security institutions must also force change from within.This requires a shift in internal culture and new incentives for members to respect democratic civil authority and promote the public interest. Senior officers need to take a firm stand against corruption. They also need to make clear that they do not tolerate the diversion of state resources in other ways - such as using military and police vehicles for private purposes.

Achieving these goals can be a matter of professional training. Indeed, in the long run there is probably no substitute for military training and broadly based education that teaches soldiers to respect human rights and abide by principles of democratic governance. National military academies do this, but they need to be tied to high professional standards for recruitment, instruction and promotion that are less prone to political interference and corruption. Perhaps even more urgent is professional training of police officers, which can do much for accountability and public trust. Achieving these goals also requires sufficient public revenue. Without appropriate equipment and decent wages, security forces will suffer from poor discipline and corruption. For police, public resources can sometimes be supplemented by innovative public-private partnerships.

Since 1990 the Citizen's Police Liaison Committee of Karachi, Pakistan, has provided free health care to police officers injured in the line of duty. Financed by businesses, the committee also recently provided gas connections to flats occupied by police officers and their families, as well as water lines, furniture, lighting and a children's park. Such public-private initiatives raise the morale of police officers -another element in building a more effective, corruption-free police force. In addition to pursuing these crucial long-term goals, democratic leaders must work to change the behaviour of security forces today -especially by punishing human rights violations and unprofessional conduct.

Professional codes of police, military and intelligence conduct and review tribunals within security services can help in this regard. So can civilian commissions that investigate possible excesses. Postwar investigations of human rights violations during civil wars in El Salvador, Guatemala and Sierra Leone, often launched by governments and civil society organizations, have been important steps towards greater accountability in the security sector. They helped expose human rights violations committed covertly -or even openly -by security forces. Over the medium and long term, judicial reform is also critical in enforcing accountability in security forces.

Police action against crime cannot promote personal security if judges can be bribed easily or if there are no prisons for convicted criminals. When judicial systems are controlled by privileged individuals whose appointments are merely political rewards, law enforcement is likely to be partial -and rule is more likely to be by law than of law. When judicial systems fail to perform basic tasks, including issuing warrants and other legal orders, police officers often must resort to illegal actions to perform regular functions. Corrupt judicial and penitentiary systems also undermine the professionalism and credibility of the security sector if they allow crimes by soldiers or police officers to go unpunished.

Other Latin American governments with long histories of military control, including El Salvador and Guatemala, have also been separating the military from the police. Such reforms need to be combined with efforts to enhance the standing and capacity of the police. Even in communities where physical abuse and corruption by the police have been the norm, efforts to build trust and confidence can foster a new relationship between the police and the people. One way is for the police to get involved in the lives of young people, ethnic minorities and low-income groups. Another is to support community policing.

Police forces with officers from diverse backgrounds tend to respond better to the challenges of diverse communities. Appointing and training female police officers in the state of Para, Brazil, increased reports of violence against women and girls to police and hospitals. In Bosnia and Herzegovina and the Former Yugoslav

Republic of Macedonia more ethnically balanced police forces are fostering trust and respect for the police. In addition, police forces should not give special treatment to certain units, such as criminal investigation and narcotics.

Such reforms take time and deep political commitment. For change to be sustained, democratic leaders must ensure that security institutions feel ownership in the process. Such reforms pose unique challenges but also yield unique benefits -for the security of citizens and the credibility of democratization. South Africa's police reforms are a notable example. After the 1994 elections, members of government and parliament acquired expertise in oversight and leadership through self-education and collaboration with unions, churches and research institutions. But a number of developments can help trigger major security sector reforms:

— *Economic constraints*: reforms result from financial pressures to downsize the military -as in Uganda and other African countries.

— *Civilian control*: a power shift occurs and the military steps down by choice or by force -as in Indonesia and many Latin American countries.

— *Western mainstreaming*: the armed forces are modernized as part of efforts to join the European Union or North Atlantic Treaty Organization (NATO)-as in many Central and Eastern European countries.

New armies: often funded and initially trained by foreign donors and influenced by civil society to respect human rights -as in Bosnia and Herzegovina, East Timor, El Salvador, Estonia, Latvia and Lithuania.

— *Scandals*: often media-driven and influential in reforming the police, intelligence agencies and civil-military relations -as in many industrial countries.

These developments are combined with committed leadership and an engaged civil society, conditions are ripe for significant democratic reforms of security forces that can reinforce broader political change -especially in countries recovering from violent armed conflict.

By establishing an environment of civic peace for national democratic institutions to develop. In the early 1990s alone, more peacekeeping missions were undertaken than during the UN's first four and one-half decades. But while this new generation of peace operations may help end violence, they alone cannot promote durable, democratic peace.

Internal tensions will never be easily eliminated when conflict and poor governance have fractured the foundations of the state. This strengthens the case for pre-emptive democratic peacebuilding, to promote peaceful resolution of simmering conflicts before they turn into wars. Where basic order has broken down, the pressures of limited time and resources produce tension between restoring civil peace and establishing democratic control.

Cambodia in the early 1990s suggests that holding national and local elections in an atmosphere of widespread violence and mistrust can unravel the peace process or legitimize the warring parties, as they did in Bosnia and Herzegovina after the Dayton Peace Accords. The military and the police have blurred roles in many developing countries. During wars the distinction breaks down altogether, with the armed forces taking responsibility for both the external and internal security of the state.

This suggests a need to identify the main security threats in wartorn societies and to devise appropriate policies for the armed forces, the police, intelligence services and other security forces. Among the main tasks include making the armed forces more manageable, affordable and professional, and clearly separated from the police. After armed conflicts, many countries in West and Southern Africa and Central America have overhauled the composition and role of their militaries. Sierra Leone and South Africa absorbed former combatants into their armed forces while reforming their militaries ' missions and orientations.

In Afghanistan it is hoped that a multiethnic army will resolve factional fighting among ethnic Tajiks, Pashtuns, Hazaras and others. Developing a civil police force -in some cases from scratch -is generally a priority in peace agreements. It is especially important for promoting civil peace after war, when organized crime, weapon smuggling and violence are rampant -and likely to surge as communities are flooded with unemployed combatants.

From El Salvador and Gaza to Bosnia and Herzegovina, Mozambique and Rwanda, the transition from civil war to civil society has been linked to broadly based police forces that are democratically accountable, impartial, depoliticized and composed of different political contingents and ethnic groups. Such forces can emerge only through effective training -particularly in the skills of community policing and other specialized training -and through better ethnic and gender balance. It may be tempting to convert soldiers to police officers, but this should be handled with care. Soldiers, especially those with human rights violations, may have methods and experience poorly suited to the police. The international community can help build accountable, effective police forces in post-conflict environments.

Until 1989 only three peacekeeping operations included UN Civilian Police units. With the end of the cold war, space opened for international assistance to provide more police aid. Besides regional and bilateral assistance, the UN Civilian Police is now a common presence in a new generation of peacekeeping, although many argue that its role requires further development. In Cambodia the UN Civilian Police provided public security and arrested suspects. In El Salvador and Haiti it helped design and train a new civilian police force - experiences recently replicated in East Timor and Kosovo.

As the United Nations assumes more complicated peacebuilding tasks involving public security, its Civilian Police and the broader development community require well-funded international police officers who are not only good cops, but experts in building institutions -police with experience setting up police academies, organizing and restructuring police organizations and fostering community policing that serves citizens rather than entrenching the power of ruling regimes.

To succeed, such interventions require support for domestic constituencies for police reform. They also require collecting accurate, credible data on domestic crime -and convincing leaders of wartorn countries that repressive policing is part of the problem, not part of the solution. Demobilizing combatants and reintegrating them into normal life is one of the most challenging priorities in post-conflict situations.

Since 1990 major postwar demobilizations have occurred in a wide range of countries: Bosnia and Herzegovina, El Salvador, Eritrea, Ethiopia, Guatemala, Haiti, Mozambique, Nicaragua, Sierra Leone and Uganda. In addition, smaller-scale demobilizations have taken place in Chad, Lebanon, Mali, Panama, Rwanda and South Africa. Such efforts require as much participation as possible so that affected groups will take ownership of reform. Many actors have a stake in the outcomes. They include demobilized combatants -male and female former child soldiers, government soldiers and guerrillas. They also include families of former combatants, communities where former combatants resettle and other groups trying to reintegrate -such as returned refugees and internally displaced people

And they include local security forces, government agencies, local and international non-governmental organizations, the United Nations and its agencies and other official donors. But because of time pressures and the vast number of people and groups involved, many of these actors have had little voice in the design of demobilization and reintegration programmes. Indeed, the process has often been led by outside agencies, muting the voices of local people. Limited participation may be inevitable in the immediate aftermath of conflict. But demobilization and reintegration programmes should be structured so that they can be adjusted over time, through inclusive dialogue with former combatants, their families, affected communities and others.

In Uganda, to test the feasibility of their reintegration, some soldiers were allowed to visit their home areas before demobilization. And interactions between former soldiers and veteran field officers helped the demobilization in Rwanda in the late 1990s.

Unsurprisingly, targeted assistance to former combatants has generated heated debate, raising issues of fairness and accountability. There are humanitarian arguments for giving former combatants special support: after demobilization, they are unemployed and far from home.

In some cases they have given years of their lives to fight for what they considered the good of their country. But they may also have been forcibly recruited into the armed forces. And they may have great difficulty re-establishing themselves in civilian life, perhaps threatening the peace process by getting involved in criminal activity or violent political opposition.

Support for former combatants can also reduce illicit trade in small arms and light weapons. Such trade - valued at $4 -6 billion a year -is an attractive source of revenue for former combatants in poor, conflict-ridden societies. In Sierra Leone these issues were taken into account when disarming and demobilizing more than 75,000 combatants since 1998, including roughly 7,000 child combatants.

In most cases former combatants are far outnumbered by returning refugees and other people displaced by war who need to be readily equipped for myriad post-conflict challenges, such as landmines. Given scarce resources, demobilization support programmes will thus have to balance helping former combatants too much and too little.

Consensus seems to have developed that special efforts for former combatants are generally necessary and justified during demobilization and resettlement -but that support in the reintegration phase should, as much as possible, be community-and area-based and part of broader development programmes. Indeed, support from communities is often crucial for the reintegration of former combatants.

Armed conflict is the worst enemy of human rights, poor people, minority rights and freedom of information. The period before a ceasefire and immediately after a war are thus critical to establishing more open, inclusive politics. Ending a war can be as destabilizing as war itself, and it is impossible to democratize political decision-making immediately. But there needs to be as much openness and participation as possible for peace and true reconciliation to take root -and for strengthening civil society and democratically minded parts of the population. To be specific, if the termination of a war is based on a peace agreement, the leading voices in shaping the country's future will be the negotiating parties and their teams.

Civilians, particularly women, are usually heavily underrepresented in peace talks. The overwhelming predominance of combatants in negotiations can seriously constrain the democratic development of these societies and reduce the long-term stability of peace. But the inter-Congolese dialogue and the greater involvement of women in peacemaking elsewhere suggest that this problem is slowly gaining wider recognition. Peacemakers must also recognize that long, deadly civil conflicts completely transform societies -whether through the displacement of local populations, destruction of infrastructure or upheaval of traditional family and social networks.

In wartorn societies such as Sri Lanka, male combatants are recruited from poor communities. For their survival, women in these communities have often transcended their traditional gender roles in terms of family, work and community. Peace negotiations and local leaders must take these radically changed realities into account when designing programmes for recovery and reconciliation. Giving a greater voice to previously marginalized groups is not only morally right, it is also practical. A growing number of peace processes address the need for strengthening democratic institutions and protecting human rights, including provisions for creating or fortifying national human rights institutions.

In 1992 a UN-sponsored peace agreement in El Salvador created the Procurador para la Defensa de los Derechos Humanos to prevent human rights violations in areas such as police conduct, prison conditions, children's rights and violence against women.

Bosnia and Herzegovina's Human Rights Ombudsman, established by the 1995 Dayton Peace Accords, has extensive powers to investigate, report, initiate and intervene in court proceedings. Given the severe human rights problems and pressures facing the judicial branch in most wartorn societies, human rights institutions are often essential in the transition to democracy by promoting international human rights commitments and providing key administrative oversight -especially in the security sector.

Many countries recovering from wars are exploring avenues for justice, such as community trials in East Timor and the gacaca process in Rwanda, that may help build public support. In addition, war crimes tribunals - and in the future, a permanent International Criminal Court -are redressing past injustices. Truth commissions have also provided a way for people to voice grievances about past atrocities -and give them a feeling that justice has been done. Since 1974 more than 20 such commissions have sought to set straight countries ' historical records, with varying objectives, structures and results. Such processes face the challenge of managing the tension between justice and reconciliation.

Governing System in Asia

Governance is a simple concept at heart: good governance is good government. The concept relates to the quality of the relationship between government and the citizens whom it exists to serve and protect. Issues of governance are at the centre of many of the most pressing challenges confronting countries throughout the Asian and Pacific region today.

In South Asia, issues of restricting the reach of state intervention and improving the delivery of basic services, such as health care and education, are high on the agenda. Economies in transition in Central and Southeast Asia are grappling with redefining the role of the state, shifting the balance between central and local power, and providing civil service employees with appropriate skills for managing a market economy. In the Pacific, issues of public sector efficiency, effectiveness, and accountability are particularly important for ensuring the long-term viability of small economies. Each nation's path to good governance is different, depending on culture, geography, political and administrative traditions, economic conditions, and many other factors. The scope of activities allocated to the public and private sectors diverges markedly. Variation in scale is also enormous. Many of the institutions and practices that work effectively in the People's Republic of China (PRC), with its 1.2 billion people, will not be relevant in Nauru, with its population of 10,000.

Yet governments share many features. They face similar responsibilities in that they need to establish a basic policy framework, provide critical goods and services, protect and administer the rule of law, and advance social equity. In executing these responsibilities, they need to perform a variety of similar tasks, such as organizing themselves to formulate and coordinate.

Governance has, therefore, political and economic dimensions. Issues of political governance include the mechanisms by which the public's political preferences are ascertained and leaders chosen. These are fundamental governance concerns, but are generally outside the scope of the Bank's work. But economic governance—sound development management—is at the core of sustainable development.

The instrumental nature of governance implies that the four governance "pillars" are universally applicable regardless of the economic orientation, strategic priorities, or policy choices of the government in question. There are four key components of governance:

— accountabilty,

— transparency,

— predictability, and

— participation.

— *Accountability* is the capacity to call officials to account for their actions. Effective accountability has two components: 'answerability' and consequences. ln is the requirement to respond periodically to questions concerning one's official actions. There is also a need for predictable and meaningful consequences, without which accountability is only a time-consuming formality.

In addition, both internal and external accountability are needed. Particularly with the dramatic improvements in information and communication technology, external accountability through feedback from service users and the citizenry can now be obtained at low cost and for a greater variety of government activities, and is an essential adjunct to improving efficiency and effectiveness of public service delivery.

— *Transparency* entails low-cost access to relevant information. Reliable and timely economic and financial information is a must for the public. It is essential not only that information be provided, but also that it be relevant and understandable. Predictability results primarily from laws and regulations that are clear, known in advance, and uniformly and effectively enforced. Lack of predictability makes it difficult for public officials to plan for the provision of services.

— *Predictability* of government economic actions is also needed as an indicator on which the private sector can rely to make its own production, marketing, and investment decisions. Most importantly, to be predictable, the application of economic regulations must be effective, fair, and uniform.

— *Participation* is needed to obtain reliable information and to serve as a reality check and watchdog for government action. Among other things, participation by external entities is needed as a spur to government operational efficiency, and feedback by users of public services is necessary for monitoring access to and quality of the services.

The Role of Civil Society in Good Governance

All, governance intervention should encourage the formation of social capital, i.e., the stock of trust and information exchange at the base of civil society. Development organizations and governments the world over widely share the views embodied in the four governance pillars, although each has its own approach in applying them. This consensus on governance has been accompanied by recognition of the costs of and damages from corruption, and the adoption by many international organizations of robust anticorruption measures.

For example, in December 1996, the United Nations General Assembly passed the Declaration Against Corruption and Bribery in International Commercial Transactions. In December 1997, a landmark convention against bribery was negotiated under the aegis of the Organisation for Economic Co-operation and Development (OECD), making bribery of foreign officials a crime at par with bribery of national officials.

Because corruption is by definition two-sided, this convergence between the emphasis on combating corruption in the developing countries and the Anti-Bribery Treaty offers a historic opportunity to reduce drastically the negative impact of corruption on development.

The financial crisis that erupted in mid-1997 quickly spread to other Southeast and East Asian economies. The worldwide repercussions of the crisis required a coordinated approach. The Bank acted, therefore, in concert with other organizations and institutions, to introduce fundamental reforms in governance and the manner of economic management. Governance-oriented interventions in crisis-affected countries Bank assistance to the countries worst hit by the crisis—Indonesia, Republic of Korea, and Thailand—has also focused on governance.

In the Republic of Korea, the Bank provided a $4 billion Financial Sector Program loan to the International Monetary Fund (IMF)-led multilateral assistance package. The loan supports the restructuring of financial institutions, combined with strengthening regulation and supervision, and with measures to liberalize the capital market and develop it further.

In Thailand, two sizeable loans have major governance components. The Financial Markets Reform Program loan of $300 million underpins fundamental reforms for transparency and accountability in the financial sector; and the Social Sector Program loan of $500 million supports, among other things, the administrative decentralization of health and education services. The years 1997 and 1998 also saw an expansion of Bank activities in countries in the Asian and Pacific region in various aspects of public institutions and the public/private interface. Of course, some interventions were under way well before the onset of the Asian financial crisis, but the crisis gave them added impetus.

Interventions have ranged from corporate governance in the Kyrgyz Republic to public administration diagnosis in Nepal; civil service reform strategies in Pakistan; governance reviews for Lao People's Democratic Republic, Thailand, and Viet Nam; anticorruption in Indonesia; urban governance in the Philippines; public sector interventions in the Pacific; and more. Bank assistance to its Pacific DMCs has broadened in scope since the formulation of the 1996 Strategy for the Pacific: Policies and Programs for Sustainable Growth.

Working in consultation and agreement with governments, the Bank has taken the lead role in the aid community as a catalyst and facilitator of policy reform and capacity building in development management, while retaining the traditional role of project financier. Economic reform programs in seven Pacific DMCs have been undertaken with Bank technical and financial assistance during 1996-1998. These programs aim at generating sustainable economic growth through the creation of a leaner, more efficient public sector, and a better enabling environment for the private sector.

Program effectiveness in improving governance and the economic policy framework is expected, in turn, to increase the effectiveness of project-based and sector-specific lending. To improve Bank interventions in the Pacific DMCs, the Bank established an interdepartmental task force to review the design, implementation, and impact of its program loans and associated policy reforms. Nineteen ninety-eight was a landmark and eventful year in many ways beyond the crisis. The Bank intensified its efforts at disseminating the lessons of international experience in public management and—most important for the future of the Bank as a broad-based development institution—managed to strengthen internal capacity significantly.

Governance issues have also started to permeate traditional sector work, as demonstrated in the policies currently being developed for integrated water management, urban development, health, nutrition, and education. The Bank's law and development activities promote legal reforms, building on empirical findings that a policy, legal, and regulatory environment, which secures property rights and enforces contracts, is supportive of economic growth and poverty reduction.

Although law and development activities have a general focus on the development of legal and regulatory frameworks that support private sector development, they take into account the need for ethnically conscious interventions into the marketly with a view to spreading market-generated wealth. People are at the heart of development; they are not only the ultimate beneficiaries, but are also the agents of development. Since development is both for and by the people, they need to have access to the institutions that promote it.

Participation, as a component of the Bank's governance policy, implies that people will have the opportunity to improve the design and implementation of public programs and projects. The Bank's Framework on Mainstreaming Participatory Development Processes defines participatory development, notes its importance to the Bank, and tells how Bank staff, in collaboration with DMC counterparts, can support it.

Additionally, it shows how participatory processes can be systematically incorporated in the Bank's business processes, and what modifications are required in the Bank's procedures, policies, and practices to mainstream participatory development in the Bank's work.

For example, the Bank's public expenditure management handbook, currently nearing completion, has benefited from the advice of technical reviewers from the World Bank, IMF, United Nations Development Programme (UNDP), and OECD. Also, the Bank has proceeded from general issues to more concrete topics.

Thus, the initial dissemination of broad problems of governance and development has provided the basis for more focused events on fiscal transparency and financial accountability. The Bank has identified six key areas of governance, for which it is acquiring an internal core capacity:

(i) participation, civil society, and social capital;

(ii) law and development;

(iii) public/private interface;

(iv) sector and project work;

(v) core government functions at the national level; and

(vi) decentralization.

Mainstreaming participation in the Bank entails modifying the conceptual framework on participation, based on lessons from the field; operational support in projects, sector work, and country strategies; work on policies, guidelines, and procedures; training and information sharing; capacity building in DMCs to strengthen participatory approaches; and networking with other development finance institutions, NGOs, and DMC-based organizations.

Predictability, one of the four pillars of governance, relies largely on a legal and judicial framework that is clear, uniform, public, and robust. Among the systemic problems found in many developing countries are delays in court hearings; poor physical infrastructure; low status of judges, and terms and conditions under which they work; weak judicial account- ability mechanisms which, in some countries, permit widespread buying of favourable verdicts; lack of trained sup- port staff and case management systems; and poor state of legal education and training.

Accordingly, assistance on specific project-related law reforms also takes into account the need for development of institutional capacity of the legal and judicial systems. Corporate governance and the public-private interface are regulatory issues in every sector, and the development impact of Bank assistance will depend to a major extent on the existence of a sound balance between the public and private interests in the sector in question.

While the public-private interface is too diverse to be amenable to meaningful generalizations, the main goal is a regulatory framework that is suited to the characteristics of the sector in question and that protects identified public interests while minimizing private transaction costs. A good regulatory framework does this by fostering accountability, transparency, and predictability in the formulation and application of the rules and regulations. This is especially necessary for issues of corporate governance of public enterprises, which must reflect the general principles of good private management as well as the interests of the state as owner, in furtherance of some public aim.

The general influence on good governance of market-based and other nongovernment mechanisms is also important. First, contestability, i.e., the possibility of market entry, can sometimes be as effective as actual competition to stimulate good public sector management.

Governance aspects of sector and project operations can be incorporated in the Bank's work through improvements in project approach and design rather than through radically different projects. Rarely will a sector strategy or a project have governance improvements per se as its central focus.

However, all sector strategies and projects should consider the possibility of strengthening accountability mechanisms, reducing the cost of information, or improving predictability—even if no particular action turns out to be appropriate to the situation at hand. Thus, more effective incorporation of governance considerations at the sector and project levels should flow from individual manager's leadership, a better-equipped staff, and career incentives consistent with the time and effort required.

Many Asian governments have developed or are starting to implement ambitious decentralization schemes. Although such initiatives hold long-term promise for more responsive and effective service delivery, in the near term there is a critical need for assistance in developing an appropriate division of labour among central, regional, and municipal governments. This is a particular concern in settings with limited administrative and financial capacity and low levels of accountability. If decentralization means only a shift in the control of resources to local institutions monopolizing task-related roles, service delivery performance may suffer from low capacity and weak accountability.

A more promising model would be to promote networks of service delivery partners, including central and local government agencies, private businesses, and NGOs. By increasing the number and diversity of partners, accountability will be increased, risk reduced, and public sector tasks better adapted to local needs. The Bank is fully committed to its transformation into a broad-based development institution, of which governance is a core dimension.

While transformation in Bank operations is well under way, to be sustainable requires, among other things, appropriate organizational arrangements, a small core of specialist staff in the various areas of public sector management and institutional development.

Governance is too important to be marginalized isolated into any single office at the Bank. It must become an integral of all analytical, lending, and technical assistance activities. Hence, at the top of the immediate agenda is the mainstreaming of governance activities into the Bank's operational departments. At the same time, the Bank is ensuring that governance considerations are appropriately incorporated into other policies being formulated and is actively monitoring implementation of the governance and anticorruption policies.

Careful and realistic assessment is needed of the costs and benefits of possible institutional innovations, in light of the characteristics and administrative capacity of the individual country. The Bank can build on recent work of other international organizations, as it pulls together knowledge about good practices and diagnostic tools in this complex area. The main efforts at external dissemination of good practice will revolve in 1999 and 2000 around a series of in-country workshops on public expenditure management, civil service/public administration, and local government, eventually covering every DMC in the Asian and Pacific region.

Improved implementation processes for governance reforms: As manuals and diagnostic tools are developed and governments set strategies for organizational development and policy reform, the second priority for medium-term improvement is the processes for carrying out these strategies. The Bank needs better processes for addressing governance concerns in its projects, and for anticipating and dealing with crosscutting governance issues affecting the Bank's project portfolio in each DMC. Too often the Bank and other development partners invest large sums to design institutional reforms that are not effectively implemented.

Promotion of Human Rights Development

Human rights may be universal, but they are not universally accepted. Human rights are seen as a threat by many groups, including man in positions of power or superiority. Rights challenge entrenched interests, just as equitable development threatens those in privileged positions. But in the longer run all can gain. Human rights and human development help build law-abiding, prosperous and stable countries.

Individual commitment and community struggle will be the critical factors for advancing rights and human development in the future-just as the have been in the past. But governments and many other actors also have vital roles. Governments have a special responsibility to lead-but NGOs, the private sector, professionals and many others in civil society have an important part to play, including making government accountable for human rights. All rights cannot be fulfilled simultaneously, and a refusal to establish priorities runs the risk of making the rights approach synonymous with a "wish list".

For many countries now bristle at external assessments, for a variety of reasons-some bad, some good. Despite the end of the cold war and the supposed adoption of an approach integrating all human rights, the external reports deal almost exclusively with civil and political rights, ignoring economic and social rights. These reviews can distort the reality of human rights struggles by groups, institutions and individuals across the world by making human rights appear to be an issue of the "West versus the rest". That is clearly not the intention of these reports, many of which involve extensive collaboration with national institutions.

But the world needs to move to the next stage-independent national assessments. National reviews should go beyond the narrow human rights focus of today's assessments. The can improve both the knowledge of human rights and the process of monitoring progress and setbacks. And the should adopt the framework of advancing rights for human development-covering all rights, not just the civil and political. An important feature of these annual assessments must be independence.

The annual reports of Pakistan's human rights commission have not only documented violations of civil, cultural and political rights but have also covered economic and social rights. The commission's chairwoman, Asma Jehangir, has emphasized the links between extreme poverty , sectarian clashes and civil rights abuses. Successive Pakistani governments in the 1990s have provided the space for these independent assessments, which are widely reported on by the print media. Brazil recently produced a national human rights report that profiles each state using human development indicators, analyses of progress in human rights and documentation of human rights violations.

Brazil is also launching local human rights observatories, monitoring instruments that are part of a network among NGOs, a university and the national human rights secretariat. Country examples such as these provide the stimulus for the global spread of independent national assessments. Many countries have "black" laws-laws that violate the human rights of particular individuals, minorities, women or other groups. Some laws are blatantly discriminator.

Institutions allied in struggles against discrimination, such as national human rights commissions and policy institutes, should publish a list of black laws. These laws should be presented to parliament, debated in the media-and changed. Action against black laws has been successful in many cases.

Including universal human rights in the constitution-and thus making them enforceable in court-has given people the legal ammunition needed to take action when their rights are violated. The political power of a strong legal judgement against discrimination should not be underestimated. In Israel an Arab family appealed against legal discrimination that had prevented them from moving into a Jewish neighbourhood.

Human Rights Committee to recognize discrimination on the basis of sexual orientation, first South Africa, and later Ecuador and Fiji, included sexual orientation in the nondiscrimination provisions of their constitutions. Delays in the judicial system are being overcome in some instances by recourse to public interest litigation, often heard by a special bench of the court, to address discriminator and arbitrary administrative actions violating rights.

Public interest litigation has been used in the supreme court of India, for example, when rights such as that to education have been violated. Increased litigation for human rights can create problems if there are too few courts or if judges, magistrates and lawyers are poorly paid. And if people have to wait for ears or even decades before their case is heard, disenchantment is inevitable.

The vital importance of an independent judiciary , efficiency is also essential. Making an independent judiciary efficient requires resources and a decentralized judicial system that brings justice close to the people.

As the Universal Declaration of Human Rights makes clear, human rights should be taught in ever school as universal rights that all people possess. Cambodia emphasizes changing social norms through earl education. Since 1994, 25,000 Cambodian teachers have been trained in the human rights curriculum. The curriculum, already taught to more than 3 million children, may turn out to be a vital investment in the country's future. Using radio, television, video-and traditional songs, skits, dramas and puppet shows-to highlight different aspects of human rights is also an important part of an education strategy , especially for illiterate citizens.

In 1995 the Cambodian Institute of Human Rights adopted an innovative approach to teaching people human rights-using television quiz shows. In 1997 the contestants were members of the military and the police force. The programmes were also broadcast on the national radio, the primary source of information. In Bulgaria a parliamentary committee has started working with television programmes, using popular entertainment to influence human rights norms. Sensitizing officials to human rights issues. Educating policy -makers, the arm , the police and other groups about human rights is essential for creating a human rights culture.

Ecuador was one of the first countries to ratify the Convention on the Rights of the Child. Soon after, it used the national electoral machinery to give children the opportunity to vote on the provisions that mattered most to them.

In Guatemala Conaviguay, a national council of Guatemalan women widowed by war, works to educate and raise awareness about the peace agreements. Mobilizing public opinion through the media. The media can mobilize public opinion by spreading awareness of human rights policies and highlighting violations.

In many countries the media already are a major force for reporting and demanding accountability. Cyber networks have brought attention to rights, disseminating information on good practices and on rights violations. A coalition of African NGOs working for the right to food and food security uses the Internet to exchange experiences and lessons. The Third World Network uses it to disseminate information and good practices on human rights.

Many institutions that work on rights do not see themselves as human rights institutions. Building a wide alliance of public agencies, civil society organizations, the media and the private sector increases the efficacy of efforts for advocacy and accountability. In some countries national human rights commissions try to ensure that the laws and regulations for realizing human rights are effectively applied.

Such commissions receive and investigate complaints of human rights abuses, resolve them through conciliation and arbitration and review the government's human rights policies and the implementation of ratified human rights treaties. For example, the Mexican human rights commission is extremely active in the rights of people with disabilities, the New Zealand commission in human rights education and the South African commission in economic and social rights.

Protecting individuals from rights abuses by public officials or institutions is a vital role of human rights ombudsmen around the world. In Slovenia the ombudsman files an annual report on the observance of human rights with parliament.

According to the 1998 report, the ombudsman has received increasing complaints against public officials, with the number rising from 2,352 in 1995 to 3,448 in 1998. In 1998 the largest share related to court and police procedures, but the biggest increases were for labour relations and restrictions on personal freedoms. According to the Inter-Parliamentary Union, of the 120 national parliaments today, nearly half have formal bodies dealing with human rights. Their mandates reflect the national context, but these bodies share the goal of ensuring that the standards set out in the Universal Declaration of Human Rights and the other human rights covenants and instruments are translated into law-and realized in practice.

In the Republic of Moldova the parliament appointed three parliamentary advocates to examine individual claims and to institute legal procedures. The are also expected to improve the legislative framework for human rights through analysis and policy recommendations. Consistent with this mission, the advocates in 1998 established an independent institution for protecting human rights.

The Centre for Human Rights reports to the legislature each ear on the observance of human rights.

In Nicaragua the Committee for Human Rights and Peace, set up in 1981, works with NGOs in seeking information and documentation on the performance of state officials. In Brazil the Committee on Human Rights receives, assesses and investigates complaints about threats to human rights. Each ear the committee organizes a national conference on human rights, with more than 400 representatives of civil society groups. All these national institutions need to be harnéssed in an alliance for promoting human rights. With each having a different comparative advantage and mandate, collaboration among them is needed to realize rights and fight against coalitions opposing progress.

The Convention on the Rights of the Child, adopted unanimously by the UN General Assembly in 1989, entered into force as international human rights law less than a ear later. It has quickly become the most ratified human rights treat in history, with 191 countries-all but Somalia and the United States-ratifying it in less than a decade. And in many countries around the world, it is already making an impact.

The Universal Declaration of Human Rights, adopted in 1948, applying equally to all children as well as adults. The Declaration on the Rights of the Child, adopted unanimously in 1959 by the UN General Assembly, providing a fuller and more precise definition of the rights of the child. The International Year of the Child-1979-during which it was recommended that the United Nations draft a comprehensive treat binding on states. The 1989 convention provides a comprehensive approach by incorporating all human rights-civil and political as well as economic, social and cultural. The "soul" of the convention is four articles setting out its overarching principles:

— No discrimination against children.

— In all matters concerning children, the best interests of the child shall be primary .

— The right of the child to life, survival and development.

— The right of the child to express views freely in all matters affecting him or her.

The Convention on the Rights of the Child has stimulated broad alliances in a wide range of countries. Similar alliances have been built at the national level to promote women's rights. In an society some groups have special needs because of who they're or because of their situation-people with HIV/AIDS, people with disabilities, refugees, homosexuals and so on. Realizing their human rights often requires alliances, such as the Disabled People's International.

The convention requires states to adopt all appropriate measures-legislative, administrative, social, economic, budgetary , educational or other-and to allocate the resources necessary to ensure effective implementation. The convention recognizes the obligations of other parties-parents and families, civil society and the international community . The fact that a child depends completely on others over the early ears underlines the importance of obligations. The needs of very young children cannot wait-whether for care, food and warmth or for loving stimulus, basic education and health care. The convention has encouraged children to speak out and defend their rights.

In Colombia the Children's Movement for Peace, nominated for the Nobel Peace prize, organized a national movement when 2.7 million children voted in a symbolic referendum on the human rights of minors. In Ecuador and Mexico, too, millions of children went to the polls and voted on their rights.

Children's rights became a principal item in all the major UN conferences of the 1990s. The convention formed the basis for other international legal instruments, such as the Hague Convention on Protection of Children and Cooperation in Respect of Inter-Country Adoption. The new ILO convention on the worst forms of child labour is another example. And several regional instruments are based on the convention, such as the African Charter on the Rights and Welfare of the Child. The convention has led to a process for formulating two optional protocols-to raise the minimum age of military recruitment and participation in armed conflicts, and to enhance the protection of children from sexual exploitation, including through greater international cooperation.

The convention paved the way for recognizing and safeguarding children's rights at the national level. Today at least 22 countries have incorporated children's rights in their constitutions-including Brazil, Ecuador, Ethiopia and South Africa. More than 50 countries have a process of law review to ensure compatibility with the convention's provisions. Bolivia, Brazil and Nicaragua have promoted the adoption of a code on the rights of children and adolescents.

Parliaments in Brazil, South Africa and Sri Lanka have enacted legislation and national budgets to more clearly identify allocations for children. In Belgium the parliament produced and impact report on children, monitoring government policy for respect for the rights of the child. In Sweden the parliament adopted a bill to ensure visibility of the child's perspective in decision-making and called for an analysis of the impact of budgetary decisions and legislation on children.

The Convention on the Elimination of All Forms of Discrimination Against Women (CEDAW), adopted in 1979, has helped realize women's rights the world over. Women's human rights are violated in three main areas:

— Discrimination in economic, political and social opportunities.

— Inequality in family life, including in marriage and in reproductive decision-making.

— Gender-based violence, ranging from violence at home to violence in the community, by the state and during armed conflict.

New policies and laws are recognizing and advancing women's human rights. But reality lags far behind rhetoric. A strategy to address the abuses of women's human rights must rest on women's empowerment-ensuring that the have greater control over their economic resources, bodies and lives.

Among the greatest challenges to recognition of women's human rights are patriarchal attitudes and traditions. To counter this requires human rights education, partnerships and persuasion from within. A coalition of progressive NGOs in the occupied Palestine territory has mounted a successful challenge to religious orthodox. Rights can be established by redress of law-national and international. Using the United Republic of Tanzania's ratification of CEDAW, courts there nullified customary law denying women the right to sell inherited land.

But in many cases national laws must be changed or written-especially for security against violence, for equal economic and social opportunity and for rights to land and inheritance. In Brazil special police forces have been trained to respond to victims of gender abuse, contributing to changes in attitudes and practices.

CEDAW brought changes to constitutions in Colombia, South Africa and Uganda. It brought new laws to China, Costa Rica and Japan. And it has been held binding in court cases in Australia, Nepal and Zambia. While CEDAW does not explicitly address violence against women, a new general recommendation was appended in 1991 prohibiting gender violence by the state and by private persons or groups.

The Vienna Declaration of 1993 was the first UN document to state that women's human rights are an indivisible and integral part of universal human rights. CEDAW's new optional protocol, introduced in 1994, contains unique procedures enabling individuals to claim remedies for violations of convention rights. Though CEDAW has many ratifications, it also has many reservations. These reservations must be removed to allow this valuable document to come to life at the national level ever where.

In all countries a critical task for public policy is to build an enabling environment that empowers people, ensures them opportunities to fulfil their human rights and, where necessary, provides support for them to do so. This is where many policies for human rights and human development come together. To generate the resources and the opportunities for fulfilling human rights, public policy has to foster a growing, efficient and sustainable economy. But public policy has any additional responsibility -it has to ensure that part of the bigger pool of resources goes to advance people's political and economic rights.

Building human capabilities of the poor, through basic health care, nutrition and education, is a primary responsibility of the government. Financing the judicial system to protect rights and improving prison conditions are among its responsibilities for advancing civil rights. The major economic ministries, such as finance and planning, need to integrate rights into the economic policy -making process. By reflecting ministries' obligations on economic and social rights in economic policy -making, the government can assess the shortfalls in meeting these rights and ways to reduce them within resource constraints.

Governments must recognize the economic and social rights of the people the serve, but it is meaningless to assert that those in poor countries must fulfil all of them immediately . Finally , the private sector also has responsibilities in creating an enabling economic environment. Chambers of commerce and other business organizations should contribute to efforts to further improve rights-not only at the workplace but also in advocating policies to address human rights violations.

Many proud civilizations are wounded by deepening poverty and marginalization-and many feel ostracized from the world community because of their lack of participation in new knowledge and global institutions. Several actions are critical for creating a conducive global environment for promoting human rights. The people in donor countries need to speak directly to the people in poor countries-by engaging in debates and decisions about the use of aid to promote economic, social and civil rights. Some donor countries are now taking the lead in focusing on civil and political rights in their efforts to promote good governance.

Australia, German , Norway , Sweden, Switzerland and the United Kingdom are among those taking a rights-based approach to development assistance. Norway recently reviewed its support to human rights efforts in the United Republic of Tanzania, Zambia and Zimbabwe.

Technical co-operation was more helpful for support to human rights institutions. Global compacts for meeting basic rights targets can also help, financed through national budget restructuring and increased international support. These global compacts call for open and accountable commitments to meeting some basic economic and social rights, such as access to education and health care.

Today's international arrangements constrain the ability of poor countries to use, adapt and develop the findings of recent research for advancing their economies and raising the living standards of their people. Because distorted research priorities focus on the problems of the rich-part of the underprovision of public goods. Some private foundations, such as the Bill and Melinda Gates Foundation, have recently given support to vaccine research for the diseases facing poor people.

In the United States a tax credit scheme for pharmaceutical companies, proposed in earl 2000, would use market incentives to redirect research efforts. The credits would stimulate vaccine research on tuberculosis, malaria and AIDS-diseases that take more than 5 million lives a ear in poor countries. The expected spending of $1 billion over the next decade is similar to what UNICEF spends on its vaccination programmes. Such public-private partnerships are the stimulus needed for other research and technology programmes aimed at the problems of poor people. There are also proposals to establish regional centres of technology, and to bring research results to poor people through the Internet and other cost-reducing telecommunications technology.

Some poor countries have made major advances in adopting new technology in some sectors. China, India and several other Asian countries have become vibrant players in the technology revolution. Such promising developments need to be built on-by the international community and by "South-South" collaboration-to address dry land agriculture, environmental degradation and the health hazards consuming the lives of poor people.

For many developing countries, better access to trade opportunities will spur growth in incomes and employment, as occurred for much of East Asia. But some of the most marginalized countries still produce agricultural products with declining terms of trade. The continue to need policy reform, technical assistance and aid inflows to diversify their economies.

While globalization shrinks the world, the distance between its richest and poorest people grows. Those who are integrated live in a charmed circle of prosperity. But for those outside, the turbulence of continued marginalization and poverty is creating a volcano of despair. Viewing global justice as a right for the poorest and the marginalized requires a moral commitment and calls for fundamental changes in attitudes and perspectives, internationally and nationally.

Some of the modern concern with human rights grew out of the struggle to protect people and their rights during war. The Universal Declaration of Human Rights was inspired in part by outrage over the traged of the holocaust and the killing and destruction of the Second World War. Preventing and reducing conflicts has two important implications for human rights. The first is the direct effect of reducing a primary source of gross human rights violations. The second is the in direct effect of freeing up resources, so that the world community can shift its focus away from peacekeeping operations and towards human development.

The key challenge is to gear international institutions-particularly the United Nations, formed with this intent-to preventing conflict. The rewards in lives saved and human development promoted are too high for continued procrastination. With global resource flows doing so little to create an enabling environment for human rights, poor people must be bewildered. Poor countries send huge amounts to rich countries to service debt. Meanwhile, rich nations spend huge sums on "peacekeeping" missions after conflicts break out, at the same time reducing resources for development assistance.

The deployment of a preventive force in the former Yugoslav Republic of Macedonia appears to be a successful example. The Organization of African Unit has also emphasized the importance of more effective earl warning systems to avoid deadly conflict. Earl warning systems are being used in Africa for the prevention of famine or natural disasters, as in Botswana, South Africa and Zimbabwe. Implementing earl warning systems for man-made disasters is a complex challenge, but deserves support in the shift to preventive actions.

Negotiating missions with distinguished international leadership can go a long way in preventive diplomacy. Bilateral aid agencies should raise concerns about the harmful effects of actions by other ministries of their governments-a protest in which the media and NGOs can participate. In particular, the should point to the damage to human rights from agreements for sales of the small arms and mines used so widely in civil wars.

The Economic Community of West African States is working with the United Nations and other agencies to reduce the proliferation of light weapons. Economic revival is likely if weapons-for-development swaps reduce tension and the expectation of conflict. Such swaps can also misfire. But when the work, as the aftermath of previous conflicts across the world has shown, the repairs and public works create a framework for economic revival.

The Security Council is seeking consensus for strengthening the legal protection of civilians. Some countries still have not ratified the basic international instruments. Many can do much more to ensure that their military and police force are trained to work within the international standards applying to war.

The modern international human rights machinery was established with the Universal Declaration of Human Rights. In the first two or three decades there was some action, much inaction and only limited achievements, in part because of the cold war. In the past decade implementation of international standards has gathered pace. The reporting procedures and monitoring strategies of treat bodies have been strengthened over the past two decades. NGOs are participating more in reporting, often by providing "shadow" (alternative) reports that complement the information provided by governments.

The treaty bodies, working through constructive dialogue, assist governments in implementing their treat commitments. Although lacking real implementation power, the often raise sensitive questions and identify the most pressing human rights issues needing remedial action. But the review process is slow and seriously under-resourced-a result of the number of countries represented, the range of issues and factual detail on which countries are asked to provide information and the limited time available to the independent experts elected to the committees.

Some African governments have used the International Criminal Court's provisions in ways that provide impressive illustrations of the actions made possible by an increasingly supportive international human rights framework. Still, much remains to be done. For example, all the crimes of the wars in Bosnia and Herzegovina and Croatia and of Kosovo are still to be accounted for. Future advances should focus not on creating new institutions but on consolidating and integrating the mandates of existing agencies.

UNICEF, for example, has incorporated a rights-based approach in its programmes and is working with many states to implement them. It is working with civil society organizations and joining forces with others to secure the rights of children. And its campaign to change social norms that "validate" honour killings of women continues its emphasis on discrimination leading to adverse economic, social and political outcomes for women.

UNIFEM's work on aspects of CEDAW and related areas is pioneering and wide ranging. UNESCO has a procedure for filing individual complaints for alleged infringements of rights to education, information, language and culture. The International Labour organization, from its inception, has set standards and put in place mechanisms for protecting workers' rights and promoting their welfare. UNDP is integrating human rights concerns into its work on human development, and its network of country offices is using an imaginative mix of advocacy and technical assistance programmes to build institutions in support of human rights.

UNDP is also creating a unique advocacy asset-a network built around the global and national human development reports. Written by national institutions, many of the national reports have already assessed the human rights situation in the country and offered policy recommendations.

UNDP's technical assistance programmes provide support for institutions of governance and organize training programmes and workshops. In all these endeavours the country offices and regional bureauxy work closely with the office of the High Commissioner for Human Rights. With most UN agencies working on different aspects of human rights, a more co-ordinated and integrated approach could offer big gains in efficiency and efficacy.

Most regions have taken human rights initiatives, encouraging action from allies and peers. The advantage of these initiatives is that the embed the advance of universal human rights in a culturally sensitive discourse. The danger is that in the name of pragmatism, the water down international standards and visions in order to reach agreement.

The regional human rights bodies reflect both achievements and shortcomings . Initiated in 1949, the Council of Europe devotes major efforts to protecting human rights and fundamental freedoms. From the beginning it included in its aims "the maintenance and further realization of human rights and fundamental freedoms. A core principle is universality of human rights, backed by promotion of "common standards throughout all member states, to the benefit of all, no matter who the are or where the are from".

Several European initiatives have extended the mechanisms for promoting human rights beyond the boundaries of the nation state. Now with 41 member states, the Council of Europe continues to work towards democratic ideals, ensuring universality of human rights by promoting common standards throughout all member states. The structures of the council include the European Court of Human Rights, which has dealt with about 4,000 cases since its founding.

The court has passed judgements against nation states in several cases-secret surveillance using telephone taps without adequate security grounds, failure to protect children abused by their parents, expulsion of foreigners in circumstances violating their right to family life. The Council of Europe has adopted resolutions on a range of human rights issues. These have included regulating the use of personal data in police records, ensuring the rights of conscientious objectors and of foreign prisoners and ensuring education on human rights in European schools.

The European Union also plays an important part in making and implementing human rights policies. One EU institution that appears to be acquiring greater importance is the European Court of Justice, based in

Luxembourg. In 1989 an offshoot of the court, the Court of First Instance, was created to hear cases brought by firms and individuals, usually involving commercial disputes. The European Court of Justice has since then dealt with legal issues among member states.

In this century, all people have the right to enjoy seven freedoms-from discrimination, from want, for personal development, from threats to personal security , for participation, from injustice and for productive work. Each of these freedoms requires a vision worth of collective effort by the nations of the world. Women and racial and ethnic groups have suffered violent discrimination. Their struggles against deep prejudices have brought many gains in freedom. But with many battles won, the war is not et over for the billions still suffering from discrimination.

The human rights and human development movements will struggle for the changes in laws, norms and institutions that must liberate those remaining shackled by discrimination. Famines wiped millions from the earth during the 20th century , mostly because of inhumanity , not nature. Such violent deprivations are now rare, but freedom from want remains a distant dream for millions of people.

The ultimate purpose of global economic growth is to provide people the dignity of being free from want, a point emphasized by the human development perspective. The frequency of torture in history provides a tragic indicator of the evil that lurks in the hearts of men. The elimination of torture, and the national and international prosecution of those who engage in it, are central to the continuing struggle for the freedom for personal security .

Many women who have been raped feel ashamed and face legal systems that reflect patriarchal prejudices. Freedom for personal security requires global coalitions for changing the laws, institutions and values that den dignity and protection to women.

The 21st century should give all people-for the first time in history -the right to choose their government and the freedom to participate in the decisions that affect their lives. Active involvement in civic institutions and unprecedented access to information and knowledge will enhance fundamental political freedoms. The arbitrary exercise of power has traditionally reinforced the helplessness of the powerless. When governments operated on the principle of the divine right of kings, rulers did not seek legitimacy for their power in an notion of justice. The struggle against such injustice demanded that social institutions be based on legitimacy, consent and rule of law.

5

Human Rights Developments in India and Pakistan

India, the world's largest democracy, has a long tradition of grassroots participation, from the independence movement earlier in this century to the well-established and widespread network of community groups, non-governmental organizations and associations of today. Its mosaic of racial, cultural and ethnic groups is governed by the democratic institutions of a sec-ular state, and its robust and active media contribute to open and lively political dialogue. Over the past 15 years, the higher courts and the Supreme Court of India have been leading advocates for the human rights of numerous disadvantaged communi-ties, such as tribal groups, pavement dwellers, street ven-dors, and fisher folk. The Government of India has intro-duced affirmative action to widen livelihood opportunities.

Comprehensive human rights legislation has also been introduced, including the Protection of Human Rights Act, which led to the creation of the National Human Rights Commission in 1993. While public awareness of human rights is growing and India's legal framework pro-tects the rights of its citizens, implementation remains uneven; there are frequent reports of custodial violence and the judicial system is facing severe backlogs. India's strong economic growth in the 1990s has brought prosperity to millions of people. The benefits, however, have not been distributed evenly. Ethnic minorities, rural and tribal populations, women and other disadvantaged groups lag behind - economically, politically and socially. Progress has been made in over-coming the ancient traditions of caste and ethnic origin.

However, many people continue to struggle against old stereotypes and communities are often affected by communal strife. Religious intolerance has unfortunately resurfaced, adding strain to India's secular social fabric. The status of women has been improving steadily, due to the efforts of a strong and well-organized women's movement. Women are participating more and more actively in government following a constitu-tional amendment in 1994 which reserves one-third of all local assembly seats for women. At the local level, programs to decentralize administration and authority are increasing opportunities for popular participation in local government, especially for women. India has also begun a campaign to reduce and eventually eliminate exploitative and hazardous child labour.

The Government of India, through the National Human Rights Commission and a wide range of human rights and community-based organizations, is actively promoting greater respect for human rights in India.

In 2001, India held steadfast to its distinction as the region's most stable and vibrant democracy even as its neighbors underwent dramatic and often violent shifts in power. With the onset of the war in Afghanistan, and as relations with Pakistan deteriorated and violence in Kashmir and elsewhere escalated, the Indian government faced heightened national security concerns. Some measures taken in response, including the cabinet approval of the Prevention of Terrorism Ordinance, came under sharp attack by various sectors of Indian civil society for opportunistically curtailing civil liberties in the name of fighting terrorism. Increased violence in the state of Uttar Pradesh, where the Hindu nationalist Bharatiya Janata Party (BJP) hopes to achieve a comeback election victory early in 2002, highlighted the dangerous results of exploiting communal and caste tensions for political ends.

Police violence, attacks on the country's minority communities including Muslims, Christians, Dalits and tribals, and violence against women continued to be serious problems, though some positive steps were taken to help better ensure women's and children's rights. Human rights defenders came under legislative assault through changes to laws and procedures aimed at restricting their ability to travel, hold conferences, and receive foreign funds. The U.N. World Conference Against Racism, Racial Discrimination, Xenophobia and Related Intolerance (WCAR), held in South Africa from August 31 to September 8, paved the way for unprecedented international as well as national scrutiny of the problem of caste discrimination.

On January 26, a devastating earthquake rocked the northwest state of Gujarat, the country's worst natural disaster in recent history. Within days at least 30,000 were declared dead and over one million were left homeless. While the government allocated equal amounts of monetary compensation and food supplies to members of all communities, Dalit (so-called untouchable) and Muslim populations did not have the same access to adequate shelter, electricity, running water, and other supplies available to others. Upper-caste families in Kutch refused to live alongside Dalits in temporary settlements built by Rapid Action Forces. As a result, hundreds of tents lay empty while Dalits were required to live in makeshift shelters. Even relief kitchens for the two communities had to be kept separate as the higher castes refused to share resources with those they considered "diseased."

According to local NGOs, several thousand Dalit homes were also left out of government reconstruction surveys. In October, Gujarat Chief Minister Keshubhai Patel resigned, in part because of criticism about the slow pace of relief and rehabilitation following the earthquake. Dalit communities continued to suffer systemic discrimination and violence.

In a number of cases, police were complicit in the attacks or used excessive force against Dalits when they organized to respond to the attacks, rendering legal protections meaningless. Violence was particularly acute in Uttar Pradesh and Bihar, and those responsible were rarely brought to justice by the authorities. On February 19, a group of Thakurs (an upper-caste community) in Lucknow, Uttar Pradesh, assaulted a Dalit laborer following a wage dispute. The perpetrators entered the victim's home and pinned him down while the employer urinated in his mouth. On June 12, assailants beat a Dalit man and then pushed his wife into a fire, burning her to death.

The incident was quickly followed by a spate of violence, including a June 14 rampage led by seven Thakurs who killed five members of a Dalit family, including three women and a ten year-old girl. In Aligarh, Uttar Pradesh in June a Dalit woman and her five children were burnt alive, allegedly by the staff of a brick kiln operating unit which had employed the woman and her husband as bonded laborers. Conditions in Bihar continued to be marred by a caste war involving rival leftist factions and upper-caste private militias. In January, fifty houses were set ablaze and four Dalits were killed in a gun battle. On February 3, rival gangs gunned down twelve Dalit youths, killing nine of them, and subsequently set their homes on fire; on April 18, militants belonging to the Maoist Communist Center killed fourteen Dalits. In August, a village in Patna was attacked, killing six Dalit women and children. Dalits also continued to face considerable opposition in exercising their political rights. On October 16 in Dharmapuri district, Tamil Nadu, an entire Dalit village was razed after Dalits dared to nominate their own candidate to the post of village council president. More than 140 houses were destroyed by members of the upper-caste community in the area, rendering eight hundred Dalits homeless.

Many were also physically assaulted during the attacks. One pregnant woman was kicked in the stomach, aborted her child, and died later that day. Police charged protesting Dalit villagers with batons and arrested more than twenty-two Dalits while the upper-caste attackers remained at-large. Social prohibitions on marriages between higher and lower-caste community members remained in place and were often reinforced through the threat of social ostracism and punitive violence. On

August 6, 2001, an upper-caste Brahmin boy and a lower-caste Jat girl in Uttar Pradesh were dragged to the roof of a house and publicly hanged by members of their own families as hundreds of spectators looked on.

The public lynching was punishment for refusing to end an inter-caste relationship. Also in August, a forty-year-old Dalit woman was paraded naked in Bellary, Karnataka after being accused of helping a fifteen-year-old upper-caste girl elope with her lower-caste fiance. Dalits were often beaten or fined for participating in religious ceremonies. On April 3 in Bargarh, Orissa, for example, a Dalit was fined Rs. 4,000 (U.S. $83.42) and beaten for entering a Hindu temple. On June 2 in Bhadkiyan, Rajasthan, an upper-caste man beat to death a sixty-five-year-old Dalit man with an iron bar for daring to pray outside the temple of the village deity. Attacks on churches and members of the Christian clergy by members of right wing Hindu groups including the Bajrang Dal, the Vishwa Hindu Parishad (VHP), and the Rashtriya Swayamsevak Sangh (RSS), collectively known as the sangh parivar continued, peaking in July and August. Christians in Orissa, Gujarat, Rajasthan, Maharastra, Uttar Pradesh and Madhya Pradesh were hardest hit. On November 26, 2000, four hundred VHP activists in Gujarat desecrated and took over a church, replacing the church's cross with Hindu idols and hoisting their signature saffron flag. The mob also drove out eighty Christian families from the area, confining them to a nearby forest until they embraced Hinduism. At St. Anna High School in Bokaro district, Bihar, a dozen armed men assaulted the principal and three nuns, and raped the school cook on December 3, 2000.

In Tamil Nadu a nun was murdered on January 21, 2001, in the state's Salem district. On January 23, in

Rampur district, Uttar Pradesh, a nun was hospitalized after sustaining serious head injuries. Two simultaneous attacks on Christian missionaries on August 6 in Madhya Pradesh and Maharashtra drew sharp condemnation from the All India Christian Council and the Catholic Bishops' Conference of India. From March 16-18, Muslim youth in Kanpur, Uttar Pradesh clashed with state police during protests over the burning of a Koran in New Delhi by Hindu radicals. When protesters began to burn an effigy of Prime Minister Atal Bihari Vajpayee, police responded with tear gas and the crowd turned violent. Police then opened fire as rioters began burning shops and hurling crude bombs. By the end of three days of riots, fourteen people were dead, dozens injured, and eighty-nine arrested. Six mosques were damaged, Muslim homes were looted, and the authorities had imposed a round-the-clock curfew. In the wake of the violence, human rights groups charged the police with using excessive force against Muslim demonstrators and looting and plundering Muslim shops and homes. In the hopes of achieving a comeback victory in assembly elections scheduled for early 2002 in Uttar Pradesh, India's most populous state, the BJP and its allies amplified calls to build a temple to the Hindu god Ram at the site of the Babri Masjid, a mosque in the city of Ayodhya whose demolition sparked the infamous 1992-1993 Bombay riots in which thousands of people, most notably Muslims, were killed.

In 2001, many feared that the re-energized Ram temple campaign would lead to more violence and bloodshed between the state's Hindu and Muslim communities. In July, a crowd of three hundred people demolished a sixteenth century mosque at Asind near Bhilwara, Rajasthan and built a makeshift Hindu temple in its place. The government took some positive steps to prosecute perpetrators of violence against members of minority religious communities. In May, the Jhabua district court in Madhya Pradesh sentenced ten men to life in prison for the September 1998 gang-rape of four Christian nuns. Prosecution of Dara Singh, accused in the 1999 murder of Australian missionary Graham Staines and his two sons in Orissa, also continued, with several witnesses testifying that Singh played a key role in instigating the murder. There was little progress, however, in many other cases, including those of individuals indicted by the Srikrishna Commission for their role in the 1992-93 Bombay riots. One exception occurred in August, however, when a special task force filed charges against former police commissioner R.D. Tyagi and seventeen policemen for their role in 1993 riots in the city. Control over natural resources continued to be the source of violence against tribal communities in Orissa. On December 16, 2000, three tribals were killed in Maikanch village, Rayagada district, in clashes with the police over the villagers' opposition to a proposed private aluminum plant in the area. A fact-finding team, which included retired Chief Justice D.S. Tewatia, claimed that the attack was pre-planned and demanded a judicial probe, alleging that an administrative inquiry ordered by the state government was a "cover-up operation."

On October 30, 2001, in Rangabhatti village, three tribals were killed and over fifty were injured when police reportedly opened fire on a gathering of four hundred tribals. The tribals were protesting against the June 24 killing of two people by an armed mob of 3,000 in Jambodora, a Dalit village. Two more people were killed by police in Raigarhar, Nabrangpur district on November 11, when over 8,000 women held a rally to protest the October 30 incident. Violence against women, including rape, kidnapping, dowry deaths, domestic violence, female foeticide, sexual harassment, and trafficking continued unabated, though authorities did take some positive steps in response. In April, the Supreme Court directed prosecutors to enforce existing laws banning the use of prenatal diagnostic techniques to determine the sex of the fetus and authorities warned doctors that their names would be removed from the register of the Medical Council of India if they were found to be practicing female foeticide. In June, authorities announced new legislative measures to safeguard women's rights, including a new Domestic Violence Prevention Bill.

There were also positive developments for children's rights. In September, the government announced that a seven-member national commission for children, headed by a retired Supreme Court judge, would be established to implement protections for children enshrined in the Indian constitution. A meeting between Indian and Bangladeshi border guards in October resulted in agreements to strengthen cooperation to stop the trafficking of women and children across the border.

According to human rights groups, about 20,000 women and children were trafficked to India from Bangladesh annually. Also in October, the state government of Rajasthan, in an attempt to make child marriage illegal, approved legislation requiring all couples to register marriages with authorities. In mid-November, the government was considering enacting a modified version of the Terrorist and Disruptive Activities (Prevention) Act (TADA), notorious for facilitating tens of thousands of politically motivated detentions, torture, and other human rights violations against Muslims, Sikhs, Dalits, trade union activists, and political opponents in the late 1980s and early 1990s.

The new proposed Prevention of Terrorism Ordinance (POTO) set forth a broad definition of terrorism that included acts of violence or disruption of essential services carried out with "intent to threaten the unity and integrity of India or to strike terror in any part of the people." It also made it a crime not to provide authorities with "information relating to any terrorist activity," and allowed for up to three months of preventive detention without charge. The ordinance came under sharp attack from civil rights groups, academics, lawyers, opposition parties, media organizations, and both religious and secular institutions. The National Human Rights Commission also maintained that existing laws were sufficient to fight the threat of terrorism. Freedom of assembly nationwide suffered following the beginning of U.S.-led air strikes in Afghanistan on October 7, with student groups and organizations protesting India's backing of the U.S.-led campaign facing increased harassment from the police.

On October 28, seven anti-U.S. protestors were killed when police opened fire on demonstrators in Malegaon, Maharashtra. Local police reportedly had tried to prevent a small group of Muslim protestors from distributing leaflets calling on people to boycott U.S.-made goods and to oppose air strikes in Afghanistan. Authorities claimed that protestors began throwing stones, leading first to a police baton-charge and then police shooting. Three more people were killed the following night when protestors tried to block the main road connecting Malegaon to the capital, Delhi. Police said they used baton charges and tear gas to disperse the crowd and only fired at protestors when that failed. The government drew sharp criticism from numerous minority groups for selectively banning the Students Islamic Movement of India (SIMI) as part of its post-September 11 actions to counter terrorism while ignoring the "anti-national" activities of right-wing Hindu groups. At least four people were killed when police opened fire on a protest in Lucknow on September 27 following the arrest of some SIMI activists. Insurgency and increased ethnic violence took a heavy toll in Assam and other northeastern states. In January, the United Liberation Front (ULFA) of Assam that advocates the establishment of a "sovereign socialist Assam" by armed force was blamed for a number of killings and bombings to disrupt elections and protest Republic Day celebrations. The group was also believed responsible for killing a ruling party leader, ten activists, and six political leaders in the run-up to elections in May. Indian federal troops killed at least five ULFA militants in response. In June, protestors opposed to any concessions to Naga rebels in Manipur burned the state legislature building and a former chief minister's home after the government extended a truce with the rebels. The conflict in Kashmir remained a flashpoint for violence, as all parties failed to protect civilian non-combatants.

On November 19, 2000, Prime Minister Vajpayee declared a unilateral ceasefire, but, shortly thereafter, Jammu and Kashmir police chief A.K. Suri announced that the ceasefire would not affect police counterinsurgency operations. Indian security personnel continued to target Muslim citizens suspected of supporting guerrillas. Arbitrary arrests, torture, and staged "encounter killings" were reported throughout the year, both when the ceasefire was in effect and after it was lifted on May 23, 2001. India, like Pakistan, continued to deny political rights and to restrict freedoms of expression and assembly in Jammu and Kashmir. At least six people were killed when security personnel opened fire on demonstrators in Haigam and Maisuma in February. On February 15 in Haigam, forty kilometers north of Srinagar, five people were killed when Indian troops opened fire on demonstrators protesting the alleged killing of pro-independence activist Jalil Ahmed Shah in police custody the day before. In Maisuma, Srinagar on February 16, one person was killed in a similar incident. In both cases the police maintained that they were firing in self-defense.

On May 10, seventeen journalists were beaten by troops of the Indian Border Security Force (BSF) in Magam. The assault took place while the journalists were covering a suicide bomb attack against a BSF camp. The officers implicated were subsequently recalled from Kashmir but as of mid-November no disciplinary action had been taken against them. July also witnessed a dramatic upsurge in violence in Kashmir with almost two hundred reported deaths in the week following the failed Agra summit between Prime Minister Vajpayee and Pakistani President Pervez Musharraf.

On July 22, fifteen Hindu villagers were killed by suspected Islamic militants in Doda district. The attacks came a day after thirteen Hindus were killed while on pilgrimage. Tensions flared up again after the September 11 attacks on the United States. On October 1, at least thirty-eight people were killed when a suicide attacker drove a hijacked government jeep to the main entrance of the state assembly in Srinagar and detonated explosives loaded in the car. The Pakistan-based Jaish-e Mohammad militant group claimed responsibility for the attack but then retracted the following day. In the weeks that followed, numerous militants and security personnel were killed in tit-for-tat attacks while tensions heated up along the Line of Control between the Indian and Pakistan-controlled portions of the territory.

Defending Human Rights

The brutal killings of two members of the Andhra Pradesh Civil Liberties Committee (APCLC) within a period of four months sent shock waves throughout the human rights community. In November 2000, T. Puroshottam, Joint Secretary of APCLC was stabbed to death by a group of unidentified men. Puroshottam had been a leading monitor of police abuses. In February 2001, Azam Ali, the district secretary of the Nalgonda branch of APCLC, was hacked to death by two sword-wielding youth. Despite demands from human rights organizations and allegations that police hired former members of armed groups to carry out the attacks, by November 2001 the government had yet to conduct any judicial inquiry. On July 7 police raided the offices of Bharosa Trust and the Naz Foundation International in Lucknow, organizations that work on HIV/AIDS prevention, arresting several staff members. Although subsequently released on bail, the staff members were charged under article 377 of the Indian Penal Code, a provision that prohibits "carnal intercourse against the order of nature." Article 377 has been used repeatedly to justify discrimination and police brutality against gay, lesbian, and bisexual individuals.

The Narmada Bachao Andolan (NBA), one of India's largest peoples' movements, continued to protest the construction of large dams on the Narmada river in central India. Protesters highlighting the impact of the project on millions of river valley residents and the government's failure to adequately rehabilitate affected families continued to face harassment, police abuse, and contempt charges. The work of rights activists was also hindered by restrictive laws and regulations. In July, the Supreme Court upheld the validity of a Union Home Ministry order requiring that organizations obtain clearance from the ministry before holding international conferences, seminars or workshops if the subject matter was "political, semi-political, communal or religious in nature or is related to human rights." On October 23, President K.R. Narayanan signed an ordinance empowering both central and state governments to suspend the passports and travel documents of any suspected terrorist, militant or "anti-national element," or any person suspected of having links with terrorist organizations.

The Role of the International Community

In August 2001, U.N. Subcommission on the Promotion and Protection of Human Rights expert R.K.W. Goonesekere presented a working results on work and descent-based discrimination, or caste discrimination, to the subcommission's fifty-third session. The presentation of the chapter, and the ensuing debate amongst subcommission experts that followed, marked the first time that caste discrimination worldwide was treated as a serious rights violation by a U.N. human rights body. The WCAR held in Durban, South Africa in September, was a watershed for the Dalit movement and for the rights of "untouchables" and other so-called lower-caste communities worldwide. The Dalit contingent of more than 160 activists, led by India's National Campaign for Dalit Human Rights, was one of the largest at the conference and drew strong international support from governments, India's National Human Rights Commission, and U.N. Secretary-General Kofi Annan.

Dalit NGO efforts met with considerable resistance from the Indian government, which maintained that caste discrimination was an internal matter and used its political and economic leverage to censor any mention of caste in WCAR documents. In the run up to the conference, journalists, anthropologists, political parties, and others in India joined an increasingly mainstream debate on caste discrimination as an issue of international concern. The conference also highlighted caste discrimination as a global phenomenon affecting many Asian and African countries.

The U.S. walked a tightrope in its relations with India and Pakistan following the September 11 attacks. India lobbied hard to ensure that the U.S.' campaign against terrorism would include militants in Kashmir. After September 11, the Bush White House accelerated the Clinton administration's moves towards closer political and economic relations with India. On September 22, the U.S. lifted the sanctions imposed against India and Pakistan in the wake of nuclear testing by both nations in May 1998, allowing resumption of military equipment sales.

The administration planned to increase funding for international military education and training (IMET) of Indian officers from $500,000 to $650,000 in the fiscal year 2002. It also planned a boost in bilateral economic assistance from $5 million to $7 million. On November 9 President Bush met with Prime Minister Vajpayee. The

U.S. renewed its offer to facilitate talks between India and Pakistan on Kashmir but made no public comments on the Prevention of Terrorism Ordinance. The U.S. Commission on International Religious Freedom urged the Indian government in May 2001 to more swiftly and explicitly condemn and counteract increasing violence directed towards Christian populations. The panel voiced concern that the government's lack of decisive action created an atmosphere that invited inter-religious violence.

The E.U. welcomed the July Agra summit between India and Pakistan. Although the summit did not reach any resolution, the E.U. urged both countries to continue their dialogue--a dialogue that seemed far out of reach by mid-November.

In its annual Human Rights Report, the European Parliament called upon the E.U. to investigate the extent to which its policies "contribute to the abolition of caste discrimination and the practice of untouchability in India" and "to formulate strategies to counter the widespread practice [of caste discrimination]." A subsequent parliamentary resolution expressed regret that the final declaration of the World Conference Against Racism failed to highlight caste discrimination.

At this writing, the E.U. and India were preparing for a second annual summit to be held in New Delhi on November 23.

On October 26 Japan announced that it too would lift sanctions against India and Pakistan imposed after the 1998 nuclear tests, citing both countries' "efforts to contribute to strengthening the international coalition against terrorism" and increased instability in the region as a result of U.S.-led military strikes in Afghanistan.

India continued to be the World Bank's largest borrower. In June 2001 the World Bank sanctioned four loans and credits to the government of India totaling U.S. $913.8 million, for a total lending of U.S. $2.5 billion for the fiscal year (FY) 2001. The U.S. Foreign Aid Bill for the FY 2002 instructed the United States executive director at the World Bank to vote against any water or sewage project in India that did not prohibit the use of scavenger labor. Though prohibited by law, the government of India employs a majority of the country's estimated one million Dalit manual scavengers for the cleaning of non-flush public latrines. In an August meeting in Delhi, Indian groups joined trade union leaders from Pakistan, Bangladesh, Sri Lanka, and Nepal to formulate a regional stance against IMF and World Bank policies that reduce jobs and increase layoffs.

Democratic Rights in Pakistan

Although Pakistan's Industrial Relations Ordinance of 1969 (IRO) provides for the right of industrial workers to form trade unions, union organizers are subject to a variety restrictions that hinder their activities and effectiveness. One of the laws that hinders trade union activity is the Essential Services Maintenance Act of 1952 (ESA) (which covers government services and state enterprises, such as energy production, power generation and transmission, the state-owned airline, and ports) and is usually invoked to limit or ban strikes, and is also used to severely curtail collective bargaining rights. Legally required conciliation proceedings and cooling-off periods constrain the right to strike, as does the Government's authority to ban any strike that may cause "serious hardship to the community" or prejudice the national interest. The Government also may ban a strike that has continued for 30 days.

Although India too has provisions that can be invoked to prevent strikes in the public sector, there are legal constraints on the arbitrary use of such provisions, and elected governments have not been able to use them as freely and easily as in Pakistan, (especially when a strike in the public sector has attracted the support of key opposition parties). And unlike in India, dismissed workers have no recourse to the labor courts in Pakistan. In the past, the International Labor Organization (ILO) has stated repeatedly that Pakistan's current law and practice violate the Government's commitments under ILO Convention 87. The ILO has urged Pakistan's Government to lift prohibitions against union activity with respect to teachers, and radio, television, railway, forestry, hospital, and other government employees, as well as to rescind the existing ban on strikes.

Pakistani law is particularly hard on agricultural workers who are denied the right to form unions and are thus prevented from striking, bargaining collectively, or making any demands on their employers. Particularly egregious is how a worker's right to quit may also be curtailed under the ESA, which critics have argued constitutes a form of compulsory labor. This is of particular importance in a country where bonded labor - especially forced child labor is a very serious issue. Although most poor countries face this scourge, the problem is particularly acute in Pakistan. Even as both the Constitution and the law prohibit forced labor, (including forced labor by children), enforcement has been very poor, and since the military takeover the situation has deteriorated further.

According to some human rights reports, children are sometimes kidnapped to be used as forced labor. According to 1996 ILO estimates, 3.3 million children between the ages of 5 and 14 years (about 8 percent of this population group) were "economically active." Of these, about two-thirds worked in agriculture. Seventy percent of the working children had the status of "unpaid family helpers." However, many observers believe that both the ILO and the Government understate the true dimensions of the problem. Some argue that Pakistani children not attending school are invariably active in the work-force - either with their families or as slaves or bonded-laborers. Shahida Jabeen, Secretary, PTUDC, states: " According to the United Nations "Education for All summit" in New Delhi, only 29% of Pakistani children were enrolled in schools, compared to the next worst level which was Nigeria with 59%." She also reports: "Brutal exploitation is rife. Over one million children work in the carpet industry, another million are employed as domestics, over 300,000 as bonded labourers in brick kilns together with many more in soap factories, small garages, shops etc."

The practice of bonded-labor in agriculture compounds the problem. A UN meet on slavery (24 May 2002) issued a depressing report on the status of bonded agricultural workers.According to research carried out for the Government of Sindh and the Asian Development Bank 1 there are some 1.7 million landless agricultural workers (haris) and sharecroppers in five districts of Sindh Province (Thatta, Dadu, Badin, Mirpurkhas and Umerkot). The report notes that most of these people are in debt bondage. While bonded labour exists throughout Sindh Province, the majority of those bonded in the north belong to the Muslim majority, while most of the bonded agricultural labourers in southern Sindh Province belong to dalit 2 (untouchable) and to tribal communities who have migrated from the drought-prone area of Tharparkar desert.

Poverty and starvation have forced these communities to accept the landlords' cash advances, and to be available for work from dawn to dusk. Bonded labourers may be detained or guarded to stop them escaping and in these situations of total ownership rape of women is not uncommon. Most are forced to provide begar, a form of forced, unpaid labour, on top of the tasks assigned against the debt. Trafficking in bonded labourers who are unable to pay their debts is a common practice among landlords.

Bonded labourers are sold by one landlord to another, usually for a price higher than the debt they had with their previous landlord thereby increasing the bonded labourer's debt. In theory, all bonded labourers should have been freed under the Bonded Labour System (Abolition) Act, 1992 and those responsible for keeping them in bondage should have been prosecuted. However, in practice the political and financial strength of the landlords in Sindh Province allows them to continue using bonded labourers with impunity. Some landlords have even successfully filed charges against bonded labourers with the police, leading to the imprisonment of some 40 haris. (Excerpts from the UN report filed in Geneva, 27-31 May 2002)

Although instances of bonded-labour (including child labour) have also been reported in India - (mainly from the states of Bihar, Orissa, and Eastern Madhya Pradesh) what is most shocking about Pakistan is how the High Court of Sindh (on 9 January 2002) dismissed 94 petitions for the release of bonded labourers declaring that they were disputes between landlords and haris (bonded labourers) over debts and should be settled under the Sindh Tenancy Act 1950. Since this judgement was announced, new petitions for the release of bonded labourers filed in the Sindh High Court have also been rejected. Whereas the Indian Supreme Court has accepted several PILs (Public Interest Litigations) filed on behalf of child-workers, and called upon the Indian government to take more concrete measures to put into effect earlier legislation calling for an end to the exploitation of children, and bonded labor, these recent court rulings in Pakistan effectively negate Pakistan's Bonded Labour System (Abolition) Act 1992 and make the struggle to rescue and liberate bonded laborers much more difficult. These court decisions are part and parcel of a political environment that is increasingly repressive.

Since the military take-over, serious (including life-threatening) impediments have been placed in the way of those fighting for workers rights, or trying to mobilize democratic forces in Pakistan. As it is, workers in Pakistan are often intimidated when they try and organize any form of economic or political resistance, now their situation is substantially worse. In 1999, Farooq Sulehria reported that a truck load of military men entered the premises of the Pakistan Trade Unions Resource Center in Lahore, and raided the offices of the Weekly Mazdoor Jeddojuhd Offices (21 Oct, 1999) soon after publication of it's first issue (19 Oct, 1999) titled: "No to Martial Law". The issue also carried an appeal to the working masses to fight against the military dictatorship. Trade Union organizations remain amongst the most active of groups trying to combat military rule, although government pressure has succeeded in intimidating some sections of the Trade Union Movement.

Earlier, when Arif Shah, the President of the Punjab Labour Federation, was assassinated by hired agents of the employers, 20,000 workers had attended his funeral the following day and pledged themselves to carry on the struggle. More recently, there has been a popular upsurge in Baluchistan. Khalid Bhatti, National Organizer PTUDC, Lahore reports how more than one hundred trade union activists and members of the Civil Secretariat Employees Association (CSEA) in Baluchistan have been arrested, and . the president and secretary general of the union were arrested and have been severely tortured. This followed an-all out strike in Quetta, Baluchistan on November 19, 2001 demanding implementation of the charter of demands accepted by the military-led government in July 2001. This union is also an affiliate of the Pakistan Trade Union Defence Campaign, and PTUDC members played an important role in this strike. Unsurprisingly, none of the major newspapers (which are generally beholden to the government) reported on the June 5, 2002 strike which shut down Quetta.

Contrary to those who saw in General Musharraf the makings of a "liberal reformer", the situation for democratic activists in Pakistan has in fact, deteriorated. In it's twenty-page report, "Reform or Repression? Post-Coup Abuses in Pakistan," Human Rights Watch stated that the Musharraf government had detained opponents and former officials without charge, removed independent judges from the higher courts, banned public rallies and demonstrations, and rendered political parties all but powerless. It's Asian director, Sidney Jones noted that "Musharraf follows a long line of generals in Pakistan who have claimed that a period of military rule is the path to true democracy. In fact, he is systematically destroying civil liberties in Pakistan." However, one of the problems facing the democratic movement in Pakistan is that some influential currents in Pakistan's progressive movement continue to be misled about the struggle in Kashmir.

Pakistan's anti-democratic forces have won so often precisely because they have managed to shift the spotlight to Kashmir. Their anti-India rhetoric has not only galvanized a section of the deeply Islamicized Pakistani populace, it has also found echoes in what is considered to be the secular or progressive movement in Pakistan.Some of Pakistan's most radical political activists think that the anti-Indian movement in Jammu and Kashmir has mass support, rather than being a pliant pawn in the hands of Pakistan's military and clerical elite (and the world-wide Islamist movement).

By legitimizing the false propaganda of the Pakistani rulers on Kashmir, some of Pakistan's human rights activists unwittingly provide a certain degree of ideological cover for the military dictatorship. This in turn, allows the Pakistani masses to be diverted from the democratic struggle, and weakens the ability of Pakistan's progressive leadership to effectively counter the forces of Jehadi militarism. Some of the most dedicated of Pakistan's progressive activists unfortunately fail to understand the dialectical consequences of the two-nation theory which by it's very logic has constantly come in the way of democratic rights in Pakistan.

The moment one legitimizes the pro-Pakistan Kashmiri separatist movement, one ends up internalizing the very sentiments that led to partition. But the partition of India was essentially anti-democratic in nature. For one thing, the creation of Pakistan had never been preceded by any free and fair democratic process, or through any popular referendum, nor had the demand for partition been raised by a political grouping that represented any genuine allegiance to democratic values. The only legitimate reason for Pakistan to break away from post-colonial India was to argue that even as India's linguistically and culturally diverse Hindus could live together in the same nation, Hindus and Muslims could not. That even as India's Hindus could put aside regional differences, even differences based on religious practice, and unite in one nation, Hindus would somehow not be able to live with the Muslims of what is now Pakistan. That even as India's Christians, Jains, Buddhists, Sikhs, Parsis and Jews could live with India's Hindus, Muslims could not.

But if it were indeed true that Hindus and Muslims could not coexist in one nation, even where there were some constitutional provisions for secularism, pluralism and democracy - then such an argument should have been applied to all of India's Muslims, not just to the Muslims of Pakistan. If it were so important to "liberate" Kashmir's Muslims, it should have been equally important to liberate the rest of India's Muslims. Pakistan has been much more sparsely populated than India - surely it could have invited India's Muslims to emigrate to a nation that presumably provides more "protections" to Muslims than does India? The fact that in spite of India's many problems, there have been no recent attempts on the part of any Indian Muslim to migrate to Pakistan must suggest that all things considered, India's Muslims prefer to be part of India - even as "minorities".

No amount of intellectualizing can change this objective reality. India's secular democracy may be flawed, even under great stress at times, but it remains a superior alternative to any state that is based on sectarian appeals to religious exclusivity. And this is what makes the pro-Pakistan Kashmiri separatist movement so suspect. Not only does the Kashmiri separatist movement fail to acknowledge the multi-ethnic and multi-religious of Jammu and Kashmir, it has never given any concrete indication of how it might be more democratic than India. For some of Pakistan's pro-democracy activists to make common cause with such a movement introduces a troubling inconsistency in their outlook, and this naturally weakens their own struggle for greater democracy in Pakistan. Some activists in India and Pakistan have attempted to finesse or obscure such contradictions by sharply denouncing Indian democracy as an utter sham, and have put an equal sign between the democratic governments of India and the military administrations of Pakistan.

India's political parties often fail to represent the interests of the common people, and more often than not, either bend to pressures from local business interests or neo-liberal elites more beholden to the agenda of Western imperial powers than Indian concerns, the answer is clearly not to replace India's democratic constitution with a constitution derived from medieval theocracy, or to replace India's elected government by a military administration. Neither can anyone seriously argue that Pakistan's military leadership is any less immune from Western imperialist pressures, or acts in the interests of Pakistan's poor and disenfranchised masses. If anything, it is quite the reverse, and that is why the US Pentagon and CIA have always preferred Pakistan's military regimes to Pakistan's democratically elected governments. While economic inequities hamper social progress throughout the subcontinent, the strength of India's democratic institutions makes it somewhat easier to research and document the problems and to articulate opposition to current policies.

By and large, it is easier in India to express dissent, and to mount more vigorous political challenges. Imperfect as Indian democracy may be, it provides opportunities for struggle and amelioration that are simply not available in Pakistan. And that is why, social indicators, even in India's poorest and least developed state, i.e. Bihar, lead social indicators in Pakistan. Pro-democracy activists in Pakistan indeed face very difficult challenges. But their task is hardly facilitated by cynically discounting the differences between India and Pakistan, or by making common cause with the Kashmiri separatists.

For instance, even 55 years after independence, there is still much that needs to be done to reverse the debilitating legacy of colonial rule in both nations. But the Kashmiri separatists can hardly provide any leadership in this regard because Kashmir was never directly administered by the British. That is why they are also least appreciative of the need to strengthen the unity of the people of the Indian subcontinent. Pakistan's pro-democracy activists are likely to make much more progress when they are able to see through the misguided agenda of the Kashmiri separatists, and overcome the India-baiting rhetoric that emanates from various quarters.

Appendix

Governance for Sustainbale Human Development (A UNDP Policy Document)

The United Nations Development Programme (UNDP) has been at the forefront of the growing international consensus that good governance and sustainable human development are indivisible. And we believe that developing the capacity for good governance can be - and should be - the primary way to eliminate poverty.

Notions of good governance and the link between governance and sustainable human development vary greatly, however, both in academic literature and among development practitioners.

So, what is sustainable human development?

We define human development as expanding the choices for all people in society. This means that men and women - particularly the poor and vulnerable - are at the centre of the development process. It also means "protection of the life opportunities of future generations...and...the natural systems on which all life depends" (UNDP, *Human Development Report 1996*). This makes the central purpose of development the creation of an enabling environment in which all can enjoy long, healthy and creative lives.

Economic growth is a means to sustainable human development - not an end in itself. *Human Development Report 1996* showed that economic growth does not automatically lead to sustainable human development and the elimination of poverty. For example, countries that do well when ranked by per capita income often slip down the ladder when ranked by the human development index. There are, moreover, marked disparities within countries - rich and poor alike - and these become striking when human development among indigenous peoples and ethnic minorities is evaluated separately.

There are five aspects to sustainable human development - all affecting the lives of the poor and vulnerable:

— *Empowerment*: The expansion of men and women's capabilities and choices increases their ability to exercise those choices free of hunger, want and deprivation. It also increases their opportunity to participate in, or endorse, decision-making affecting their lives.

— *Co-operation*: With a sense of belonging important for personal fulfillment, well-being and a sense of purpose and meaning, human development is concerned with the ways in which people work together and interact.

— *Equity*: The expansion of capabilities and opportunities means more than income - it also means equity, such as an educational system to which everybody should have access

— *Sustainability*: The needs of this generation must be met without compromising the right of future generations to be free of poverty and deprivation and to exercise their basic capabilities.

— *Security:* Particularly the security of livelihood. People need to be freed from threats, such as disease or repression and from sudden harmful disruptions in their lives.

UNDP focuses on four critical elements of sustainable human development: eliminating poverty, creating jobs and sustaining livelihoods, protecting and regenerating the environment, and promoting the advancement of women. Developing the capacities for good governance underpins all these objectives.

What, then, is governance? And what is good governance?

The challenge for all societies is to create a system of governance that promotes, supports and sustains human development - especially for the poorest and most marginal. But the search for a clearly articulated concept of governance has just begun.

Governance can be seen as the exercise of economic, political and administrative authority to manage a country's affairs at all levels. It comprises the mechanisms, processes and institutions through which citizens and groups articulate their interests, exercise their legal rights, meet their obligations and mediate their differences.

Good governance is, among other things, participatory, transparent and accountable. It is also effective and equitable. And it promotes the rule of law. Good governance ensures that political, social and economic priorities are based on broad consensus in society and that the voices of the poorest and the most vulnerable are heard in decision-making over the allocation of development resources.

Governance has three legs: economic, political and administrative. Economic governance includes decision-making processes that affect a country's economic activities and its relationships with other economies. It clearly has major implications for equity, poverty and quality of life. Political governance is the process of decision-making to formulate policy. Administrative governance is the system of policy implementation. Encompassing all three, good governance defines the processes and structures that guide political and socio-economic relationships.

Governance encompasses the state, but it transcends the state by including the private sector and civil society organisations. What constitutes the state is widely debated. Here, the state is defined to include political and public sector institutions. UNDP's primary interest lies in how effectively the state serves the needs of its people. The private sector covers private enterprises (manufacturing, trade, banking, cooperatives and so on) and the informal sector in the marketplace. Some say that the private sector is part of civil society. But the private sector is separate to the extent that private sector players influence social, economic and political policies in ways that create a more conducive environment for the marketplace and enterprises.

Civil society, lying between the individual and the state, comprises individuals and groups (organised or unorganised) interacting socially, politically and economically - regulated by formal and informal rules and laws.

Civil society organisations are the host of associations around which society voluntarily organises. They include trade unions; non-governmental organisations; gender, language, cultural and religious groups; charities; business associations; social and sports clubs; cooperatives and community development organisations; environmental groups; professional associations; academic and policy institutions; and media outlets. Political parties are also included, although they straddle civil society and the state if they are represented in parliament.

The institutions of governance in the three domains (state, civil society and the private sector) must be designed to contribute to sustainable human development by establishing the political, legal, economic and social circumstances for poverty reduction, job creation, environmental protection and the advancement of women.

Much has been written about the characteristics of efficient government, successful businesses and effective civil society organisations, but the characteristics of good governance defined in societal terms remain elusive. The characteristics?

— *Participation*: All men and women should have a voice in decision-making, either directly or through legitimate intermediate institutions that represent their interests. Such broad participation is built on freedom of association and speech, as well as capacities to participate constructively.

— *Rule of law*: Legal frameworks should be fair and enforced impartially, particularly the laws on human rights.

— *Transparency*: Transparency is built on the free flow of information. Processes, institutions and information are directly accessible to those concerned with them, and enough information is provided to understand and monitor them.

— *Responsiveness*: Institutions and processes try to serve all stakeholders.

— *Consensus orientation*: Good governance mediates differing interests to reach a broad consensus on what is in the best interests of the group and, where possible, on policies and procedures.

— *Equity*: All men and women have opportunities to improve or maintain their well-being.

— *Effectiveness and efficiency*: Processes and institutions produce results that meet needs while making the best use of resources.

— *Accountability*: Decision-makers in government, the private sector and civil society organisations are accountable to the public, as well as to institutional stakeholders. This accountability differs depending on the organisation and whether the decision is internal or external to an organisation.

— *Strategic vision*: Leaders and the public have a broad and long-term perspective on good governance and human development, along with a sense of what is needed for such development. There is also an understanding of the historical, cultural and social complexities in which that perspective is grounded.

Interrelated, these core characteristics are mutually reinforcing and cannot stand alone. For example, accessible information means more transparency, broader participation and more effective decision-making. Broad participation contributes both to the exchange of information needed for effective decision-making and for the legitimacy of those decisions. Legitimacy, in turn, means effective implementation and encourages further participation. And responsive institutions must be transparent and function according to the rule of law if they are to be equitable.

These core characteristics represent the ideal - and no society has them all. Even so, UNDP believes that societies should aim, through broad-based consensus-building, to define which of the core features are most important to them, what the best balance is between the state and the market, how each socio-cultural and economic setting can move from here to there.

UNDP is faced increasingly with post-crisis situations and disintegrating societies. For them, the issue is not developing good governance - it is building the basic institutions of governance. The first step is towards reconciliation - building society's ability to carry on a dialogue on the meaning of governance and the needs of all citizens.

Relationships between governance and human development

Each domain of governance - the state, the private sector and civil society - has a unique role in promoting sustainable human development.

The state

In countries where electoral processes exist, the state is composed of an elected government and an executive branch. The state's functions are manifold - among them, being the focus of the social contract that defines citizenship, being the authority that is mandated to control and exert force, having responsibility for public services and creating an enabling environment for sustainable human development. The latter means establishing and maintaining stable, effective and fair legal-regulatory frameworks for public and private activity. It means ensuring stability and equity in the marketplace. It means mediating interests for the public good. And it means providing effective and accountable public services. In all four roles, the state faces a challenge - ensuring that good governance addresses the concerns and needs of the poorest by increasing the opportunities for people to seek, achieve and sustain the kind of life they aspire to.

The state, of course, can do much in such areas as upholding the rights of the vulnerable, protecting the environment, maintaining stable macroeconomic conditions, maintaining standards of public health and safety for all at an affordable cost, mobilising resources to provide essential public services and infrastructure and maintaining order, security and social harmony.

State institutions can also empower the people they are meant to serve - providing equal opportunities and ensuring social, economic and political inclusion and access to resources. But people can be empowered only if their legislatures, electoral processes and legal and judicial systems work properly. Parliaments of freely and fairly elected members representing different parties are crucial to popular participation and government accountability. Effective legal and judicial systems protect the rule of law and the rights of all. Open elections mean public confidence and trust - and so political legitimacy. States should also decentralise political and economic systems to be more responsive to citizens' demands and to changing economic conditions.

In developed and developing countries alike, the state is being compelled to redefine its role in social and economic activity - to reduce it, reorient it, reconfigure it. The pressures for change stem from three sources:

— The *private sector* wants a more conducive market environment and a better balance between state and market.

— *Citizens* want increased accountability and responsiveness from government, as well as greater decentralisation.

— *Global pressures* from supranationals and worldwide social and economic trends are challenging the identity and nature of the state.

The private sector

The state is a big force for development - but it is not the only one. Sustainable human development depends in part on creating jobs that provide enough income to improve living standards. Most states now recognise that the private sector is the primary source of opportunities for productive employment. Economic globalisation is fundamentally changing the ways in which industries and enterprises operate. In many developing countries, private enterprise must be encouraged and supported to be more transparent and competitive in the international marketplace.

Equitable growth, gender balance, environmental preservation, expansion of the private sector and responsible and effective participation in international commerce cannot be achieved by the market alone, however. States can foster private sector development that is sustainable by:

— Creating a stable macroeconomic environment.

— Maintaining competitive markets.

— Ensuring that the poor (especially women) have easy access to credit.

— Nurturing enterprises that generate the most jobs and opportunities.

— Attracting investment and helping to transfer knowledge and technologies, particularly to the poor.

— Enforcing the rule of law.

— Providing incentives for human resource development.

— Protecting the environment and natural resources.

Civil society

Civil society also has to protect the rights of all citizens. As the state and the private sector are being reshaped and their relationships redefined, civil society is changing in important ways. Unresponsive government and unrelenting economic and social pressure have undermined some traditional civil society organisations and strengthened others - and in many cases forced people to organise in new ways. Civil society is thus more than just society. It is the part of society that connects individuals with the public realm and the state - it is the political face of society.

Civil society organisations channel people's participation in economic and social activities and organise them into more powerful groups to influence public policies and gain access to public resources, especially for the poor. They can provide checks and balances on government power and monitor social abuses. They also offer opportunities for people to develop their capacities and improve their standards of living - by monitoring the environment, assisting the disadvantaged, developing human resources, helping communication among business people.

More fundamentally, civic networks ease the dilemmas of collective action by institutionalising social interaction, reducing opportunism, fostering trust and making political and economic transactions easier. Well-developed civic networks also amplify flows of information - the basis for reliable political, economic and social collaboration and public participation of civil society members. These relationships and social norms make up a nation's social capital.

Civil society organisations do not always pursue the qualities of good governance. Nor are they always the most effective development agents. That is why states, while recognising and protecting the democratic rights of civil society organisations, must also ensure that the rules of law and values that reflect societal norms are adhered to. Democratic institutions, particularly local ones, can be important in ensuring that all in society have a voice, as well as ensuring that there are transparent and fair ways to reach consensus.

Like private enterprises, civil society organisations need adequate capacities to fulfill their potential. They also need an enabling environment, including a legislative and regulatory framework that guarantees the right of association, incentives to facilitate support and ways for civil society organisations to be involved in public policy-making and implementation.

Strengthening the enabling environment for sustainable human development thus depends not only on a state that governs well and a private sector that provides jobs that generate income. It also depends on civil society organisations that make political and social interaction easier and that mobilise society to participate in economic, social and political activities.

The global context

The transformation from command to market-oriented economies, the emergence of democratic political regimes in the former Soviet Union, the rapid development and global proliferation of new technologies, the pervasive spread of telecommunications systems, the growing importance of knowledge-based industries and skills and the continuing integration of the world economy through trade and investment - all these have created the foundation for a new age of sustainable human development. But all carry risks as well. Is it to be a breakthrough or a breakdown?

Changes in the world's economic, political and social systems have indeed brought unprecedented improvements in human living conditions in both developed and developing countries. Consider the profound breakthroughs in communications, transport, agriculture, medicine, genetic engineering, computerisation, environmentally friendly energy systems, political structures, peace settlements. The list goes on.

But these changes also bring new uncertainties and challenges as the world steps into the 21st century. Signs of breakdown are everywhere: disintegration of families; destruction of indigenous societies; degradation and annihilation of plant and animal life; pollution of rivers, oceans and the atmosphere; crime, alienation and substance abuse; higher unemployment; and a widening gap in incomes and capabilities. Not a pretty picture.

The trend towards globalisation deserves special attention. It is manifest in the growth of regional blocs that cooperate in such areas as trade and legal frameworks, in the power of intergovernmental bodies such as the World Trade Organization and in the spread of transnational corporations. Globalisation has profound implications for governance the final impact of which we cannot yet determine. First is the increasing marginalisation of certain population groups. Those who do not have access to the technological/information revolution are in danger of becoming part of a structural underclass. Second is the erosion of state sovereignty as transnational bodies increasingly mediate national concerns and press for universal laws. Third is the increased globalisation of social and economic problems, such as crime, narcotics, infectious diseases and the migration of labour. Finally, international capital and trade are decreasingly accountable to sovereign states.

Governance can no longer be considered a closed system. The state's task is to find a balance between taking advantage of globalisation and providing a secure and stable social and economic domestic environment, particularly for the most vulnerable. Globalisation is also placing governments under greater scrutiny, leading to improved state conduct and more responsible economic policies.

Because each domain of governance - state, private sector, civil society - has strengths and weaknesses, the pursuit of good governance requires greater interaction among the three to define the right balance among them for sustainable people-centred development. Given that change is continuous, the ability for the three domains to continuously interact and adjust must be built-in, thus allowing for long-term stability. UNDP's Initiatives for Change recognises that the relationships among government, civil society and the private sector:

> are key determinants in whether a nation is able to create and sustain equitable opportunities for all of its people. If a government does not function efficiently and effectively, scarce resources will be wasted. If it does not have legitimacy in the eyes of the people, it will not be able to achieve its goals or theirs. If it is unable to build national consensus around these objectives, no external assistance can help bring them about. If it is unable to foster a strong social fabric, the society risks disintegration and chaos. Equally important, if people are not empowered to take responsibility for their own development within an enabling framework provided by government, development will not be sustainable.

Developing countries must ensure that everyone can participate in economic and social development and take advantage of globalisation. They must build a political system that encourages government, political, business and civic leaders to articulate and pursue objectives that are centred around people and a system that promotes public consensus on these objectives.

What role can UNDP play in this?

We are already doing much. As of 1995 a third of our resources were allocated for governance. Ongoing development cooperation in management development and governance, including cost-sharing, amounts to about $1.3 billion. Management development and governance allocations vary significantly across regions. In Africa, the Arab States and Eastern Europe and the CIS, the largest total contribution (UNDP and cost-sharing) is allocated to aid management and coordination. Within the Asia and the Pacific region, however, the largest allocation is for economic and financial management, while the Latin America and the Caribbean region tends to emphasize planning and support for policy formulation. Within global and interregional programmes, the largest allocations are those dealing with planning and support for policy formulation, decentralisation and strengthening civil society.

UNDP policy for governance programming is driven by three major forces:

— *Our mandate*: We support the implementation of declarations and agreements reached at global UN conferences, many of which have specific references to governance. The most recent mandate for governance is Executive Board decision 96/29 in which the Board endorses the mission statement.

— *Our mission*: To promote sustainable human development.

— *Our comparative advantage:* We have institutional strengths that, together, set us apart from other external partners concerned with governance issues:

— *Impartiality* - We can work as an agent for change with all actors.

— *Customer orientation* - We pursue our mandate within national priorities.

— *Long time frame* - We view development from a long-term perspective and seek to maintain a presence in programme countries.

— *Experience* - We have 50 years of experience in capacity development.

— *Trust* - UNDP has won the trust of governments and other partners in programme countries.

— *Universality* - Field presence in 137 countries ensures ongoing dialogue, learning and cooperation.

In seeking to promote good governance within its programme countries, UNDP is drawing on its experience, backed by a clear mandate. We recognise, however, that the pursuit of programmes supporting good governance in dynamic, unpredictable environments is a complex process that carries risks. A well-developed and understood strategic vision and policy can help to get the most from our efforts and reduce the risks by providing a framework and guide for programme initiatives.

UNDP may be called on to support many types of governance-related programmes. To maximise our resources, however, we must target our assistance and build our core competencies in a few key areas. Based on our understanding of the role of governance in sustainable human development, our mandate and our comparative advantages, UNDP has identified five priority areas for governance programming that will best achieve our goals:

— Governing institutions

— Public and private sector management

— Decentralisation and support to local governance

— Civil society organisations, and

— Governance in special circumstances.

Different environments will require different programmes, and different entry points and types of programmes. The challenge for UNDP will be to take a systemic and strategic approach to governance that meets national priorities.

Governing institutions: legislature, judiciary and electoral bodies

UNDP support can, in principle, be directed to all three branches of government - executive, legislative and judicial - and the processes needed to establish and operate them. Sound national and local legislatures and judiciaries are critical for creating and maintaining enabling environments for eradicating poverty. Legislatures mediate differing interests and debate and establish policies, laws and resource priorities that directly affect people-centred development. Electoral bodies and processes ensure independent and transparent elections for legislatures. Judiciaries uphold the rule of law, bringing security and predictability to social, political and economic relations. Human rights organisations help ensure that governing institutions uphold national laws and internationally recognised conventions.

UNDP only recently became involved with legislative and judicial systems. Even so, demand for our assistance in these areas has been high. Because of our impartiality and the trust it engenders, we have a considerable comparative advantage over other organisations - and can also help greatly in coordinating external resources.

Given our limited resources, our often close relationship with governments and the importance of the legislature and judiciary in influencing equity and poverty, UNDP should aim for a strategic role in this area. Our primary task is to help develop a country's capacity to strengthen its governance. UNDP should, therefore, first help government create a framework and strategy for institutional reform. This should include the relationship between state institutions and the private sector and civil society.

Support for institutional development of legislatures may include help in setting up effective parliamentary (or similar national and local) structures, systems, processes and procedures as well as training parliamentarians in their roles and legislative procedures. The Inter-Parliamentary Union in Geneva is a valuable partner in this effort, particularly in needs assessment, advisory services and capacity development. Collaboration with Parliamentarians for Global Action in New York, an NGO that assists in policy advice and advocacy, is also being sought.

Support for legislatures also includes assistance in strengthening electoral processes, including support for electoral commissions, electoral legislation, voter registration and electoral registers. UNDP has played an important and expanding role in electoral processes, in some cases complemented by our institutional strengthening efforts. When UNDP is approached for direct support for electoral processes or elections, country offices should contact the Electoral Assistance Unit in the UN Secretariat for guidance and support. An agreement outlining the mutual roles and responsibilities of UNDP and the UN is available. The International Institute for Democracy and Electoral Assistance (IDEA) is an intergovernmental partner outside the UN system that can also provide advice and technical support. There are also experienced regional institutions, such as Parlatino (Parlamento LatinoAmericano).

Judiciaries can be supported in establishing systems of justice and laws, ombudsmen and human rights oversight bodies and security systems. Judicial and legal reforms that may be supported by UNDP include improving the structure, organisation and administration of court systems; training judges, magistrates, lawyers and support personnel; making access to justice easier by improving subordinate court systems; removing legal barriers to full participation of women, minorities and civil society institutions; and providing specialised assistance in legal education on constitutional and electoral law and laws related to human rights. Partnerships with experienced local and international organisations will be important. Issues of human security and crime are dealt with by the Crime Prevention Division of the United Nations. For questions on human rights and to obtain advisory services, contact the UN Centre on Human Rights in Geneva.

Public and private sector management

One of UNDP's greatest strengths is management development, particularly in developing national capacities. We have learned from our vast experience that constructive change has three requisites: laying out a clear vision of goals and of how to reach them; identifying and supporting people who can lead and help reach those goals; and developing strong, effective and accountable managerial capacities and institutional structures to implement change.

Leadership, policy development and managing change

Support for leadership development and managing change cuts across UNDP governance efforts. Effective leadership, essential for successful good governance programmes, is particularly important when countries are undergoing complex or systemic change involving civil society and private actors. Effective leadership entails developing the capacities of everyone who can increase political commitment to sustainable human development. It also includes the ability to bring together public and private actors to define sustainable development goals and strategies that are centred around people and the capacity to manage systemic change in unpredictable situations. Countries also need professionals who can translate political vision into sustained programmes for good governance.

UNDP should seek to develop national capacities to articulate goals, policies and strategies, especially those that are long term and support good governance, with an emphasis on processes that elicit broad national support and consensus. To that end, UNDP can support national institutions that develop the skills of leaders in initiating and managing processes that are systemic and complex and that involve stakeholders and beneficiaries from government, the private sector and civil society. This support will include assistance for training in planning and implementation, building national competencies and developing approaches to public-private partnerships. Gender-specific concerns will merit particular attention.

Moreover, UNDP has concentrated on strengthening management in three areas that are vital to sustainable human development - reform of the civil service, economic and financial management and urban management.

Civil service reform

Reform of state institutions so that they become more efficient, accountable and transparent is a cornerstone of good governance. Effective reform requires political commitment, which should include the support of the private sector and civil society. UNDP's experience with and technical knowledge of public administration reform and management of development has ranged from pioneering work in national technical cooperation assessments and programmes to support for comprehensive civil reforms. In many countries UNDP has sought key partners and coalitions that are politically strong, found suitable entry points, initiated a policy dialogue that brings together stakeholders and beneficiaries and introduced reform in a phased, systemic manner.

Many needs can be addressed: formulation of strategies; assessment of capacities; reform of governance rules and procedures, including those for the market and the most vulnerable; review and restructuring of functions and networks; improvement of systems, especially those concerned with planning, management, information and new technologies, budgeting and expenditures, statistics, reporting and accountability; reform of wage and incentive structures; private-public partnerships; and decentralisation. The central issues of sustainability - ownership, fiscal discipline, incentives, political support and external aid - would also be addressed. Gender concerns should be built into all of these tasks.

Economic and financial management

Good governance includes both procedural and substantive elements; so too does the management of economic and financial matters. Countries need to establish relationships between the state, the private sector and civil society and develop frameworks that provide incentives for broadly based and sustainable growth. Crucial elements for sustainable human development include macroeconomic policies, management of the external sector (trade, aid, investment and debt), market regulation and privatisation, social safety nets and resource management. Sound policies and practices in economic and financial management will contribute significantly to an enabling environment for sustainable human development.

While the Bretton Woods institutions and several bilateral donors have greater resources at their disposal to assist developing countries in this area, UNDP can and should bring issues of sustainable human development and poverty into the centre of policy discussions, make macroeconomic decision-making more transparent, and influence resource allocations. Because of its impartiality, UNDP can be called on to help develop national capacities to negotiate with external partners and mobilise resources in line with national priorities. UNDP can also draw on its comparative advantages to support national capacities to improve efficiency, accountability, transparency and cooperative relationships in all sectors.

UNDP also has extensive experience with aid coordination and management. This provides an important opportunity for UNDP to influence policies in support of sustainable human development.

UNDP can help countries involve civil society and the private sector in policy development and management of development resources, and can enhance the transparency and accountability of economic and financial management processes. It can also help bring business, government and civil society together to address issues of poverty, gender, sustainable livelihoods and the environment. The creation of an enabling environment to attract private investments and nurture enterprises - using appropriate laws, fiscal and monetary policies and stable long-term development strategies - is a priority.

More specifically, UNDP can provide support to build capacity in economic policy analysis, formulation and management, budgeting, economic administrations (customs, debt management and so on), regulatory frameworks and national accounting. The capacity to coordinate and manage aid and debt is also important in the overall management of development resources. By taking the lead in aid coordination processes, UNDP can also advocate its approaches, influence policy and help mobilise resources for national programmes. UNDP can help manage the integration of countries with economic and trading blocs, and can help countries take advantage of the information and knowledge revolution. Not least, UNDP should help governments introduce economic and financial policies that empower and benefit women, the poor and others who may be marginalised, and that protect the natural resource base.

Urban management

Urban populations in developing countries have mushroomed over the past 40 years. This relentless growth is irreversible. The effective functioning of cities and towns is essential for equitable, sustainable growth. Urban management involves multisectoral activities that cut across UNDP's focus areas of poverty alleviation, environmental improvement, gender equity and sustainable livelihoods. UNDP is uniquely placed to provide leadership and to assist countries in developing partnerships with agencies in the UN system. UNDP's Urban Management Programme, developed and managed in partnership with the United Nations Centre for Human Settlements, is the largest multidonor technical cooperation programme in urban development.

Urban management issues include environmental and land management, municipal finance, maintenance of urban infrastructure, regulatory frameworks for the informal sector, urban shelter and services and, of course, poverty alleviation. Gender issues should be mainstreamed throughout urban management programmes.

UNDP agency partners in these priority areas include the Department for Development Support and Management Services (DDSMS), for civil service reform and financial management; UNCTAD, for policies and management of trade and debt; the World Bank, for financial and budgetary issues and investment in civil service reform and urban programmes; the United Nations Centre for Human Settlements, for follow-up to HABITAT II and technical cooperation in urban areas; and the Group of Cities Associations, for cooperation of mayors. In addition, several regional institutions have a wealth of experience.

Decentralisation and support to local governance

Decentralising government - from the national level to regions, districts, towns, municipalities, rural areas, settlements and communities - enables people to participate more directly in governance processes and can help empower people previously excluded from decision-making. In this way a country can create and sustain equitable opportunities for all its people. Closer contact between government officials and local communities and organisations also encourages the exchange of information that can be used to formulate development programmes that are tailored to local needs and priorities, and thus are more effective and sustainable.

UNDP and other UN agencies have extensively promoted decentralisation, accumulating considerable experience along the way. UNDP has supported many public management reform programmes focused on decentralisation and local institutional strengthening. A leading example is the Local Initiative Facility for Urban

Environment (LIFE) to promote dialogue among municipalities, non-governmental organisations and community-based organisations to improve the quality of urban environments in low-income settlements.

UNDP offers many services at the country, regional and global levels to help countries build capacities for decentralised governance. These include systemic institutional analysis and generation of decentralisation policy, strengthening local authorities, direct support to civil society organisations concerned with local governance issues, support to rural institutions and management, implementing local pilot projects and evaluating, documenting and disseminating decentralisation experiences. An example of such support at the global level is the Decentralised Governance Programme.

In addition, UNDP should help improve urban government and administration in ways that not only ensure coordination among agencies but also promote partnerships among local communities, non-governmental organisations, the private sector and urban governments to respond to the problems facing urban populations.

The logical agency partners for all of the above efforts are the United Nations Capital Development Fund, DDSMS and the World Bank.

Civil society organisations

Civil society is the well-spring of the social capital - people working together for common purposes - that is essential for good governance. Civil society organisations can fill the vacuum left by the slimmed-down state, and can advocate and monitor reforms that foster sustainable human development.

Civil service organisations that are involved with development complement (rather than replace) the state. UNDP considers collaboration with these organisations important because of their responsiveness, innovation, direct relationship with the poor, capacity to stimulate participation and articulate local views, cost effectiveness, local accountability and independent assessment of issues.

In many developing countries, however, such organisations are weak. They lack capacities in issues analysis, advocacy and outreach, networking, management and revenue raising. In addition, they need to be more accountable and responsive to and more inclusive of their stakeholders. Some also operate within tight legal and regulatory environments.

UNDP's traditional partner has been government, although it is developing its partnership with civil society. Our ability to work with government remains one of our main comparative advantages. In many programmes we can capitalise on government trust of UNDP to encourage interaction and cooperation with civil society and the private sector, even (or particularly) when sensitive issues are involved.

UNDP's first task may be to bring government and civil society together to discuss policies and programmes and to help create a safe and impartial space that encourages trust and lasting relationships. In fact, UNDP should encourage partnerships with civil society organisations to support national efforts and to plan and implement UNDP-supported programmes. UNDP may then support national efforts to improve legislation and administrative and tax frameworks for these organisations and assist in improving government's relationship with them.

UNDP may also consider helping these organisations develop their capacities to plan, manage and implement activities effectively and accountably and to research, advocate and monitor issues of sustainable human development (including poverty and gender) in ways that build on our experience in reaching the poor, marginalised and disadvantaged. UNDP can also help civil society organisations network, cooperate and share information for social and development purposes and participate in aid coordination and management. UNDP also has a role in what can be termed "civic education": helping national civil society organisations define and implement country-specific programmes that build social cohesion, help resolve conflicts, increase people's awareness of their rights and responsibilities and nurture participation in development and governance. Assistance in collecting and disseminating relevant information on issues of governance and sustainable human development in an impartial way may also be worthwhile.

Governance in special circumstances

There are two categories of countries: crisis countries and transition countries. The social and political stability associated with good governance are fundamental to sustainable human development. During crises, systems and institutions that protect the vulnerable are the first things to be destroyed and must be restored. But good governance is by nature preventive. By valuing development assets and building social cohesion and consensus, it can help reduce vulnerability to - and even the likelihood of - disasters and conflicts.

UNDP's comparative advantage lies not in its humanitarian response and relief but in its long-term development presence and its ability to respond to complex and multifaceted development challenges. In crises where a rapid and coordinated response is required, UNDP must work closely with UN and donor partners with greater experience in emergency situations and with greater resources. UNDP, however, can play a role in planning for development needs while other agencies concentrate on immediate needs. Moreover, UNDP's ability to work with and bring together government, civil society and the private sector can be valuable both during and after a crisis.

There is no universal approach for responding to crises. UNDP must identify the most suitable entry points and respond quickly and flexibly. While good governance programmes generally can reduce the risk of crises, there are specific efforts that UNDP can support before, during and after them.

Impending crisis

UNDP can initiate reconciliation and consensus building and build national capacities to avoid, manage and mitigate crises. It could also regularly gather information on indicators that signal a pending crisis. National human development reports are important in identifying potential trouble. UNDP should also develop a network of people and institutions from which it can obtain development information and with which it can cooperate during crises.

During a crisis

UNDP can support both macro and local planning initiatives and reconciliation. If the state collapses, UNDP may launch participatory programme planning and development for specific needs, such as area, city, regional and food security planning. It should also aim to develop basic governance, management and coordination capacities. During a crisis, partnerships with civil society organisations - both formal and informal - can prove invaluable. These organisations can be crucial intermediaries - supporting participatory planning and reconciliation, and implementing small-scale development initiatives.

Post-crisis

UNDP should assess governance-related requirements, give priority to rebuilding those strategic capacities that have the greatest impact and help identify and coordinate needs for resource mobilisation. This could include assistance to rebuild such core institutions as the executive, legislative and judicial branches of government.

A second category of countries - called transition economies - are those that are moving away from central planning, which attempted to achieve social equity through heavily subsidised state-led development. These subsidies were, in fact, unaffordable, and the failure of this development model has required often painful transitions to market-oriented economies. Most transition economies are also moving towards more open (or democratic) political systems. In many cases economic reforms have faced multiple challenges, including global economic recession (resulting in less trade, aid and investment), environmental degradation (which threatens human well-being), low savings and investment, rocketing unemployment and social disintegration (resulting in soaring social ills and crime). Even so, these countries - including newly independent countries of Central and Eastern Europe, republics of the former Soviet Union and Mongolia - have made remarkable advances and possess substantial untapped capacities.

UNDP efforts in many of these countries have emphasized interventions that build on people's high education levels and help them gain access to outside knowledge, information and experiences, which help them develop capacities that reflect reform priorities. Reforms are also systemic, at times integrating many interrelated processes and generally emphasizing good governance and a stable macroeconomic framework. Developing democratic and accountable institutions (including political parties, free trade unions and the media) are critical. Support to emerging private and civil organisations, particularly to develop management capacities and accountability, are priorities. So too are aid coordination, capacity building to help define goals and policies, support to social security and productive capacities and management of natural and financial resources. Because the needs are so great, UNDP has placed special emphasis on leveraging its resources to mobilise further funds.

Contextual factors relevant to governance programmes

Several contextual characteristics may affect which types of governance programmes are more or less important - and more or less likely to have an impact:

— Socio-economic indicators including education, access to basic needs and the role of women.

— The economy: its base, growth and type; financial dependence on external resources, including aid and debt; and degree of integration with the global economy.

— Human capacities and sustainability.

— Natural resource base and trends in the environment.

— Cultural, religious and ethnic diversity and structures, conflict or polarisation and internal means of resolving conflict.

— Indigenous values, networks and knowledge.

The manifestations and mix of these factors vary greatly among and within regions. For example, in many countries in Asia, Eastern Europe and Latin America public sector and market reforms have created conditions for high growth and expanded opportunities. Even so, some people are becoming increasingly marginalised. Sub-Saharan Africa, by contrast, remains saddled with huge debt, economic stagnation and rapid population growth, causing overexploitation of the natural resource base. Reforms are being undertaken at a time when official development assistance has leveled off and the benefits of globalisation have largely bypassed the region.

The success of governance programmes and projects greatly depends on the way they are designed and implemented. The underlying principles of UNDP's implementation strategy are finding suitable entry points and partners for policy dialogue; responding quickly to national needs while keeping a long-term view; creating opportunities for government, the private sector and civil society to interact to achieve policy and programme consensus; implementing programmes in ways that are nationally led, sustainable and that develop strategic capacities; and coordinating development and UN resources.

Throughout programming, the country office should bear in mind the UNDP mandate, our comparative advantages and approaches to good governance, the socio-economic environment of the country and the country type.

Participatory approach

Without the full involvement of major stakeholders and beneficiaries in design and implementation, programmes are not sustainable. Numerous participatory methodologies are available. UNDP Management Development and Governance Division has helped to further and test one methodology, called *process consultancy*, for developing participatory programmes while also developing social capital. The outside expert's role is to support and help build consensus. The methodology helps UNDP country offices and experts to initiate that consensus building, cultivate an awareness of the importance of governance, identify key agents of change (reformers, leading thinkers, civic leaders and so on), develop goals and strategies and organise capacities for change. The methodology can be applied in all UNDP programme countries. Process consultancy, combined with a *programme approach* and *national execution* (which support development of national capacities to meet national goals), can serve as a powerful tool for developing capacities to reach collective targets. This is one proven way in which UNDP provides training, management development and governance programming. Other effective approaches are available. Guidelines for process consulting and other approaches are available from the Management Development and Governance Division.

Identifying entry points

At the beginning of the programming process, UNDP should identify and consult key people in government, civil society and the private sector who will be involved in governance programmes. In that way it can assess national needs and identify areas for support. Any dialogue should be impartial and bring together national stakeholders to reach consensus, develop political will for change and understand the importance of good governance. Documents and studies (such as national human development reports) and regional strategies could be used to provide analysis, options and methodologies, and to stimulate dialogue. Synergies and linkages should be sought between governance, poverty, sustainable livelihoods, gender and the environment. This should lead to a country cooperation framework document that clarifies national goals and strategies and identifies possible areas for UNDP support, along with appropriate entry points and partners.

Experience shows that UNDP is most effective when it is able to respond quickly and flexibly to unfolding needs and opportunities, while retaining a long-term view on sustainability. At times UNDP must be willing to take risks to take advantage of fast-evolving opportunities, some of which may be directly related to governance - for example, national elections, changes in government bodies, annual planning and budgetary discussions, national campaigns and conferences on specific themes. Some of the most effective governance programmes, however, have been initiated through other entry points - such as poverty, gender, the environment and integrated rural and urban programmes.

Developing strategic capacities

UNDP's approach to capacity development is based on two important principles. First, it asks, "capacity development for *what?*" and advocates that the answer be closely related to people-centred sustainable development. Second, it claims that *how* capacities are developed influence the *what* as well. UNDP advocates that capacity development design take into consideration the key characteristics of good governance - participatory, transparent, equitable, accountable and strategic vision.

The success of good governance programmes depends on developing capacities to articulate goals and manage change. UNDP emphasizes the importance of sustaining and expanding existing capacities and targeting high-impact capacities for assistance. Criteria for strategic interventions include the impact on policies, development resources and the enabling environment, particularly to eliminate poverty; whether key leadership and managerial capacities will be strengthened; and whether support will broaden participation. Because most governance programmes involve, for example, judicial systems, financial management systems, parliamentary systems and decentralised governance systems, a systems approach to capacity development - which places institutions and people in processes that perform specific tasks - is most appropriate.

UNDP support for *building capacities for national information systems* and linkages to regional and global networks is a cornerstone of its strategy to develop capacities in priority areas. Such linkages support national decision-making by helping countries tap into an array of local, national and global knowledge and experience, and to build a global network of experts to support governance-related programmes. Guidance on design issues is available from the Sustainable Development Network Programme and the Management Development and Governance Division of the Bureau for Policy and Programme Support.

Institutions in each region will receive support for regional and subregional networks. At the global level, UNDP's Management and Governance Network (MAGNET) will be the global node for national and regional networks. MAGNET, which is managed by Management Development and Governance Division, includes a consultancy roster and UNDP governance documents that can be found on the Internet.

Feedback on impact is an important device for future programme design and implementation. UNDP is working to develop capacity targets, benchmarks and indicators of progress and success that are tailored to measure the success of governance programming.

Coordination and the role of the resident coordinator

UNDP can take steps to improve the impact of the governance programmes that it supports and to ensure that the UN and external partners support national priorities in a coordinated way. For example, it can become the lead agency in collaboration and country-based aid coordination for one or more aspects of governance programmes; provide an impartial forum to discuss issues related to governance and to help forge local partnerships; provide data and electronic information services on national governance programmes to all development partners; help governments package and negotiate governance programmes for resource mobilisation; and help coordinate UN responses and programmes in support of national goals or in answer to crisis situations - or both.

Division of responsibility within UNDP

UNDP has responsibility for governance programmes at three levels: the country, the region and the world.

UNDP country office

Leadership by country offices is crucial, since most of UNDP's resources are available at the country level. The UNDP country office is responsible for identifying, developing, implementing and monitoring programmes and projects that develop consensus on national goals and strategies and then develop relevant capacities. Coordination and resource mobilisation are also vital. These responsibilities have important implications for a proactive office: UNDP offices may need to organise themselves to analyse changing needs and respond rapidly to emerging opportunities. Some offices have a team focused solely on governance programmes. More important are the abilities within country offices to identify effective entry points and implementation partners, identify partner institutions that can monitor and assess trends and develop a network of people and institutions that can help in initiating consultation and development of programmes.

Regional support to programme countries

Regional programmes add value and support to UNDP country initiatives in one or more ways. They help define regional governance policies and strategies, facilitate sharing of regional experiences, establish regional networks and centres of excellence, provide flexible and rapid regionwide support to develop national programmes, undertake regional briefings and training, conduct regional studies of trends and identify and pilot new approaches in countries that may also be applied regionally. Each of the UNDP regional bureaux has prepared (or is developing) regionally tailored governance strategies.

Global support to programme countries

UNDP supports a number of global projects to support good governance including those on institutions of governance, decentralisation and urban management.

UNDP Governance Task Force. Chaired by MDGD\BPPS, the task force facilitates UNDP governance policy and interbureau activities; shares information and provides guidance and feedback on global programmes; and responds in a coordinated way to interagency and UN conference requirements.

BPPS Management Development and Governance Division. MDGD, working within the framework of the BPPS Global Programme, has three main responsibilities: developing corporate-level policies, tools, instruments and methodologies based on country experiences; researching issues of priority to UNDP; and supporting UNDP country offices for programme development and backstopping. MDGD is developing competencies in such areas as institutions of governance; decentralisation and local governance; civil society; urban management; economic and financial management; aid management and accountability; and capacity development methodologies. In other related areas MDGD is developing partnerships and a comprehensive roster of consultants who can be recruited rapidly. MDGD strategy calls for close collaboration with other BPPS divisions dealing with the macroeconomic framework, poverty, gender, the private sector and the environment. MDGD will collaborate closely with the United Nations Capital Development Fund in local government programmes. The fund is concentrating its resources in the poorest countries to provide modest capital grants and microfinance that support local and community institutions of governance.

Office of UN Services, Emergency Response Unit. The Emergency Response Unit provides resources under TRAC line 1.1.3 for the development of strategic frameworks and capacity development of national institutions to prepare for, mitigate, manage or prevent crises. Where possible, available resources should be programmed during the preparation of the country cooperation framework.

Partnerships

UNDP will build partnerships with agencies in the UN system as well as with institutions and networks outside the UN system to implement its governance policy. UNDP is chairing the UN systemwide Sub-Task Force (of the Interagency Task Force on Enabling Environment) on Capacity-building for Governance with representatives from 18 UN agencies and programmes. The mandate of the Sub-Task Force is to promote integrated follow-up to UN conferences by building on best practices of existing interagency cooperation. UNDP is also taking the lead in the governance sub-group of the Secretary General's Initiative for Africa. Partnerships with specific agencies in the UN system are identified in chapter 2 of this document.

UNDP will also use the expertise and experience of global, regional and national institutions and networks outside the UN system. Collaborative agreements have been signed or are being developed with several global institutions and networks including International Union of Local Authorities (IULA), Inter-Parliamentarian Union (IPU) and International Institute for Democracy and Electoral Assistance (IDEA).

Bibliography

Akash, M.M.2000. *Right-Based Approach to Development and Right to Land.*

Alston, Philip.2000. *Towards a Human Rights Accountability Index.*

Anand, Sudhir,and Amartya Sen.2000. *Human Development Progress Indicators.*

An-Na 'im,Abdullahi A.2000. *Human Rights in the Arab World -A Regional Perspective.*

Coomaraswamy, Radhika.2000. *Women 's International Human Rights.*

Dias, Ayesha. 2000. *Human Rights,Environment and Development:with Special Emphasis on Corporate Accountability.*

Flinterman, Cees, and J.Gutter.2000. *The United Nations and Human Rights:Achievements and Challenges.*

Ghosh, Jayati.2000. *Rules of Economic Integration and Human Rights.*

Goldstone, Leo.2000. *Proposals for Human Rights Benchmarks.*

Goonesekere, Savitri.2000. *Human Rights Systems in the UN.*

Green, Maria.2000. *Human Rights Indicators:An Overview of the Field.*

Hassan, Bahey El Din.2000. *Egypt Human Rights Report.*

Liebenberg, Sandra.2000. *A Country Study of South Africa -Human Development and Human Rights.*

Mehra, Malini.2000. *A Comparison of International Trade, Human Rights and Environmental Agreements.*

Muntarbhorn, Vitit.2000. *Child Rights:A Decade of the Con-vention on the Rights of the Child and Beyond.*

Muntarbhorn, Vitit.2000. *Human Rights and Human Develop-ment:Thailand -A Country Study.*

Mutua, Makau.2000. *The African Human Rights System:A Critical Evaluation.*

Normand, Roger.2000. *Separate and Unequal:Trade and Human Rights Regimes.*

Olcott, Martha Brill.2000. *Regional Study on Human Develop-ment and Human Rights -Central Asia.*

Oloka-Onyango, Joseph.2000. *Human Rights and Sustainable Development in Contemporary Africa -A New Dawn or Retreating Horizon?*

Osmani, Siddiq R.2000. *Human Rights to Food,Health and Education.*

Pinheiro, Paulo Sergio,and David Carlos Baluarte.2000. *Study on National Strategies -Human Rights Commissions,Ombuds-men,Specialized Agencies and National Action Plans.*

Rodas-Martini, Pablo.2000. *The Debate on Labour Standards and International Trade:Technically Inconclusive and Politically Explosive.*

Rosero, Rocio.2000. *Human Rights and Human Development in Ecuador.*

Sarkar, Lotika,Vina Muzamdar,and S.P.Sathe.2000. *Country Study -India.*

Sen, Amartya,and Sudhir Anand.2000. *Human Rights and Human Development.*

Shiva Kumar, A.K.2000. *Measuring Progress in Human Develop-ment:Tracking Inputs,Assessing Efforts,Evaluating Outcomes.*

Transparency International.2000. *Justice and Corruption.* Report 2000

Vizard, Polly.2000. *The Evolution of the Idea of Human Rights in Western and Non-Western Thought.* Country and regional studies

---.2000b. *TNC 's, Codes of Conduct,Self-Imposed Codes and Human Rights.*

Index